JOHN HOWELLS

CHOOSE LATIN AMERICA

A GUIDE TO SEASONAL AND RETIREMENT LIVING

Illustrated by Noni Mendoza

GATEWAY BOOKS

San Francisco

Printed in the United States of America

Gateway Books
66 Cleary Court #1405
San Francisco CA 94109

Edited by Patrick Totty

Cover designed by Ed McElligott

Maps by Barbara Sewards

LIBRARY OF CONGRESS
CATALOGING CARD
NUMBER: 86-22929

Contents

preface

Recently, Don Merwin and I co–authored a book on economical living and retirement in Mexico (CHOOSE MEXICO, Gateway Books, San Francisco) in which we advised Americans how they might live in Mexico as residents or retirees on as little as $400 a month. How to live *well* on $400 a month. We conceived the book as a guide for those lucky souls who manage to arrange their lives so they may travel and spend full or part time in the adventure of living in a foreign country. It can be done, and you needn't be a member of the "jet set" to do it.

The book has been very successful, and it became obvious that other books were needed to expand the choices for the long–term traveler or retiree looking for the adventure and stimulation of living in a foreign country. How to do it economically, safely and comfortably, as a full–time or part–time resident. This book enlarges the scope of travel/retirement possibilities, adding Central and South America to the menu. The author brings you his experiences and knowledge gained from over 30 years of living and traveling in Latin America.

The countries, cities and towns discussed in this book are not the only ones in Latin America where a traveler or retiree might find his ideal living adventure. They're just best according to my personal notions of what a "good" place to live might be. I've tried to present choices where you might feel the most comfortable and still enjoy the fun of living in a foreign country. But this lifestyle isn't for everyone. Whether or not you decide to retire in Latin America, there are things to be learned from this book. If you end up viewing our neighbors to the south with a different perspective, and if you gain an insight into why I feel attracted to Latin America, I'll have done my job.

This book is designed as a guide for those individuals who feel a need to enhance their lives with foreign travel. It's for those who want to experience foreign living. It's for the school teacher on sabbatical, the construction worker with winter unemployment, the executive who can take a leave of absence. It's for the self–employed individual who can trust his business to others while he enjoys life *now* instead of waiting for that "someday" which may never come. It's for people like me, who hate winter and are searching for inexpensive ways to have an extra summer every year.

But equally important, this book is for the retired couple searching for an affordable, interesting life after leaving the workplace. It's for those who are nearing retirement age and are casting about for possibilities as to what their eventual lifestyle could be.

What are your dreams and goals for retirement? Do they include buying a condominium in a senior citizens' complex somewhere in Arizona or Florida? Do they involve withdrawal from life, growing old in the passive company of others who have abandoned the adventure of living?

Perhaps you feel you have no alternative but to stay put, braving the heat of summers, huddling around the fireplace in the winters. Somehow you'll manage those enormous fuel bills this winter only to face exorbitant electrical costs for next summer's air conditioning. Must you always be looking forward to next spring? Are you constantly aware of the diminishing number of springs you have left in your storehouse of seasons?

Most people face exactly this kind of future and this style of retirement. Many feel they have no choice. Others lack a feeling for adventure and don't care to even envision alternatives. And some actually look forward to this kind of retirement; it seems to be a perfectly natural way of life. This book is not for them.

A few--those who bother to read this book--demand a little more from life than resignation to their "declining years." Once you are fortunate enough not to have to work, these years should be enjoyed to the maximum. They shouldn't be "declining years" but, rather, the "years of opportunity." For the first time in your life, you have the time and the opportunity to do all those exciting things you've always dreamed of.

If you aren't yet retired, then this is the time to begin making your plans. Now is the time to think about "trying before buying" with creative experiments in quality living. CHOOSE LATIN AMERICA presents some alternative ideas about where to experiment and how to go about making these plans.

"Traveling around the world is easy to talk about," you mutter under your breath. "I'm lucky just to be able to stay here and be able to meet the utility bills. And, if the house weren't paid for, I couldn't even afford time off from work! So don't talk to me about retiring in some exotic paradise!"

The truth of the matter is, there are places in the world where you *can* travel and/or retire, where you *can* live well, all for less than many people spend just for rent at home. That doesn't mean you have to move lock, stock and VCR to some foreign country. You can, of course, but some feel that a yearly *temporary* home in a foreign country is a better idea. Take a look at Chapter 16, "Can You Afford It?" before deciding that foreign living is out of the question financially.

To tell the truth, I happen to enjoy California, and hate to miss the summers there. Winters, well, these are something else. So, my individual choice is to spend winters in Argentina or Uruguay (where it is summer in December, January and February) then enjoy a second summer in June, July and August back in America. But no law says I can't change my mind and go to Mexico next winter instead of Argentina. Mexico is a great place for the winter. So are Costa Rica and Chile. How about Brazil? Where to go? How to do it? Plenty of Americans choose to live in Mexico, Guatemala, Costa Rica, Argentina, Uruguay and other parts of Latin America. They've discovered that life can be easy, if not luxurious, on a limited budget of less income than many couples receive in Social Security payments. Look at it this way: An average Latin American wage earner would feel blessed to have the income equal to what we might consider an inadequate Social Security check.

This book will argue that you can spend all or part of each retirement year in Latin America, live a full, exciting life, yet not spend all of those savings that your nephew plans on inheriting so he can buy a convertible.

Let us be very clear about one important point: CHOOSE LATIN AMERICA is not a travel book, although it may well be useful when traveling in Latin America. I won't recommend hotels or restaurants. I won't quote air fares or schedules. That's the job of the many excellent travel publications such as Fordor's SOUTH AMERICA ON $25 A DAY, MEXICO ON $25 A DAY, or Rand McNally's SOUTH AMERICAN HANDBOOK. The book you have in your hand is just one of the tools you need when trying to decide where you would like to live or to retire. You are urged to frequent the library and study travel books, history books, guidebooks, anything you can get your hands on, in order to make an intelligent decision as where to live or retire. Maybe you're interested in hunting or fishing. Then pick up a book that tells you where in Latin America you may catch or shoot the biggest of whatever you are after. Camping and RV travel? Several publications (some free) tell you all about it. If I could get all of the pertinent information about Latin America into one book, you couldn't afford to buy it. You couldn't carry it home from the bookstore.

A final note is on the use of the word "American" when referring to citizens of the United States and Canada. You often hear a semantic game when someone taunts, "We're *all* Americans." This leaves an impression that people in Central and South America resent our appropriation of the term *American*. The truth is that when referring to United States or Canadian citizens, Latin Americans almost unanimously say *Americanos*. When people ask me where I'm from, I always answer, "California." They usually smile and say, "Oh, *Americano*, eh?" But you never say you're from *America*, instead you are an *Americano* from *Los Estados Unidos* or from *Canada*. The people down south consider Canadians to be *Americanos* also (much to the chagrin of many Canadians), even though they are fully aware that our two countries are separate. The point is that *Americano* is a convenient term for an English–speaking inhabitant of North America.

The word *gringo*, by the way, is not an automatic insult in Latin America. It's like calling an Irishman a "Mick," or a native of Indiana a "Hoosier." It all depends on the tone of voice. Most Latin American countries have nicknames for their nationalities. For example, the Costa Ricans call themselves *Ticos* (because of an odd way they have of pronouncing diminutives, i.e. saying "momen*tico*" instead of the usual "momen*tito* for "just a minute"); the Nicaraguans are *Nicas*; people from Buenos Aires are *Porteños* (because Buenos Aires is famous as an ocean port). So we become *gringos*. Actually, it's easier to say than the formal Spanish term *estadounidense* ("Unitedstatesian"). Try pronouncing that a few times, and you will be happy to call yourself a gringo. So, don't be miffed if someone calls you a "gringo" or a "gringa." In this book I use the terms *gringo* and *American* interchangeably to mean any English–speaking inhabitant of America. I hope I'm not insulting anyone by this. As an aside, it's always been interesting to me that I have *never* been treated rudely because of my citizenship, not even by individuals who disagree vigorously with some U.S. policies. On the contrary, I've talked with gun–toting revolutionaries in Central America who begged me to take the message home that "we like the American people, but we don't like your government's treatment of us." More on this later in the book.

(*NOTICE:* It is impossible to keep up with changes in governmental regulations concerning immigration and visa requirements. Even though every endeavor has been made to ensure that the facts in the book are correct, you are cautioned to secure authoritative advice from the consulates of whatever country you are considering visiting.)

ACKNOWLEDGMENTS

Special thanks go to Sherry Pastor for her patience and invaluable support, and to my good friends Don and Judith Merwin for their kind assistance in this project. Especially, I wish to extend my appreciation to Paul Gillette, whose unselfish sharing of knowledge, advice and encouragement made all of this possible. In loving memory of Dorothy, Bob, Evan and Owen.

CHAPTER 1

Is Living/Retiring Abroad Practical?

Many think so. According to the latest government statistics (based on reports from U.S. Foreign Service posts), 1,829,870 U.S. citizens live in foreign countries. This does not include U.S. Government employees (either military or non–military) or their dependents. This doesn't mean that there are 1,829,870 *retirees* living out of the country, because many of these Americans abroad are working for multi–national or foreign companies. But hundreds of thousands are retired; hundreds of thousands are part–time residents. If you choose to try overseas living, you will have company.

The Social Security Administration mails more than 300,000 checks out of the United States every month to all parts of the globe. However, as with all statistics, this one needs some analysis. First of all, you don't have to be native–born, or even a U.S. citizen to draw a Social Security check. Many recipients are foreign workers who have earned their retirement working in the United States and who have returned home to enjoy their old age. As an example, the latest figures show 269 monthly checks going to Nicaragua and 337 to El Salvador—I seriously doubt that 600 U.S. citizens would choose these countries as ideal retirement locations! The second point is that many, if not the majority of U.S. citizens living abroad insist on having their Social Security payments deposited in their hometown bank instead of risking postal and currency problems of foreign countries. For example: while the U.S. Foreign Service lists 20,000 U.S. citizens living in Costa Rica, there are only 1,191 Social Security checks going there. My guess is that most of those checks are going to Costa Ricans who have returned home to collect their benefits.

Besides the 20,000 U.S. citizens in Costa Rica, the U.S. Foreign Service reports 35,000 in Brazil (13,800 in Rio, 13,364 in São Paulo, etc.); 7,145 living in Buenos Aires; 5,927 in Santiago, Chile; 12,912 in Bogota, Colombia; 6,600 in Guatemala City; 10,000 in Lima, Peru; a whopping 275,000 in Mexico. They even list 15 gringos living in Afghanistan. However, Afghanistan is not on my list of recommended countries.

I checked with the nearest Canadian consulate, but was unable to get any definitive figures on the number of Canadian citizens residing abroad, but you can be sure they are proportionally the same. As a matter of fact, a trip to Acapulco during the dead of winter will convince you that half of Canada is down there soaking up tropical sunshine by day and tequila sunrises by night. Makes one wonder who's watching the store. Canadians, particularly French Canadians, learned long ago how to escape 20 degree–below winters. (They don't need guidebooks, they just go.)

So, you can see that almost anywhere you might want to go in this world, you will find North Americans. This could be an important point for you to consider. Later we'll discuss the need to examine your psychological makeup to see how dependent you are on English–speaking social situations. Chances are you need to have social contacts who speak your language from time to time, at least for casual friendships.

HOW MUCH MONEY DO YOU NEED TO LIVE ABROAD?

Clearly, this question has no satisfactory answer because everyone's lifestyle is different; needs and expectations vary widely. It's like asking the question: "How much money do you need to live in North America?" If you are used to driving a Mercedes, eating in expensive restaurants, having house servants and a gardener, your needs are going to be much greater than a couple who drive a pickup and eat at home all the time.

In researching our book CHOOSE MEXICO, we sent out hundreds of questionnaires, asking foreign residents how much they spent per month to live in that country and how much they thought a couple needed to live in a small two–bedroom house or apartment––

for rent, food, clothing, entertainment. Our personal experiences of living in Mexico correlated perfectly with the replies to our questionnaire. Four hundred dollars a month seemed to be what most people felt was a minimum for a decent living in Mexico. Some spend much more because they have large houses and several servants. A few spend less, just as some people spend less while living at home. Research on this book clearly indicates that inexpensive living and retirement spots in other parts of Latin America are also affordable with the same monthly outlay. Some situations would require careful budgeting to make it within the $400 minimum. Realistically, $600 might be a better minimum in some countries. Economic conditions are subject to change of course, but at the moment of writing, this $400–to–$600–a–month minimum figure for long–term living or retirement in most places in Latin America is possible.

It's important to keep in mind that the $400–$600 figures are the *minimum* needed to maintain a decent lifestyle. From there, you have to adjust to your style. We all know people who spend more than that on booze or new clothes. Also, the estimated living costs don't allow for an automobile or imported luxuries. You'll have to figure these according to your tastes and pocketbook. I solve the automobile problem by using public transportation, then renting a car for special occasions.

ESTIMATING YOUR PURCHASING POWER ABROAD

Why is it that the U.S. dollar goes so far in foreign countries? How is it possible that an income that borders on poverty here will allow you to live comfortably elsewhere? Are things really that cheap overseas?

The answer is that things aren't cheap, it's just that the United States and Canada are expensive. The Union Bank of Switzerland puts out a very interesting booklet which compares wages and living costs in various countries. They point out that North America is just about the most expensive place in the whole world. It takes more dollars to put food on the table, pay the rent and clothe a family in the United States than in Europe, and much, much more than in most of Latin America. On the other hand, wages are higher here, higher by far. We spend more and we earn more. Where our advantage comes is the high demand for the dollar and the favorable foreign exchange rate for dollars. This exchange rate is the secret to inexpensive living overseas.

The best way to understand the power of your currency is to study the charts of wages and prices here. These statistics were compiled from questionnaires, from the *United Nations Statistical Report*, and from the Union Bank of Switzerland's booklet on worldwide price and wage statistics.

First, take a look at average wages paid for various occupations in North America, and see if there isn't something comparable to the type of work you do, or to the salary you earn. Then check out wages world wide. (Remember that these wages are after deductions for taxes, Social Security, hospitalization, etc.) If, for example, you are used to earning the wages of an electrical engineer, clearing let's say, $26,000 a year, then see what your colleagues earn elsewhere. In this case, we find that in Buenos Aires a similar job would pay $7,400. An automobile mechanic in Houston who gets by on $20,700 finds that Mexico City auto mechanics earn only $2,500 to support their families. You get an idea of how much income people abroad have to spend on their living styles. This will give you a clue as to how far your income would go overseas.

Caution: Don't assume that all wages are directly proportional to the standards of living both here and abroad. For example, an automobile mechanic in Houston lives on a much higher social and economic level than his counterpart in Latin America. Manual labor doesn't carry the status in Latin America that it does here. Construction workers in Rio de Janeiro who earn $900 a year obviously can't live in the same style as a construction worker in Los Angeles who earns $26,000. Many skilled workers here enjoy union–negotiated wages and benefits that are unheard of in some other countries. But a couple with a Social Security check of $600 a month ($7,200 a year) earns two and a half times the salary of a teacher in Buenos Aires, or more than three times the wages of a toolmaker in Mexico City, or twice the average family's income in Costa Rica. By comparing your net income with other trades and professions, you arrive at some idea of where your $7,200 a year will allow you to live comfortably. One other caution: the cost of living is only part of the decision; more important is the quality of living in a particular country.

Comparative Costs in the Americas

	Wage Levels	Food Prices	Apt. Rents	3-Mile Taxi
Houston	113	$295	$390-530	$6.30
New York	142	362	1,050-1,630	5.50
Bogota	19	173	300-490	4.50
Buenos Aires	20	141	90-210	1.60
Caracas	46	173	550	1.60
Mexico	17	196	240-310	1.40
Panama	33	246	550-800	2.00
Rio de Janiero	18	132	150-190	1.40
Sao Paulo	23	124	190-210	1.60

Price and wage levels, Zurich=100.
Food: monthly outlay for small family.
Apartment: unfurnished 3-room.

Comparative Wages in the Americas

	Chicago	Buenos Aires	Mexico	Rio	Bogota
Mechanic	20,700	2,300	2,500	1,600	2,900
Electrical. Eng.	25,200	7,400	7,000	10,300	7,200
Toolmaker	21,900	3,100	2,300	2,100	3,500
Secretary	17,800	4,200	3,800	3,900	6,000
Bank Teller	15,500	6,000	3,600	4,300	5,100
Saleswoman	6,900	1,700	2,200	1,000	2,200
Construction	21,500	1,400	2,400	800	1,900
Teacher	17,000	2,800	2,500	2,400	1,900
Manager	43,100	4,800	5,900	19,800	12,500

NOTE: These wages are in dollar equivalents of take-home pay, after taxes, health insurance, social security, etc. Also note that the social status and living standards of some professions are different from those in the United States.

WHERE TO LIVE ABROAD?

Most Americans, when considering travel and living abroad, look toward Europe, for that is the font of our culture, our heritage, the land of our ancestors. We are barraged with travel articles and travelogues with scenes of London, Rome, Madrid and Athens, to the point that when we actually make our visit, it is almost anticlimatic, because we know the scenes by heart. In the back of most travelers' minds is the fantasy of spending a summer in a Paris apartment, or in a cottage on the Costa Brava, maybe owning a place in the Greek Isles. Many consider retirement in Europe and many actually do retire there, carving a stimulating, full life from what might otherwise be a dreary existence at "home." Yet, except for a few countries, you will find the cost of living not much less than in the United States or Canada––perhaps even a bit higher. Still, when most people talk of living or retirement abroad, the implication is Europe.

Of course, many Americans know Mexico, and know it well. It's nearby, easy to visit, and definitely a foreign country. Many Americans have elected to live and retire there––more than a quarter of a million of them. But few Americans can picture what the rest of Latin America may be like. They envision countries crowded with people, overflowing with slums, beggars, and suffering revolutions every other month. When and if American tourists decide to make travel arrangements for South America, they typically select a whirlwind, 10–day tour to see Machu Picchu, Copacabana and the Amazon, with perhaps a layover in Bogota (where someone steals their luggage), then on to the Panama Canal and home. The notion of staying in Latin America long enough to actually know it seldom occurs to any but the most adventurous travelers.

But for those who venture outside the confines of the 10–day tour, a pleasant discovery is in store. Most of Latin America, particularly South America, is far from crowded; underpopulated is a better description. For example, in the temperate countries of Argentina, Uruguay and Chile, the population density is about a tenth of that of France and one–twentieth that of Britain. The birthrate is about half to one–fifth that of Mexico's and just a little higher than Canada's. One can drive through miles of open, lush agricultural land which lies fallow because there are neither people to farm it nor demand for the produce.

The small towns in the temperate zones are neat and prosperous, looking very much like small towns and villages in America or

Europe. The cities are modern, clean and fashionably middle–class, yuppies and all. Many cities are startlingly European in appearance and customs, with broad avenues, thriving small businesses, and continental cuisine served in restaurants that open late and stay packed until dawn. In some countries, you see little apparent poverty and low crime rates. The reasons for this are discussed later in the book.

WHY LATIN AMERICA?

Friends have asked me, "If Latin America is so great, why is it that all those people want to come up here?" And in Latin America they ask a variant of the same question: "Why is it that all you gringos want to come down here, while so many of us want to go up there?"

It should be obvious, but let's belabor the obvious for a moment. Most parts of Latin America are pleasant––easy living for anyone with even a few dollars in his pocket. As we point out in this book, with $400 a month a family can live quite well. But, if you don't have $400 a month, if you must work seven days a week to make a living, then beautiful surroundings mean little. The cold and dreariness of Detroit, or the urban violence and bone–chilling winds of Chicago don't look so bad when a person knows it's possible to earn more in a couple of hours work "up there" than he earns all week long in his native country.

"But," you might argue, "money doesn't buy happiness." They reply, "Just give me the money–– I'll do my own shopping!" A few years ago, I taught English to foreigners in an adult education program in California. I developed an exercise to teach the notion of the English subjunctive tense. I made flash cards with a series of sentences which the students would read to each other, each beginning with either "If you saw..." or "If you had..." The other student would then complete the sentence, starting off with: "I would..." One very interesting card said, "If I had a million dollars, I would..." I could almost predict what the answers would be by the nationality. Japanese students would say something silly, like, "I would buy a Rolls Royce for every day of the week, and a diamond ring for each of my toes." An Italian or French student might say, "I would buy a house." A student from India would say, "I would spend it to help the poor." But the Mexican or Costa Rican student almost always

16

would say--with a sad look in his eye--"If I had a million dollars . . . I would go home."

Okay, will all readers who plan on retiring to their home towns as soon as they make a million bucks, please stand up? Aha! I thought so!

BEWARE OF STATISTICS

You'll find some statistics on Latin America in this book. Study the figures and analyze them carefully, but beware. I'm always suspicious of conclusions drawn purely from statistics. This bias comes partly from my academic background in social science and my experience with some ludicrous conclusions drawn from statistics. My suspicions were confirmed when newspapers and televisions announced that researchers, through the use of statistics, arrived at the astounding conclusion that Pittsburgh is the best city in the United States in which to live, and Yuba City, California, the worst. In this same study, St. Louis also ranked in the top 10. St. Louis? Pittsburgh? If I didn't know and like Yuba City, I would have suspected that the United States is in pretty bad shape if Pittsburgh and St. Louis are the best in the nation!

Some books on retirement rank countries by their desirability as retirement locations by comparing statistical rankings on the cost of living, taxes, transportation, civil freedoms, and so forth. One study ranked the little European country of Andorra as the most desirable, followed by the Bahamas, and so on with Costa Rica coming in sixth place and the United States 12th in desirability. The United States, by the way, was beaten out by Puerto Rico, which took a coveted 10th spot in the derby!

Another statistical study ranks the United States first, and Andorra 20th. Yet another study ranks the United States *41st* in a study of quality of life of 107 nations. I presume they were using the same statistics but with different criteria to arrive at these findings. Still, Andorra consistently ranks quite high as a potential retirement spot--if you look just at statistics. This strikes me as funny, since Andorra is a tiny country of 36,000 inhabitants, with only one road going clear through it. Its larger cities are towns solidly packed with shopping centers and discount stores. Andorra's entire national population is less than Fayetteville, Arkansas, or about the same as Coon Rapids, Minnesota (pop. 35,286).

It turns out that Andorra is quite prosperous, with low taxes, little unemployment, low crime, and all that, because it's a duty-free country with hordes of bargain hunters from neighboring countries flocking there to buy cheap imported goods. In the winter, there is snow and bitter cold. Winter or summer, the main road is continually jammed with traffic of out-of-country shoppers. It's a pretty little country, I can assure you, and well worth a visit provided you time your border crossings to avoid peak traffic and hours of waiting in line. I suppose you *could* retire in Andorra, if you don't mind crowds of shoppers and traffic jams that permit fascinating cobwebs to grow between your steering wheel and windshield. All things considered, I think I'd rather retire in Pittsburgh. On the other hand, I've never visited Coon Rapids, Minnesota; that might be a possibility. It could not be much colder in the winter, anyway.

Statistics will show that living almost anywhere in Latin America is inexpensive. Yet, there are other factors which will be discussed in this book that do not show up in statistics, factors such as climate, crime and political unrest. For example, statistics on temperatures may look good, but insects and rain could make the place unbearable. Crime statistics on Latin American countries are either unreliable or unavailable because few government agencies keep the statistics. And political unrest can't be measured except at ballot boxes, and in some countries, elections are meaningless. Therefore some countries will be discussed in more detail, simply because they are the more desirable places to live. Other countries will be touched upon only briefly, because few Americans find them pleasant or safe.

CONTACTING RESIDENTS AND RETIREES

Since the publication of CHOOSE MEXICO, the most frequent request made of me is that I supply names and address of residents living in foreign countries. Some readers feel a need to contact someone there, to ask for information or assistance in relocating.

First of all, when I conduct my surveys and interviews with foreign residents, I assure them that their identities will be protected. To include someone's name in a book going out to thousands of strangers would be truly unfair. My friends could be flooded with requests for information and assistance. To expect even the most gracious and helpful person to reply to hundreds of letters from people they don't know is totally unrealistic. (I can't even get my own kids to answer my letters.)

The same thing applies to retiree organizations. There are some very active ones in places like Guadalajara and Costa Rica, but like all volunteer organizations, the leadership changes frequently, and so do mailing addresses. Even if the addresses were current, the clubs aren't set up to answer any but routine communications. Understand, their concerns are with club members, not with people who simply want information or to become pen pals. The truth is, many people already living in a foreign country have no reason to go out of their way to encourage more immigration. Some even want to keep their paradise as their own personal discovery.

The second most requested information is a list of real estate agents. Again, I have to stiff–arm this one. I know some reputable real estate agents, yet I refuse to go on record as endorsing one over another. And, even if I were sold on an agency's honesty and reliability, the agency could change hands by the time a reader picks up this book. Furthermore, a real estate agent can't do you a bit of good until you have investigated thoroughly the place you wish to live. You might buy a piece of property sight–unseen in the United States, but you would be a fool to do this in a foreign country.

In countries like Mexico or Costa Rica, where there are North Americans all over, making contact with residents is rather easy once you are there. But some people feel that they can't make a move without having a specific place to zero in on. The answer in this case is to subscribe to one of the newspapers listed in the bibliography and look for contacts there through display ads, classified ads or news stories. You'll find current retirement clubs and real estate agents' addresses. You'll learn what kind of business and personal services that are offered for foreign residents. You'll find housing rentals and sales. My approach would be to place an ad myself, stating when I was arriving, the type of housing I need, or the kind of assistance desired, and then sit back and wait for a reply. The local residents read these papers thoroughly. If they have a place for rent or sale, they'll be delighted to contact you. But don't expect to find many long–term residents with the time or inclination to enter into involved correspondence with perfect strangers. It doesn't happen that way in your neighborhood, or down south, either.

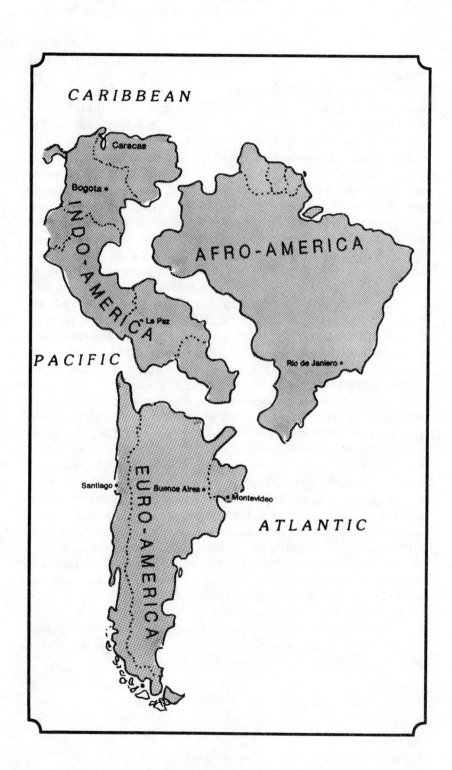

CHAPTER 2

What is Latin America?

Latin America is a convenient term for all of the Spanish, French or Portuguese–speaking countries in the Western Hemisphere. Because the United States and Canada share a common culture, speak the same language, read the same books, watch the same movies and television––often sharing the same world views––we commonly make the error of assuming everything "south of the border" is also one culture, one people. This is a mistake. The more than 25 entities of "Latin America" are individual and unique, each in its own way.

Like the United States and Canada, however, some Latin American countries are more closely related than others, culturally, racially and economically. For this reason, I choose to divide Latin America into four sections. These divisions were suggested to me by my good friend Luis Alberto del Bo, an economist and professor at the University of Cordoba, Argentina. They are arbitrary ideas, convenient and perhaps oversimplified, and for all I know, previously used by other writers. Left out of this book (to be included in a future one) are the Latin American countries of the Caribbean.

The first logical section I call *Euro–America*: Argentina, Uruguay and Chile, those countries with almost pure European peoples and culture. The next section, I call the *Middle Americas*: Mexico plus the seven Central American countries of Guatemala, Belize, Honduras, El Salvador, Nicaragua, Costa Rica and Panama. These countries are connected by road and rail, trade, ideas and people moving more or less freely. The third section I call *Afro–America*, referring to Portuguese–speaking Brazil and the mixed–language Guianas. The fourth and final division I call *Indo–America*, because its people are heavily indebted to Native Americans for cultural and racial heritage. These divisions are admittedly rough and in no way imply, for example, that Africa was the sole contributor to Afro–American culture, or that Caracas or Bogata are "Indian;" or that Buenos Aires isn't uniquely "Argentinian."

Each of the sections has its own special living/retirement advantages and disadvantages, as far as Americans go. Later, we will investigate each for possible living and retirement spots.

BUT, ISN'T IT EXPENSIVE?

Many people are skeptical that it is possible for a person to live in Latin America for less than $1,000 a month. Recently I read some statistics in a Sunday newspaper travel section claiming that a dinner for two in Buenos Aires with wine and tip costs $49 for two people. Hotel rooms were quoted at about $140 a day for a "nice" hotel and $60 for an "ordinary" room. How can you live inexpensively with prices like that?

No question that you can easily find hotels charging that much, and if you looked hard enough, you might find a restaurant that expensive (although, for the life of me, I can't think which restaurant that might be, and I know Buenos Aires rather well). But, as is the case even in the United States, there are several levels of prices and living standards. Some tourists think nothing of paying $140 a night for a hotel room or $49 for dinner. But few can afford it for many nights in a row.

The answer is that living as a resident or as a tourist are two separate conditions, whether at home or abroad. Let's look at one example of how to test economical living as a resident in a foreign country. This is an excellent way to see if you might like it, and to pick up some language skills at the same time.

Let's try $600 a month. In San Jose, Costa Rica, for $600 a month you can enroll in a language school to study Spanish. This money not only includes tuition for a four–hour–a–day class, but also covers room and board with a Costa Rican family, and even your laundry! They'll even pick you up at the airport. See Chapter 20 for details about schools.

Let's talk about expenses for a moment. You don't have to be told what it costs you to live in your home town. You probably grumble about the cost of living, and remember with fondness the days when you needed help to carry $20 worth of groceries out of the supermarket. Things have changed, haven't they? Some people I know think nothing of shelling out over $200 a month to heat their houses in January, and breathe a sigh of relief when summer comes and their air-conditioning energy only costs $150 a month. Many families in Latin America manage to live on less than what my friends pay just to heat or cool their houses. When you consider that a saleswoman in Buenos Aires clears about $142 a month, or a school teacher in Rio de Janeiro around $200, you can see how valuable dollars are down there and how far they can go. Since you are bringing dollars and changing them into local currency, you are in a great position financially.

People in most parts of Latin America will shake their heads in astonishment if you tell them your expenses for maintaining a household, keeping gasoline in your autos (have to have more than one car per family, right?), or putting food on the table. Many Latin American families count themselves fortunate if they earn as much per year as you pay just in income taxes! We're not talking about poor people, we're talking about ordinary middle-class people who live at relatively the same level as middle-class Americans live here. I use the term *relatively* because there are some items we take for granted that are considered luxury items down there; automobiles, for example. An ordinary small car such as a Datsun or Ford might be too expensive for a working-class family, whereas the typical U.S. family needs several cars to survive.

Just for fun, total what it costs to make payments on a couple of autos, to maintain them, and to keep them insured each year. If you're like many North Americans, you are spending a large part of your income just trying to get to work so you can afford to make your car payments. In most parts of Latin America, public transportation is excellent. It has to be, because everyone depends on it. Buses go zipping along every few minutes. Even remote roads back in the provinces have regular bus service. A bus ticket in Buenos Aires costs about a dime and the subway a little more. In Mexico City, a subway is a fraction of a penny. Taxis will take you dozens of blocks for such a low fare that you wonder how they can afford to buy gasoline. The point is, people aren't forced to use private transportation. This leaves more resources to spend on food, clothing and entertainment.

BUT, IS IT SAFE?

Is there crime in Latin America? Of course there is. There has never existed a society without crime. Whenever you have laws, someone is bound to violate them. Is there crime in North America? Don't ask.

An interesting thing happens when I tell someone in Latin America that I am from California. They usually smile and say something like: "Everyone says California is the prettiest part of the United States!" But when they ask what part of California I am from and they hear the answer: "San Francisco," a look of horror sometimes crosses their faces.

"My God," they reply in astonishment, "how can you stand to live in such a dangerous place? Aren't you frightened?"

It turns out that reruns of the TV show "Streets of San Francisco" are very popular on Latin American television, played almost nightly on one TV channel or another with dialogue dubbed in Spanish. People in Latin America (Europe, too) are often surprised to learn that San Francisco is part of California. Many have a vague notion that somewhere in the U.S.A. is a province known as "San Francisco" and it is populated entirely by criminals and victims who chase each other over hills and sidewalks in reckless orgies of murder and mayhem. When I explain that I've lived in the San Francisco area for years without ever seeing a holdup, a shooting or a stabbing--let alone a pickpocketing--they give me an odd look, as if I were covering something up. I explain that while I'm sure things like that happen, it's extremely rare and that I don't personally know anyone who's ever been robbed, or shot or stabbed. When I tell them that I feel as safe on the streets of San Francisco as I do on the streets of Montevideo or Santiago, the reaction is a polite but disbelieving nod of the head.

Don't misunderstand, while some places in Latin America are very safe, there are other places where you must be cautious. The same is true in the United States. Although I've never been molested in New York or Miami, I certainly take more precautions there than I would in Seattle or Phoenix.

Although the travel/retirement spots most highly recommended in this book aren't in areas of extreme poverty, you shouldn't make the mistake that many Americans do, of equating crime with poverty. Criminals rarely rob because they're poor; robbing is simply much easier than working. When you see some humble Indians standing around on the street, they aren't necessarily planning to steal from you. If they were dishonest, they probably wouldn't be poor. In the poor countries you find that the smaller, more close-knit the community, the more family ties there are among the people, and the less crime. Stealing and robbing carries a danger of punishment, but there is no punishment quite as devastating as the wrath of a grandmother, the scorn of your cousins, aunts, uncles and godparents. So smaller communities are always the safest.

In the large cities, where the European traditions of late-night restaurants and entertainment prevail, you will find the streets thronged with people until long after midnight. Restaurants in some large cities don't even open until 10 p.m. and are full until after 4 a.m. You can get valid clues as to the safety of the streets by observing who is out at night. When you see parents and little children strolling along the boulevard at midnight or a crowd of children leaving the movies at 11 p.m. to traverse dark streets toward their homes, then you know that the safety level is quite high. This isn't true in all large cities in Latin America. Some can be quite as scary late at night as some North American cities.

Another interesting thing about crime in most Latin American countries, is that the level of violence is much lower than in the United States. Up here, such crimes as muggings, rapes, armed robberies are appallingly common, while violence in Latin American crime is *not* the norm. There, such crimes as pickpocketing and burglary—crimes where the criminal and victim don't come face-to-face—are the more common transgressions. Fortunately, these are the kinds of crimes that can be avoided simply by taking precautions.

Another factor is our cavalier tolerance of drug dealings and the need for addicts to steal in order to satisfy their habits. Most South American governments are fiercely anti-drug, and quite intolerant of addicts or drug-related crimes. The police can be extremely harsh in their treatment of petty criminals and "street people." The result of these attitudes is a remarkably low level of juvenile delinquency and crime in many countries. The absence of juvenile gangs and graffiti is striking—except for political graffiti, which is accepted almost proudly as evidence of democracy. (In a few countries even political graffiti is still a very serious offense.)

Yes, I do feel safer in most areas of Latin America than I do at home. But without question, there are places down there that are not as safe as home. For example, in cities of Panama, Colombia, Bolivia, Peru or Brazil, I would advise you to keep a wary eye about you. But this is not to say that you should avoid visiting these countries. If you allow fear of all possible disasters to rule your life, you won't go anywhere and you'll not enjoy much out of life. So, keep your wallet in your front pocket and don't carry a purse or bring your good camera. If you take proper care, the worst that can happen is a small loss, which you can afford, and which you can figure as part of the price of a marvelous sight–seeing trip. But be careful! I'm convinced that the life expectancy of a camera left on the front seat of your auto at a tourist spot in the United States isn't any longer than at a similar place in South America. Maybe even shorter, because thieves in the United States seem much bolder, more desperate to me. I'm also convinced that an aware person has little to fear. In more than 30 years of living and traveling in all parts of Latin America, I've *never* had anything stolen.

Later on, this book will tell you how to avoid being a victim of petty thievery.

WHAT ABOUT POLITICS?

What of the political situation? Many interesting political changes (for the better) have occurred recently, and more are probably on the way. There has been a general switch from rigid military governments to democracy in Latin America. After World War II, right–wing coups and military takeovers (often with United States encouragement) toppled one democratic government after another until there were 21 dictatorships and only three democracies in Latin America. Now the tide has turned to the point where the exact opposite is true. Only three or four governments can be called true dictatorships. Suffice to say that a new climate of political stability and economic growth provides an exciting background for today's Latin American life.

Yet, even in the countries where the military still rules, the tourist or the retiree is rarely ever bothered by authorities. That is, unless one meddles in politics. Visitors have no right to become involved in politics, in any country they visit. Until you become a citizen, you have no business telling people how they should live, or what kind of government or economic system they ought to have. The U.S. government does quite enough of that as it is. It's an interesting phenomenon that while the U.S. government is sometimes harshly criticized, its citizens are almost always received warmly.

This shouldn't be surprising, because the same thing occurs in all countries. For example, while many Americans may feel that Russia is "the empire of evil," individual Russian tourists would rarely be treated rudely because of their nationality. Should one stop you on the street to ask directions, chances are you would answer his questions most graciously.

I have definite thoughts about military governments, ideas that have formed from my life in a democracy. Therefore I am ever amazed at how many citizens of South American countries actually like the military. Older people, particularly, tend to miss the stability and enforced calm of a military government. I manage to keep my political opinions to myself unless specifically asked, and even then I'm reluctant to express them.

CHAPTER 3

South America: An Unknown Continent

"Nothing important happens in the Southern Hemisphere," goes the saying among diplomats. After all, the major wars, arms races, saber rattling and threats of mutual destruction, all happen in Europe, the Middle East, North America or Asia. All in the Northern Hemisphere. In the event of a nuclear confrontation, it's going to be the Northern Hemisphere where radioactive fallout will circle the globe on the jet stream. Nothing big ever happens in the Southern Hemisphere. Then, on the other hand, maybe there's something to be said for a continent where they don't fight "world wars" and don't threaten each other with hydrogen bombs and guided missiles. At least, not yet.

Most of the earth's land masses are north of the equator. Most of the industrial nations of the world lie north of the tropic of Cancer. What do we find south of the equator? There's Australia, some small island countries, the smaller portion of Africa and most of South America. Since the bulk of the South American continent stretches far below the equator, we find a vast amount of land in the temperate zone, just as most of inhabited North America is in the temperate zone. For example, Buenos Aires and Santiago are as far south of the equator as Los Angeles is north. This means a similar climate--mild winters and moderate summers. The *pampas* of Uruguay and Argentina have about the same rainfall patterns as Illinois, making them fertile and green with agricultural abundance, but green all year around, with no ice or snow.

As you go north, crossing the tropic of Capricorn and approach the equator, the climate becomes tropical, sometimes hot and steamy. Here, the climate is determined by altitude, with pleasant year–round climates where the elevation is over 4,000 feet (there's a one–degree drop in temperature for every 300 feet of elevation). But even on the equator, at sea level, temperatures often aren't as unbearable as you might imagine. For example, in the Amazon Basin, which is right on the equator, the average temperature is 81 degrees and the highest recorded temperature is just a little under 91 degrees. Warm, muggy perhaps, but a piece of cake compared to Houston or St. Louis summers. Other places, such as Guiana, however, can be *hot* and muggy. Climates and temperatures vary greatly even in the tropics.

Throughout South America, it appears that temperate climates are the ones that attract Americans. Partly because these climes seem most familiar to us, and partly because living conditions seem "safer" than in the lowland tropics. A general rule is that the more tropical the place, the less "civilized" and prosperous it is. That is, poverty and crime rates seem higher in countries with tropical heat and oppressive humidity. Why this is so escapes me. There is also a relationship between democratic governments and higher standards of living. My observation is that the more wealth a country has, the more its citizens want to have control over the government. Democracy, it seems to me, is the inevitable result of prosperity. Feel free to argue the other way around if you so please.

So what does South America have to offer? To answer that question would require a volume in itself, because the land mass is huge and astonishingly varied. For some reason, looking at a map doesn't tell the story of the size of the countries. After traveling in Europe and crossing several frontiers in a single day, it comes as a shock to travelers to realize that what seems like a short trip in South America can end up being a three–day trip by Pullman car.

Dense rain forests of the Mato Grosso grade into forested mountains and high plains and then back down into broad stretches of incredibly rich farmland, South America offers any kind of climate and topography imaginable, from glaciers to jungles to deserts.

The people too, are the most varied to be found anywhere. You can find Jivaro headhunters in the Peruvian–Brazilian jungles, and Welsh farmers in Patagonia. Blacks in the Guianas speak a dialect of West Africa, while Bolivian Indians still use the language of the Incas. The peoples of Argentina are a mixture of Italian, Spanish, German and British. Brazil has influences from Africa, Portugal, and other European countries as well as primitive natives in the Mato Grosso jungles-- natives who fiercely resist the mainstream of Brazil's culture, sometimes with bows and arrows.

This variation in geography, climate and people makes South America a great choice for full or part-time residency and retirement. You may choose your ideal situation. For those interested in starting a new career, opportunities abound. Most South American governments welcome Americans who wish to bring their energies, enthusiasms and know-how to the country. Some offer enticements to make settling in their country attractive. It seems that we North Americans have a reputation as "movers and doers." I recall a conversation not long ago in Argentina in which we were all suggesting possible solutions for some of South America's economic woes. One man suggested, "If we only could rent the country out to the Americans and the Japanese for two years, they'd have things going full blast in no time at all."

What is there in South America? The answer is: Just about anything you have in the United States or Canada, only more of it! There are lakes in Argentina that are just as pretty as any in Maine or Wisconsin. You'll discover cities as modern and cosmopolitan as any in the world, and rustic villages, picturesque and pleasant as you might find in Europe. The marvelous thing about living there is that you have the opportunity to travel on the spur of the moment, to make trips others only dream about. You can visit the Amazonian jungles and in the same week be exploring Inca ruins in Peru. Once you've expended the money to get to South America, the big bite is out of the way; transportation within the continent itself is relatively inexpensive.

WHY SOUTH AMERICA?

I can think of three excellent reasons: One is that living or retiring to South America is affordable; the second is climate; and, finally, the people of South America are decent and friendly. Even if South America weren't such a bargain financially, it would still be a great place to spend at least part of your life each year. Allow me to present the reasons many Americans include South America in their travel and retirement plans.

When it's winter in the United States, when grimy snow and frozen slush cover sidewalks and gutters, a benevolent summer sun shines on South America. Birds sing, flowers bloom, children build sand castles on the beach—while men in Chicago pull heavy overcoats around their throats, trying to escape the cutting wind. Oh, yes, there's that three-week vacation in Cancun or Acapulco for a brief respite from the cold, dark winter, but then it's back to the battle of you and your utility bills against the winter. Winter always wins.

It isn't just a matter of staying warm. There are places—Florida, Arizona, California—where you'll rarely freeze in winter. It's usually warm, often shirt-sleeve weather in the middle of the day, but it's still winter. It's dark until after breakfast and the sun goes down early, disappearing into darkness and winter's gloom by five o'clock in the afternoon. Why do depression and suicides peak during the Christmas season? Some scientists maintain that the long, dark nights of winter and brief hours of daylight tend to upset the biological clock in some people, causing chemical imbalance in the bloodstream. Depression, gloom and lethargy is the result. The explanation is that the body secretes a hormone known as melatonin during periods of darkness, and this hormone is known to cause emotional changes in many people. The most recent medical term for this condition is Sunlight Affective Disorder (appropriately shortened to "SAD").

During my days as a graduate student in anthropology, I became convinced that mankind originated in the tropics, where it was not necessary to grow a fur coat, and where sunshine gets equal billing with darkness. So, it comes as no surprise to me that some of the highest suicide rates in the world are in the countries of the far north, such as Norway, Sweden and Russia. There, tropics-evolved human beings are forced to adapt to the frozen, dark nights. Haven't you noticed how much happier and exuberant people are during the summer?

TWO SUMMERS A YEAR

In the Southern Hemisphere seasons are the reverse of ours. When you leave dead winter in Minneapolis and fly to Buenos Aires, you suddenly find yourself in the middle of summer! You can feel it the moment you step off the airplane. People step briskly with exhilaration at being alive on such a nice day. They smile for no reason other than that it's summer. As you walk out into the balmy summer air and hear birds singing, see trees blooming and butterflies flitting about joyfully, you know the difference between just being warm and being in summer.

Are you one of those people who spend the winter wondering if spring is ever going to arrive? How many summers do you have left in *your* life? Count them, and then figure that for every delightful June and July you have coming to you, you also have a frigid December and January to suffer through. Suppose you could trade a December for an extra June this year, wouldn't it make good sense to do it? Give up a January and a February out of your life in return for an extra July and August? Don't you feel that you owe it to yourself? I do.

You can enjoy two summers a year, simply by incorporating South America into your retirement or long-term travel plans. You could also do it by going to South Africa, New Zealand or Australia, which are also south of the equator and have reversed seasons. But South Africa? I should think not under present circumstances. Australia or New Zealand? It's expensive getting there, the cost of living is higher than in South America, and there are age restrictions on immigration and retirement.

HOW MUCH INCOME WILL I NEED?

From the statistical data taken from studies by the United Nations and the Bank of Switzerland plus queries and interviews by the author, we find that the average middle-class family in Montevideo earns about $415 per month after taxes. In Buenos Aires, the standard wage for a bank teller would be about $500 a month; for a school teacher, about $233. A family in Rio de Janeiro feels comfortable with an income of $400, and could possibly afford a servant on that salary; part time, anyway. In the United States or Canada, you wouldn't even reach the lower rungs of poverty levels on that kind of money.

A modest house in Mendoza, Argentina—two bedroom, two baths and a garage—will sell for $15,000. Or you could rent it for only $150 a month. A luxury villa on the "South American Riviera" at Punta del Este might cost you $40,000, but you couldn't buy anything similar up here for less than $800,000! Or a luxury apartment can be yours for about $600 per month, an ordinary one much less.

How much you need to live in South America depends on your lifestyle and how you go about it. Of course you could do it on a minimal income, say, $200 a month. Many families do, you know. But, although this lifestyle is comfortable for the local people, Americans would find it a bit humdrum. They need stimulation, frequent trips to the beach, to the mountains, to the cities. On $200 a month, you would have to do all of your cooking at home, wash your laundry by hand and hang it in the backyard to dry You'd have to raise chickens and plant a garden to supplement the food budget. That's not exactly the lifestyle I'm looking for, how about you?

FOUR TO SIX HUNDRED DOLLARS A MONTH

From the research I've conducted, through surveys and interviews, I find that most respondents agree that $400 a month is the absolute minimum figure a couple would need to live comfortably in such urban areas as Montevideo, Buenos Aires or Santiago. This amount would just barely get you by. Let's add a couple of hundred dollars to this for safety. On $600 you can afford to eat out a couple of times a week, and possibly afford someone to do part–time cleaning of your apartment. However, you certainly shouldn't think about travel/retirement if you don't have a "cushion" to back you up. Emergencies happen abroad just as they happen at home, and you ought to be prepared for anything.

These figures are based on renting an apartment for $125 to $150, about average for cities like Buenos Aires, Montevideo, or Santiago. Food bills and household expenses shouldn't go over $200 a month. A meal for two in a typical restaurant, with soup, salad, wine and dessert will set you back around $6––maybe $4 in an economical restaurant or $10 in a more elegant establishment. Bus and train transportation is reasonable. Taxis are cheap, auto rentals reasonable. Some countries, such as Venezuela, are higher–priced; these figures don't apply there.

Yet, it must be stressed that conditions change. Politicians could begin manipulating money supplies and currency, which could alter the economic advantages of the U.S. dollar. I don't see this happening in the near future, but you must keep on top of exchange rates and trends.

GETTING THERE

An important item is the cost of getting there. This must be amortized over the length of your stay. From the West Coast, the cheapest round–trip air fare to Buenos Aires, that I'm aware of, is about $800. From the East Coast, a bit less. Transportation costs must be considered in figuring your monthly expense. Airline specials come up often; watch the Sunday travel sections of the larger newspapers for bargain fares.

For a stay of three months, the cost of, let's say, a $600 ticket adds another $200 per month to your retirement or vacation budget. If you are starting from a base of $400 to $600 a month, and add the $200, you are only talking $600 or $800 a month. That's still cheap. Eight hundred dollars barely rents an apartment on my block.

I urge that you add a safety factor in your finances, and maintain $200 a month over and above your estimated costs, for emergencies, for luxuries. Should $600 or $800 a month seem steep, you might consider purchasing our book CHOOSE MEXICO, RETIREMENT LIVING ON $400 A MONTH (Gateway Books, San Francisco). If $400 seems steep, well . . . maybe you should hang on to your job for a while longer.

Living in South America clearly is not for everyone. For one thing, you will need a higher degree of fluency in Spanish than you might in other parts of Latin America. For another, you would be faced with winter months there during June, July and August. (Not harsh winters, no worse than California or Florida, but winters nonetheless.) And finally, Americans tend to become homesick, most need to return home for a "culture fix" from time to time. It's a long way from home.

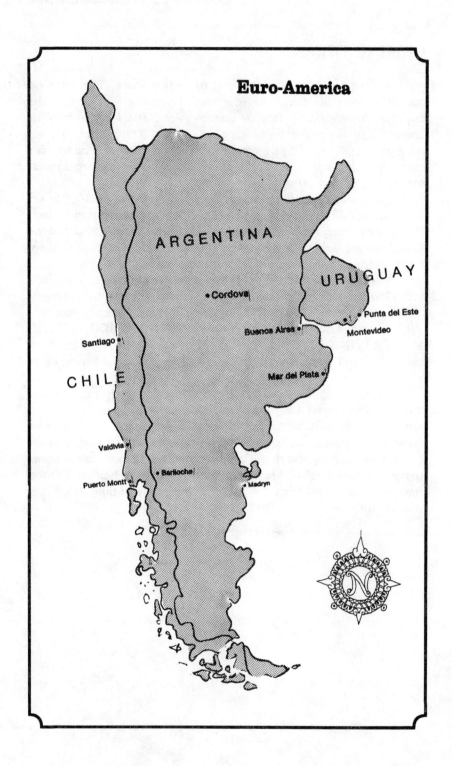

CHAPTER 4

Euro-America

Although South America is a huge continent, it isn't a single, accessible landmass like North America. The United States and Canada have little in the way of natural barriers to impede communications and transportation. Up here, you can jump into your family station wagon and drive almost anywhere you please, from Alaska to Panama, from the Atlantic to the Pacific. Trains and buses can take you almost anywhere you might want to go. Not so South America.

It isn't simply a matter of technology, since road building techniques are rather basic, requiring minimal equipment that's available almost anywhere. Obviously, road construction technology in South America isn't any less advanced than that in Panama, Guatemala or El Salvador. The problem is that there are physical barriers, plus subtle political and cultural barriers that have the effect of stopping communications. A few years ago, radio and television were astounding technological developments, yet today they are so commonplace that almost anywhere you travel in North or South America, you find TV antennas sprouting from even the most dismal hovel, and satellite dishes generously scattered about. Electronic communication technology may be mysterious, but it is also ubiquitous.

The dream of easy access between the continents suddenly halts at the Darien Gap in eastern Panama. An impassable, swampy jungle stops all but the most intrepid from entering South America from the north. A few years ago some 4–wheel drives pushed across the gap in a daring publicity stunt, but at the cost of millions of dollars and several lives. The stunt has probably been repeated since, but certainly as an adventure and not as a regular route. Except by airplane, travel from Panama to Colombia requires an ocean voyage. Once you land in Colombia you have but three paved exit roads out of the country: one which makes its torturous way into Ecuador; and two that enter Venezuela. No paved roads leave east or south from Venezuela to enter the rest of South America. Just that one highway connects Colombia, Venezuela and Ecuador with the rest of the continent. That's isolation.

As you travel south, your movements are limited by some rather formidable barriers. Swampy river basins, impenetrable, almost unexplored jungles and bone-dry deserts, all combine to isolate one section of South America from another. The majestic Andes range the 4,000-mile length of the continent with very few passes permitting east-west travel. Even within some countries, travel is quite difficult. For example, I've met many Americans who've traveled the Amazon River as tourists, but I've yet to encounter a resident of Rio or Sao Paulo who even thinks about visiting that part of his country.

Other reasons for the cultural differences between sections of South America can be found in historical events. Shortly after the European discovery of the Americas, the pope intervened between Spain and Portugal and mediated a division of the new lands. This brought the Portuguese into the picture, with their different language, and their practice of using African slaves. Then, wave after wave of settlers crossed the ocean, fleeing historical developments such as war, economic disaster, and industrial chaos in Europe. As these newcomers settled in, barriers of geography, politics and language prevented ideas and customs from spreading from one place to another. Each population developed its own ways of living isolated from and little influenced by next-door neighbors.

These natural and cultural barriers delineate the three divisions of South America that I call Indo-America, Afro-America and Euro-America. In each division you find distinct differences in economic systems, racial make-up, food, philosophy, world views, sometimes language. Each division has its own advantages and disadvantages for an American who might wish to live there.

EURO-AMERICA

The southern part of South America, or Euro-America, consists of the countries of Uruguay, Argentina and Chile. These three
countries are insulated from the north by swamps, deserts, rivers or
jungles. While the geographical barriers between Uruguay and Brazil
are not that great, language and cultural differences are. Even though
the Andes physically separate Chile from Argentina, the history and
settlement patterns of these two countries are similar, making Chile
almost as European as Argentina and Uruguay.

Perhaps the most important reason Euro-America developed
differently from the rest of South America is the time frame of its
development. That is, all three countries experienced heavy European immigration at the same period of history, centuries after the
rest of the continent had already been settled. Because of the timing
and the circumstances of this immigration, all three countries developed pretty much the same ways of behaving and thinking. The customs and values the newcomers brought with them were those of 19th
Century Europe. Notions of equality, democracy and the work ethic
of the industrial revolution contrasted sharply with traditions in countries of South America which were settled 300 or 400 years earlier.
There, a world view consistent with medieval Spain or Portugal is
pervasive, where a feudal, elite society tends to be the political and
economic force. None of this is to say that there aren't very European sections in other countries, or that there aren't any Native
Americans in Euro-America. But by and large, you'll find a 19th and
20th century European outlook dominant in the south of the continent.

Euro-America can be best explained by reviewing a bit of history. Almost 500 years ago, when Spain began colonizing the "New
World", the big interest was minerals, particularly gold, silver and
precious stones. At that time, Spain was basically a feudal, agrarian
nation. It didn't need to import food, so it didn't make sense to
develop an export agricultural base in South America. Gold and silver were the names of the game. Argentina and Uruguay seemed to
have little to offer in the way of minerals of any kind, so Spanish
settlers quickly turned up their noses at these rich but useless agricultural lands. Chile offered rich deposits of copper, and these were
mined fairly early. But copper had little demand compared to the
rich deposits of gold and silver in Peru, Bolivia, Colombia and Mexico. So Spanish colonists ignored the southern part of South Amer-

ica, heading instead for the easy pickings of Indo–America and Middle–America––anywhere gold and silver could be extracted easily from the earth.

Other good reasons reason for ignoring Uruguay, Argentina and Chile were the fierce indigenous tribes who defended their lands from the Spanish with surprising skill and vigor. This helped convince the Spanish that these lands weren't all that great for settlement in the first place. Indians in Peru, Bolivia and Ecuador were much easier to manipulate. In Uruguay, the Indians valiantly fought off Europeans for over 200 years. It wasn't until the 1700s that Spanish managed to plant a colony there with some degree of safety.

In Chile and Argentina, Indian wars continued up until the late 19th Century, when the military succeeded in destroying the Indians during the "Campaign of the Desert" from 1879 to 1883. This "War of Extermination," as it was also known, was so successful that today you find practically no influence of Native America in Euro–America. Lest we become hypocritical about this tragic racial injustice, we should remember that during this same period in the United States, our armies were busily exterminating our own Native Americans to make room for *our* white, European settlers. Cochise, Geronimo, Chief Joseph, and Sitting Bull were doing their best, but modern technology won out in North America as well as South America. Although we didn't quite succeed in slaughtering all our Indians, It was not that we didn't give it a try. We managed to herd the survivors onto wastelands and killed those who tried to escape. This effectively kept the Native Americans out of our gene pool and off of the good farming lands.

There are very few blacks in Euro–America, in contrast with Afro–America and Indo–America. The reason for this is that the earliest settlers neither owned nor needed slaves. For slavery to be practical, you need labor–intensive agricultural projects like sugar cane or cotton, the kind of work that makes slave labor profitable. Cattle production, and later grain, didn't require so many workers; maintaining slaves would have been non–productive. The occasional black you see in Euro–America is usually an immigrant from Brazil or Peru.

For almost 300 years after it was settled, Buenos Aires––today the largest city of Euro–America––remained little more than a military garrison and a smuggling port. Spain prohibited the colony from overseas trade. Then, with independence from Spain in 1816, trade restrictions were lifted and a new era began. About that time in

Europe, the consequences of the Industrial Revolution and the accompanying social problems began putting pressures on the populations there. Displaced workers and farmers began emigrating, anywhere they could. Of course, the preferred countries were in the New World, where land was plentiful and chances for a new start in life were possible. At the same time, a world market for wheat and cattle developed, while new shipping technology made it practical to ship food to a newly industrialized Europe.

The people fleeing Europe came mostly from Italy, Spain, Germany, Yugoslavia, Holland and England; all European countries were sending their excess population to the New World. The United States and Canada were the goals of most. But of course, when these emigrants heard of the richness of Argentina, Uruguay and Chile, cheap land and a chance to become wealthy, many of them detoured south. Italy contributed by far the most immigrants, followed by Spain, Portugal, Germany and other southern European nations. British settlers were also interested in cattle and agriculture, and even a share of North Americans relocated as farmers, technicians and business executives. The only British community in the world outside the Commonwealth that is larger than the one in Buenos Aires is in South Africa.

The countries I call Euro–America are almost totally European, both culturally and racially. Although they speak Spanish as national languages, the culture is less that of Spain than a melange of southern European ideas and customs. There are places in Euro–America where Italian is the second language. British colonists hold onto their language, and there are areas where German is spoken extensively.

CHAPTER 5

Argentina: The Cultured Giant

There is a good–sized Argentinian community living in Los Angeles, and another in New York. An interesting thing about those Argentinians who emigrate to the United States is that they are almost always successful in business or in their jobs. For foreigners, they seem to adapt unusually well to our system and soon find their way into the better neighborhoods and are seen driving expensive automobiles. If you ask them what they like best about the United States, they will almost always reply: "The United States is so much like Argentina that I feel perfectly at home."

They particularly adore Los Angeles because the climate is almost identical to that of Buenos Aires. The main difference is that Los Angeles and other parts of California receive practically no rain in the summer time, whereas Argentina gets a normal share, enough to keep the countryside looking green and pretty year round. And it should be noted that there is never a wisp of smog in the crystal–clear air of Buenos Aires. (In Spanish *Buenos Aires* actually means "good breezes.")

Argentina is like California in several other ways. It is geographically similar in that both are long and proportionally narrow, encompassing climates from the near tropical to permanent snow on the higher peaks. And of course, skiing and winter sports are excellent in both places. Both have beautiful mountain ranges with thick forests and deep–blue lakes contrasting with stretches of desert and hundreds of miles of uncrowded beaches. Both have vast extents of rich farming land as well as cosmopolitan cities. Argentina has all of this, but some things on a much grander scale. Argentina is huge.

The eighth largest country in the world in square miles (1.07 million square miles), Argentina ranges from subarctic Patagonia to the tropical forests of the Chaco. Imagine for a moment that you could superimpose Argentina in an analogous position in the northern hemisphere. One end would start about where Puerto Vallarta is in Mexico and the other end would stretch all the way to Alaska. You can understand why the climates are varied.

Now, California is a large state. It is three–fourths the size of France, and almost 2.5 times the size of England. Yet you could put *six* hunks of land the size of California into Argentina's borders, with room left over for Indiana, Illinois and more. California is one of the richest pieces of real estate anywhere when it comes to agriculture, but it pales in comparison with the enormous potential productivity of Argentina, with its millions of acres of rich Pampas soil, most of it uncultivated. It's often said, without too much exaggeration, that Argentina could feed the whole world if all of its farmland were put into production.

Yet, despite the fact that Argentina is more than six times the size of California, despite all its untapped resources, Argentina has almost the same population as California! Very uncrowded. People down there say, "One of the problems here is underpopulation. If only we could get more immigration, put the Pampas into full production..." How strange this sounds to ears that have been used to hearing gloom and doom of over–population!

With fewer than 30 million people for this huge country, almost half of them choose to live in Buenos Aires and its environs. This leaves the rest of the country *really* unpopulated.

What is it then, according to Argentinians, that makes Argentina so much like the United States? Several things. One is the high standard of living. The working man in Buenos Aires lives pretty much like his counterpart in the United States or Canada, with excellent health care and educational opportunities, in some ways superior to that available in the United States The cities are clean, modern, but unlike the United States, enjoy excellent public transportation. The small towns, for the most part, remind one of small towns in the U.S.A., particularly California or Oregon. All of this comes as a surprise to travelers who expect exotic, picturesque villages as in Mexico or Brazil. A North American would have no problem adjusting to either city or country living in Argentina. The major lifestyle difference is that a middle–class family seldom owns a second or third automobile. On the plus side, they aren't oppressed by additional car payments, or insurance premiums, or gasoline bills, or repairs, or teenagers collecting tickets and crumpled fenders. With excellent public transportation systems, they don't need these things.

Another similarity between Argentina and North America is the physical composition of the people. Eighty percent of the U.S. population is of European descent. An even higher percentage of Canada's peoples are European. But, in Argentina, European influence is even higher than in the the United States or Canada. In fact, only 3 percent of all Argentinians are *not* European. This 3 percent is divided among Asian, African, Arabian and Native American. When you see a brown face on the streets of Buenos Aires, you can make a good guess that it belongs to a tourist or a foreign worker. Since there are practically no minorities, it isn't surprising that racial prejudice is lacking. Racially different people are seen as exotic or curious, not as objects of animosity, fear and suspicion as is too often the case in the United States.

This European construct is interesting in another way: The majority of Argentinians are Italian. Italian influence almost overwhelms the Spanish in some areas, and many children learn to speak Italian in the home before they learn Spanish. Italian food is standard restaurant fare, with pastas replacing potatoes, and table wines are routinely served with meals. Music, slang, clothing, surnames, and some architectural styles are overtly Italian. Germany and England are also heavily represented. These two countries have contributed their blond, blue–eye genes to Argentina as well as their unique architectural styles. You commonly see a house which looks as if it belongs in the Black Forest sitting comfortably between a cottage from Wales and a glass–and–steel ultramodern out of Barcelona. Fortunately, neither Germany nor Britain has contributed much in the way of their remarkably unremarkable cuisine. On the other hand, because of the lack of ethnic diversity, good oriental and non–European restaurants are almost non–existent.

In the south of Argentina, you find towns with such unlikely names as *Rawson*, *Madryn* and *Trelew*. Don't sound Spanish, do they? Actually, they're Welsh. This part of Argentina was settled by immigrants from Wales in the late 1800s. To this day, some people there still speak Welsh. Most homes wouldn't look out of place in the more modern parts of Wales, nor would these Argentine citizens look unusual on the streets of Swansea or Cardiff.

In the Andean region around Bariloche, there is so much German, French, Italian and English spoken, and the architecture is so Alpine, that it's easy to imagine that you're in Switzerland. Precisely trimmed landscaping, spotless streets, Swiss chocolate shops and restaurants with steep–peaked roofs, mountain chalets, and snow–covered crags in the background, all contribute to this impression of Swiss Alps. The restaurant menus bring you back to Argentina, however, with their *parilladas* of juicy porterhouse, Italian sausages, chops and kidney, served with generous portions of pasta al pesto and delicate Chilean wines.

MILITARY GOVERNMENT AND DEMOCRACY

When people hear the word "Argentina" they often receive a flash impression of military dictatorships, fascist demigods, and political repression. We've seen the play "Evita," watched TV specials on Juan and Eva Peron, read newspaper and magazine accounts of Juan Peron's activists and the excesses they committed back in the 1940s and 1950s. Our media reported with much horror (and some exaggeration) all of the terrible things that happened under Peron.

The U.S. government disapproved of the Peron administration and did everything it could to make things uncomfortable for it. They hated it when he returned from exile in 1973 to take over the country after some years of turmoil. But Peron had little chance to prove himself because he died after only nine months in power. Anarchy broke loose in Argentina, to the point where many were relieved when the military finally resumed power. Thus began an era of suppression of democracy and human rights that received Uncle Sam's tacit approval and overt aid for eight years. We congratulated the military usurpers, sent them millions in military assistance, and lent them economic and social experts to try and make the dictatorship succeed. The military fell under the impression that anything it did would have our approval, and assumed that we would at least remain neutral in its move to take over the Malvina Islands (Falklands) by force in 1982. This was a fatal mistake. The military announced, through state controlled news and television, that Britain had attacked Argentina for no reason, and that the country was forced to fight back. Suddenly, to their horror, they realized that the people of the United States would never support them against Britain. But it was too late. Britain took full advantage of our satellite intelligence and refueling stations to help it to a comparatively speedy victory. Without our help, it's doubtful if the British could have won, certainly not without a long, drawn out war of attrition.

When the citizens of Argentina discovered the truth about the tragic war, they finally stood up to the military, took back their country and eventually put the generals on trial. Some of the top officers of the former dictatorship are now serving prison terms.

Argentinians learned a lot from this experience. Today, they are determined to take politics away from the military and to give civilians total control. They elected a brave and honest president who has performed some rather heroic deeds in gaining the upper hand for democracy. He retired hundreds of generals and ranking officers, and put the armed forces into the hands of loyal, non-political, professional soldiers. He prosecuted the officers who led the repression of political dissidents and those who bungled the Malvinas war. President Alfonsin gained the respect of even those who voted against him, and appears to be on his way to outstanding success. My firm belief is that Argentina will never again accept the military dictatorship route.

But, what was it like living under the military? How would it affect, let's say, an American who was living there, or who owned a business there?

As an average American, I detest the idea of a dictatorship of any sort, right-wing or left-wing, so I have to admit surprise at the reaction of the people who went through it. Many, particularly older folks and the well-to-do, actually thought the dictatorship was a good idea! "It was very calm," they explain, "I felt very safe when there were soldiers on the street corners with their guns. No crime." And finally, many people felt that the alternative was worse than a military government. As one Argentinian put it, "We don't care what kind of government we have, as long as we have a strong leader. But it's nice to be able to change the leader when we aren't satisfied; that's where the military government failed, it didn't allow for change."

Evidently, the military kept a fairly low financial profile while it engaged in other excesses. This was easy to do, since it controlled the press and airwaves. From what I can tell, corruption in the military wasn't blatant as is the case with some other Latin American nations, and the military didn't get involved too deeply in actually running the government (this was left to civilian ministers). Law and order seemed to be the primary interest of the military, plus suppression of dissent, which it did with a vengeance during the early part of the regime.

The answer to the question of what was it like living there is that while most people didn't like the notion of a non–democratic government, most of them were also relieved to be rid of the nuisance of the terrorists. Bombings, robberies and kidnappings had become so commonplace that a trade–off between security and freedom seemed reasonable to a majority. I would suspect that many "law and order" Americans would have felt very comfortable there. However, I refused to even visit the country until democracy was restored. I feel pretty good about it now.

To better understand the Argentina of today, it might serve us well to discuss the Juan and Eva Peron years. Peron came to power (in an election, not a coup) during the closing days of World War II. It was a dramatic period of economic growth. Argentina was in an enviable position as a food producer for warring nations, and the country was riding the crest of a wave. Peron took advantage of this economic boom and of his personal popularity with the workers to launch the country into some rather dramatic social experiments.

Peron, encouraged by Eva Duarte Peron, pushed on boldly. But he was opposed by the military, by the Catholic church, by business and industrial interests, by the large agricultural families, by the wealthy and near–wealthy, by the news media, and by the government of the United States. His only real support came was from labor unions. They were in the majority and Juan and Eva knew how to get their votes. At Evita's urging, Peron granted women the right to vote, thus ensuring majorities at all elections. Next, factories, railroads and businesses were taken over by the government. Inefficiency and corruption became legion. Employees, protected by strict labor laws that made it practically impossible to fire them, began to loaf on the job. Farms and ranches were taxed heavily, until the cost of doing business cut into their competitive position in world markets. Still, the working classes loved the Perons because their lot became better, while the upper classes grew poorer.

Today in Argentina, you find few who are neutral on the subject of Peronism. Either there is a love or a hate expressed when the subject arises.

What is left to Argentina in the aftermath of the Peron years is positive: good schools, fine medical care for all, a prosperous working class which aspires to become middle class, and practically no poverty. Unions are still very influential there, still very political, yet lack the notorious corruption that characterize union movements in many Latin American countries. They still accomplish many of their goals through legislation rather than negotiation, but the years of military oppression and the voters' memories of labor excesses have cut into the unions' power considerably. This became obvious in the first elections held after the military retired. Workers deserted the Peronist party and voted for middle–of–the–road candidate Alfonsin. The truth is that the Argentine worker, like his American counter-part, thinks in terms of social mobility and considers himself only temporarily a worker. With a little luck he could move up to the upper classes. As in the United States, the opportunities are there.

The absolute standard of living is probably higher in Argentina than any other country in the Western Hemisphere with the excep-tions of Canada and the United States. Taking into consideration the decaying cities, growing ghettos and sectional poverty in the United States––Argentina might possibly have a higher overall standard of living than the United States. I have no statistics to support this; it's simply my impression based on many months of observation and talk-ing to people. No matter what, Argentina is certainly a place where North Americans can feel comfortable.

The Argentina of 45 years ago kept plenty of bad company among world governments: Nazi Germany, Fascist Italy and Falangist Spain as well as other nations under iron–fisted governments. Yet today, Spain, Germany and Italy are models of democracy and stabil-ity. Argentina has joined the democracies of the world and it too, is a pleasant place to visit and in which to live.

WHAT DOES IT COST TO LIVE IN ARGENTINA?

It's essential to understand that in any country, the cost of liv-ing can vary enormously, depending on who is managing the econ-omy and how. This is particularly true of Latin American countries. A few years ago, before triple–digit inflation and devaluation, it would have been prohibitive to spend more than a week or two visit-ing Argentina. The peso was held at 10 to the dollar, making it highly overvalued. Dollars were so cheap that Argentinians routinely flew to the United States for their vacations because it was much cheaper to shop and have a good time in Florida than go to Mar del Plata (the Argentinian version of Miami Beach). But once the government let the peso float to its true value, the dollar skyrocketed in value and the peso plummeted. Prices for those who held dollars fell to an astounding, almost embarrassing low.

It's possible, although not probable, that the reverse can happen in the future. For this reason, anyone living or investing in Argentina should keep a sharp eye on the currency trends. See the chapter on inflation to learn how to protect your capital and how to take advantage of these trends. Remember that for every loser in currency fluctuations, there is a winner. Having one foot in a foreign country and the other in the United States or Canada gives you a tremendous advantage in this respect.

REPRESENTATIVE WAGES AND PRICES

The following figures were obtained by personal observation during 1985 and 1986 in Argentina, through interviews and surveys conducted in the country and by statistical information found in the publications of the United Nations and from the Union Bank of Switzerland.

The people interviewed almost without exception agreed that it would be a joy to have $600 a month to spend on living. The average family has about $375 a month of spendable income, so you can see that anything over that puts you in an enviable position. Listed below is a table of wages for various occupations, to give you an idea of what the people earn, and where you would be on their scale of wealth.

Bank teller .... $300–$500
School teacher .... $150–$250
Contractor .... $500–$1,000
Plumber .... $450–$800
Policeman .... $250–$300
Gardener $150
Salesman .... $250–$300
Factory worker $200
Minimum wage .... $ 68
(take–home pay, monthly)

Listed below are some random prices from Buenos Aires. Costs will be a bit less in the provinces, perhaps a little higher in Mar del Plata.

Double room with bath in clean, modest hotel
(equivalent cost in U.S. $35) .... $10–$15

Rent two bedroom apartment in middle–class neighborhood, walking distance to bus line and shopping
.... 150–$200 month.

Purchase two bedroom apartment in above average
middle–class neighborhood, walking distance to good
transportation and shopping $15,000

Transportation:

Bus fare for trips up to 5 miles .... 10¢
Subway fare .... 15¢
Taxi trip of 15 minutes $1.50

Food and Grocery shopping:

Meal in an average restaurant ...... $3.00–$6.00
Tomatoes, lb. .... $ .50
Potatoes, lb. .... $ .50
Zucchini, lb. .... $ .25
Lettuce, head .... $ .10
T–bone steak, lb. .... $ .90
Lamb chops, lb. .... $ .50
Filet of sole, lb. .... $ .60
Chicken, lb. .... $ .60
Beer, 12 oz. .... $ .20
Table wine, liter .... $ .40
French bread, 2–lb.loaf .... $ .24
Provolone cheese .... $ .80
Average monthly food bill for
family of three $150–200
Average monthly wage for a maid
(8 hrs a day) $100
Average utility bills for
family of three .... $ 20

Clothing:

First–quality shoes
of Argentine leather .... $20–$30
Top–quality men's suit
or sport coat and slacks .... $60–$100
Woman's dress suit
or cocktail dress .... $30–$60

Medical care:

Doctor's office visit $8
Home visit $10
Hospital stay, per day $30
Cost of appendectomy $150
Dentist bill for cleaning teeth,
X–ray $10

CHAPTER 6

Where Americans Live in Argentina

According to the latest report from U.S. Foreign Service posts, there are over 7,000 U.S. citizens living in Argentina. Certainly, there are many more British than that, plus an unknown number of Canadians who work and live there. Unlike some Latin American countries, it is perfectly all right to work in Argentina once you obtain your residency papers. Of course the 7,000 figure probably doesn't take into consideration the number of U.S. citizens who are not actually residents, but who spend the 90 permissible days in Argentina as tourists and then either fly home or go across the river to Montevideo for a few days and then return for another 90 days. (Tourist visas are good for four years with multiple entries.)

There are several excellent choices for pleasant living in Argentina, depending on whether you prefer the stimulation of the city, the glamour of a beach resort, the quiet isolation of the country or the brisk air of a ski resort. Big towns, small towns, country--they're all there for you to choose.

BUENOS AIRES

Buenos Aires is often called "the Paris of South America," and for good reason. Much of Buenos Aires, particularly the older sections, do resemble Paris: buildings with wrought–iron balconies, tree–lined streets, broad boulevards and parks--all contribute to a sense of old–fashioned elegance. Very European, very cosmopolitan. However, the inevitable modern glass–and–steel buildings have a way of slipping in among the older architecture, imposing a sense of "progress" and reminding one that this is indeed a bustling city. Buenos Aires also has much of the excitement of Paris. There are hundreds of sidewalk cafes, elegant shops, smartly dressed women strolling the avenues in the latest European fashions and sophisticated businessmen hurrying about with briefcases under their arms.

Yet there is a significant difference between Paris and Buenos Aires, as far as I am concerned. The difference is the exuberant friendliness of "Portenos" contrasted with the cool, almost haughty reserve of Parisians. While I have never been treated rudely in Paris, I've not been overwhelmed with friendliness either. But in Buenos Aires, just stop someone on the street to ask for directions, and you will think it is his single mission in life either to answer your question or stop someone else until your problem can be solved. You might end up with three or four people waving their hands in animated debate over what is the best way for you to find whatever you're looking for. Like as not they'll accompany you to make sure you don't get lost. In Paris, a request for directions is usually answered with vague shrug. When someone there offers to go with me, I suspect a sting in the offing.

Another difference is that most Parisians are understandably tired of tourists. They are underfoot continually––crowding restaurants, cafes and shops, and generally making nuisances of themselves––upsetting the precisely balanced French sense of order. But in Buenos Aires, tourists are rare curiosities. Besides, a coolly balanced sense of order is definitely not the Argentinian way! One gets the impression that Argentinians love confusion, that their Italian heritage demands excitement and stimulation. You notice this immediately in restaurants, where the noise level is extraordinarily high, with people conversing at full volume, laughing and enjoying dinner to the fullest. In Parisian restaurants, people seem to whisper, as if continually discussing something shameful. Parisian waiters stand about like haughty robots, noses in the air, separated from their customers by a wall of professional reserve. In Buenos Aires the waiters are part of the scene, talking loudly, joking with customers, sometimes joining in animated conversations and political discussions at the tables they are serving. (According to the record book, the last time a Parisian waiter was known to have smiled was in June 1973 when a customer from Omaha poured catsup over his *cordon bleu.*

The waiter was severely reprimanded and drummed out of the waiter's union that very day.)

It has been said that there is no such thing as a bad restaurant in Buenos Aires, and I believe it. The only complaint that I can make is that the portions are much too large and impossible to finish, although I manage somehow. It's a city of 24–hour activity, with many of the better restaurants not opening until 10 p.m. and remaining packed until dawn. The streets seem to be alive with people at any hour of the day or night. A big puzzle for me is trying to figure out when they ever sleep. I've been invited to people's homes for dinner at 9:30 p.m. (the customary hour when dining at home), but dinner seldom hits the table until 11 p.m. Then, after a typical leisurely meal, ending with champagne and French pastries, the children go out to play in the park while the dinner guests sit around and discuss politics and the current economic situation. Often dinner parties last until two o'clock in the morning! (Yes, children are permitted to play outside after dark, just as we were when I was a child. It's that safe.)

Buenos Aires has much of the excitement of New York when it comes to restaurants and theaters. Theaters dot the avenues and are very popular, with the latest stage plays from London and New York translated into Spanish and many local playwrights presenting their works. There may be more theaters in Buenos Aires per capita, than anywhere in the world.

POLLUTION AND CRIME

A big plus is that, despite being one of the world's largest cities (12 million people, including suburbs), Buenos Aires has very low levels of two problems that plague most large cities: pollution and crime. One reason for the clear skies is a constant breeze that sweeps across the pampas and the enormously wide Rio de la Plata to scour the city clean. Another reason is that excellent public transportation tempts people to keep their automobiles at home, leaving the streets to buses and taxis. For a large town, it is the easiest I've seen to drive in, mostly because of the low numbers of private automobiles in daily use. True, the taxi drivers get paid by the trip, and therefore drive like taxis anywhere in the world, yet they know what they are doing and manage to avoid accidents and slow–witted drivers like me.

The question why the city has such a low crime rate is an interesting one. Some say that Buenos Aires has never had a high rate of crime, while others claim that the years of military occupation reduced the number of criminals and dissuaded others from choosing crime as a career. My belief is that traditionally strong Argentinian family ties have a great effect on delinquency and crime. Whatever the reason, one feels remarkably secure almost anywhere in the city, day or night. Parents think nothing of letting children to walk to and from neighborhood movies, returning home well after dark, or to let them play outside after nightfall. Something that impresses me as a barometer of respect for private property is the number of bicycles I have seen left leaning against a wall or lamppost in downtown Buenos Aires without being locked. Outside of the city, almost no one bothers to lock up a bicycle. This is interesting because an unlocked bike in some U.S. cities would have a new owner in about 12 minutes or less.

Don't get the wrong idea, there *is* crime in Buenos Aires. No society in the world manages to be crime free. It's just that the level of crime in Buenos Aires is extraordinarily low for a large city. Buenos Aires gives me a secure feeling that I don't find in many U.S. cities, and certainly not in some Latin American cities, such as Lima or Rio.

BUENOS AIRES, THE CITY

While parts of Buenos Aires retain a Paris–like charm, other parts are being modernized with steel–and–glass buildings. What seem to me to be beautiful, gracious old buildings from the Victorian age are ruthlessly destroyed to make room for the sleek and modern. Not that the result isn't pleasant, it's just that I have a reverence for the old, and am quick to criticize the Argentinians for not sharing this reverence. But it's all a matter of perspective. To people with roots in Italy, England or Spain, where a building isn't really considered "old" or "historic" unless it was built at least 500 years ago, something only 100 years old isn't really old, it's simply old-fashioned. Since the country was largely unsettled until the turn of this century, there are almost no traces of colonial architecture. So from the Argentinian's viewpoint, a building from the 1890s, with its fancy turrets and balconies, and other gew–gaws, is simply garish, tasteless and ugly. It's not old enough to be historical. A cleanly designed modern apartment building is much preferable, to their way of thinking.

Happily, the center of Buenos Aries hasn't fallen victim to urban decay or urban renewal as have the cores of most American cities. In North America we've all but abandoned our downtown areas in favor of huge shopping complexes in the suburbs. We cannot conceive of "going shopping" without taking our automobiles. Convenience of parking and the speed with which we can complete our tasks become more important than selection or quality of the merchandise.

Not so in Buenos Aires. Shopping is a leisurely, enjoyable event. Crowds of people stroll along the fashionable downtown malls where large and small stores, shops, boutiques, restaurants and businesses of all kinds remain open late for the convenience of all. If you want to buy a pair of shoes, or a suit, or a television set, you aren't restricted to a few choices in a single shopping center. The selection is bewildering, with store after store tastefully displaying quality merchandise, competing for your business.

The downtown section is fashionable, and the business, financial and commercial heart of the city is much the way it was in urban America many years ago. Instead of being ringed with slums and decay, as we are accustomed to up north, the edge of the downtown area is simply the beginning of residential neighborhoods. Both modest and affluent apartment buildings circle the center of the city, and distinct neighborhoods with shopping and restaurants begin to take shape. There is no stigma attached to living "downtown," in fact, there are several prestige areas not many blocks from the financial center. Housing projects for low–income families tend to be found farther out, away from the "downtown" area, the reverse of the arrangement found in the United States.

Farther away from the center, as you reach the suburbs, the emphasis is on smaller buildings and single family homes, although there are many government–built highrises even on the edge of town. Because of all the low–cost housing provided by the government, there aren't any discernible slums, so working–class neighborhoods don't look drastically different from more affluent areas. For some reason, there isn't the vandalism or destruction that characterizes low–cost housing complexes in the United States. Everything looks well–cared for, the result of obvious pride on the part of renters.

One explanation for this high–maintenance factor is that Buenos Aires families don't move as frequently as we do in North America. When they decide that they like a neighborhood and rent or buy a place, it's usually forever. So they tend to take as much interest and pride in a rental unit as if they owned it. When my sister–in–law returned to Buenos Aires after 23 years' absence, she found almost all of her friends and school chums still living in the old neighborhood, some in the same rented houses where they were born.

The northern part of Buenos Aires is the most affluent, but even there prices aren't out of range for a retiree or long–term visitor on a limited budget. Small apartments can be purchased for as little as $16,000, or rented for $150 to $200 a month (and up, of course). Closer to the center and in the southern part of town, a two–bedroom apartment can be bought for as little as $10,000, or rented for $100 and up. (The less expensive rentals might not be entirely satisfactory for many Americans, however.) A subway system crosses the city in several directions and is surprisingly clean and efficient. And for those living in the extreme north or far south, a rapid transit rail system runs frequently and is inexpensive. An auto is a weekend luxury in Buenos Aires.

The place to look for apartments is in the daily newspaper *El Clarin*. You might try placing a classified ad yourself, using the phone number of your hotel. My recommendation is to stay in a small hotel, preferably family–operated, where the staff will be happy to assist with phone calls if your Spanish is inadequate. You'll get plenty of action from a newspaper ad, because the "want ads" are read thoroughly. If you're looking for an unfurnished apartment, make sure it includes a stove and refrigerator, because often "unfurnished" means exactly that. If you prefer a house, you'll have to go for the suburbs, and expect to pay more. Buenos Aires is a city of apartment dwellers.

You might also consider boarding with a family. This is an excellent situation in any Latin American country, because of the unique opportunity to enter into everyday living situations and learning what it means to be a resident of the new country. For sharpening your language skills, there is no better way than a situation where you're forced to communicate. Often you'll find families with children who are studying English and who would love to have a guest with whom they can practice. If you can't find a suitable home in the newspaper, ask your hotel desk clerk to help you compose an ad for the *Clarin*. If your hotel's employees are too busy for that sort of thing, look for another hotel. A good hotel clerk in Buenos Aires doubles as travel agent, financial advisor, interpreter and friend. (I always take solar calculators, digital watches and similar items as gifts for helpful hotel personnel.)

Almost everyone we interviewed in Buenos Aires agreed that a nice apartment should average around $150 a month, and that a family of three could eat very well on $200 or less a month. Add to that the expenses of utilities (inexpensive), clothing and entertainment, and we find that it's possible to live as inexpensively in Buenos Aires as in any large city we've ever seen.

MAR DEL PLATA

If Buenos Aires is the Paris of South America, then Mar del Plata is clearly the Miami Beach. A city of 360,000 permanent inhabitants, it has no excuse for existence other than tourism and retirement. During the summer season (our winter, of course), up to 2 million tourists swell Mar del Plata's population, turning it into a large city, indeed. Hotels, hostels and boarding houses of all categories abound, so finding accommodations isn't too difficult, although you may have to look around a bit without reservations. Advance reservations are a good idea, yet renting a room you haven't seen can be disappointing.

Mar del Plata rears abruptly from a broad plain that ends at a beautiful stretch of Atlantic beaches. Modern, immaculate, and relatively inexpensive, the city attracts Argentinian vacationers and retirees alike. Unlike Miami, Mar del Plata is a calm, relatively crime-free city. I feel as safe on the streets there as I do in Buenos Aires. High-rise apartment buildings and condominiums dominate the town since everyone who can possibly afford it owns an apartment here. Even those who can't afford it own them. There are some good restaurants, but also some mediocre ones. That's to be expected where there are so many tourists.

This is a very popular retirement town for Argentinians. As you might expect, a number of Americans have selected it for their living and retirement adventures. Even though many like Mar del Plata for year-round living, this wouldn't be my choice, because it gets cold in the winter, just as cold as California beach towns. Not freezing, of course, and for many Argentinians and North Americans, it is a delightful winter playground. But for winter-haters—even those pampered by California winters—it's still winter. Mar del Plata is an ideal "second summer" place for someone who can't live without having the ocean handy. And it's obviously okay to live here all-year round, as do the retired Argentinians who make up most of the 360,000 permanent residents. Because there are so many apartments, there are always some available for rent during the season, and off–season you can get one for a song. The easiest way to find one is to look in the classified ads in the Buenos Aires *Clarin*, before you go, or check the local newspaper when you arrive. Many rental agents in Mar del Plata do nothing but sell and rent apartments. You'll find a great selection. Rents are a bit higher than in Buenos Aires, as are restaurant meals, but not by much, because the absentee owners are always anxious to keep their apartments occupied while they're not using them. The way the economy has been, many really can't afford to own the apartments in the first place, and they'll do almost anything to keep them rented.

The downtown beaches are incredibly crowded. If that bothers you, walk or take a taxi about a mile or two either north or south and you'll find plenty of empty beaches. The water is a bit cold for my taste, but then I'm a real coward when the water is less than tepid. A problem here, for those who like servants, is that there is so much employment for local people that it's hard to find someone willing to toil as a domestic. Argentina in general is not a place for servants anyway. When you hire them, they tend to be bossy and hard to please.

Because the town is on the South Atlantic, continuous ocean breezes keep things pleasant even in the hottest part of summer. At night it's seldom too warm to be comfortable in a sport coat or jacket. People do tend to dress more in the evening here than anywhere else in Argentina. It's interesting to go to the casino in the evening and see the dignified dress and decorum of the gamblers. Jackets and ties are the rule for men, and women love to wear their finery. The casino atmosphere is totally different from a gambling casino in Las Vegas or Atlantic City. Here, casino noises are hushed, people whisper, bets are placed in silence, and winnings or losses are taken with restrained emotions. None of this "seven come eleven, baby!" or "daddy needs new shoes!" stuff for the South Americans. It takes some of the fun out of gambling.

There are golf clubs, polo grounds, heated saltwater pools for those who scorn beach swimming, night–clubbing and fishing excursions. While a few full–time North Americans can be found here, there aren't enough to count on for making a large network of English–speaking friends. Like all resorts, the population floats. Be prepared to brush up on Spanish if you're going to stay more than a few weeks.

BARILOCHE, THE SWITZERLAND OF SOUTH AMERICA

For many who love to ski, there is only one place in South America: San Carlos de Bariloche. Two famous runs, *La Catedral* and *El Tronador*, tower high in the Andes above Bariloche. It takes three different lifts to get to the top, about an hour in all, and then it's a long, long downhill run during the winter months of June, July and August. Since those are my favorite months in the northern hemisphere, I've never been to Bariloche during ski season, but I've been assured that the winter weather is superb. I can vouch for the delightful Bariloche summer weather (in December, January and February). It boasts the most beautiful mountain scenery you'll ever hope to see anywhere.

Bariloche sits at the edge of a lake of blue, perfectly clear water. It is so pure that they don't bother to add anything to it for the city water system. It's piped directly from the lake to your home. On the other side of the lake is a wall of mountain peaks that are trimmed with snow all year, mirrored in the azure blueness of the water, like a cliched picture postcard. This is just one of many, many lakes in the area, each prettier than the last.

The town itself is a study right out of the European Alps, with steep–roofed chalets and timbered buildings that would do credit to any Swiss or Black Forest setting. Lovely restaurants with German and French names nestle among boutiques and chocolate confectioners along a main street where ski stores and clothing merchants compete for space. German, French and English are heard so often along the streets and in the restaurants that they seem to have equal time with Spanish. The town is a favorite goal of backpackers from many nations and it is often colored by bands of Gypsies who sell handmade jewelry and flowers made of dyed wood shavings that look prettier than real flowers.

The main commercial section is two–streets deep, running alongside the hill, overlooking the lake. Bariloche isn't a large place at all, with 70,000 listed as its population. This is difficult for me to believe, because the main business section is only a handful of blocks long, and the town itself looks like it shouldn't have over about 30,000 people. The only explanation I have is that they must count all of the surrounding area as part of the town and may include tourists in their census. During the ski season, accommodations are scarce, indeed, but the rest of the year rooms, chalets and apartments are available. Check the local newspaper for summer rentals. Also the Tourist Office, which is located in the picturesque Civic Center, keeps a rental list of chalets, houses and rooms in private homes.

As you leave town in any direction, the scenery becomes even more spectacular, with lakes and forests overshadowed by the lavender and purple Andes in the background. It's along the side roads that skirt the lakes where the prettiest chalets are found. With the present real estate situation in Argentina (see Chapter 16), these country homes are a real bargain. Perhaps these are for the affluent skiing enthusiast who can afford to jet down from the Northern Hemisphere, where it's summer, to get in some winter sport on the slopes. I suppose there are some people who want two winters a year. To each his own.

For people who want to escape northern winters, yet not swelter in heat and humidity, Bariloche is an ideal spot for enjoying that extra summer. Because it is so far south of the equator, summer days are quite long, with sunsets late and colorful, and evenings delightfully cool. Actually, Bariloche is farther south than Australia and several hundred miles farther south than the southern tip of Africa. Here is where you can savor summer to the maximum, in naturally air–conditioned comfort.

An interesting side trip, which I highly recommend, is to take a bus tour across the Andes into Chile. It leaves the Bus Norte terminal in Bariloche at 8 o'clock in the morning and arrives in Puerto Montt, Chile, at about 4:30 in the afternoon after a fantastically scenic drive over a low pass that crosses the Andes. For part of the way the road is gravel. Of particular interest are the stands of giant bamboo, and the profusion of ferns and fuschia trees that grow in this low and humid part of the Andes. In a way, the lush rain–forest atmosphere reminds me of the Olympic Peninsula in Washington State.

To return to Bariloche, the best way is by a combination of boat and bus. You catch the Andina del Sur bus in Puerto Montt at 8 o'clock in the morning, which takes you to Lake Todos los Santos, just a few miles west of the Argentinian border. There you board a boat for a three–hour cruise. You arrive at the Peulla Hotel, on the east side of the lake, in time for lunch. Most people stay the night at Peulla, having spent the day exploring wooded paths alongside the river and enjoying the scenery. Next day you board a bus that climbs over a low pass through snow–covered crags on its way to Lake Frias, and another boat ride. After 20 minutes of cruising amid beautiful scenery, you board a bus that takes you to Bariloche. Total time on this run is about 12 hours, so breaking it into two days and an overnight stay takes the fatigue out of the trip. Be sure to make your reservations through a travel agent so you are assured of a return ticket, otherwise you may have to wait several days for a return reservation or else fly back. The plane fare turns out to be only about twice the cost of a bus and the flight takes about an hour.

Several national parks of extraordinary beauty await your pleasure, uncrowded and delightful to visit. They can be explored by auto, hiking or horseback. San Martin de los Andes is a good place to stay while exploring Lanin National Park, known for beautiful lakes and forested mountains, with the snow–frosted Lanin Volcano looming in the background. San Martin de Los Andes, on the edge of a sparkling lake, is a place where you might want to spend a few months relaxing in the mountain sunshine. The best place for information about rentals in this area is back in Bariloche at the Tourist Office, which deals in rentals for the entire area. Employees of local shops and businesses often know of chalets for rent.

MENDOZA, THE OASIS OF THE ANDES

Argentina is famous for its wines, which are ranked quite highly by connoisseurs of vintages. The source of most of the best Argentine wines is Mendoza and its productive vines, 1,000 kilometers (623 miles) west of Buenos Aires at the foot of the Andes. For good wine, the moisture in the vineyards must be just right, so that the sugar content of the grape can be controlled. Because rainfall in Mendoza is slight and sunshine is predictable, and because local irrigation systems are so efficient, it's easy to control the factors that go into producing the perfect wine grape. Vintages from Mendoza are not only excellent, they don't vary greatly from year to year as do those from most other of the world's best growing areas. Most of the better wines you will drink in Buenos Aires come from Mendoza. Don't miss a wine–tasting tour here, for in addition to intriguing insights into the mechanics of wine–making, the samples are generous.

The same irrigation water flowing from high in the Andes that has turned the province into a famous wine area has also turned the city of Mendoza into a virtual oasis. It is lush with fruit trees and vineyards, and is heavily planted with gardens and flowers.

The mountains rise high behind the city, incredibly high, looming blue–black in what appears to be a perpendicular wall in the distance. In the winter, and sometimes into summer, snow dazzles on the peaks. If you fly over the Andes at this point, you can gain an appreciation of just how rugged, how majestic they can be. To me, this has always been an emotional sight––impossibly steep canyons, soaring peaks, forbidding crags, like an artist's imagination of what mountains might be in a dream. It's possible to cross the Andes by auto and by bus for a visit to Santiago, Chile. I understand some buses have hostess service and even serve breakfast aboard. Those who have taken the trip say the scenery makes the 10–hour trip worthwhile.

The Tourist Office in Mendoza is located at the airport, but there's also one at the bus terminal on Avenida San Martin. People there can help you locate a hotel, apartment or house rentals. Very few Americans can be found here, so Mendoza is for those fortunate adventurers who have developed their Spanish skills and are ready to put them to the test.

By the way, almost all Argentinians who've taken academic courses in high school and college have studied English, but seldom have the opportunity to hone their skills by talking to a real live English speaker. Once they get over their embarrassment, and realize that you aren't going to make fun of them, most delight in trying to communicate in English. Even if your Spanish is still rudimentary, often it isn't as difficult to communicate as you might think, provided you know a smattering of words, and your friend remembers some English. You aren't going to discuss Wittgenstein's theories of predicate calculus, but you'll have loads of fun exchanging information about your families, your jobs, and other more mundane topics.

CORDOBA, THE AREA OF SURPRISES

Northwest of Buenos Aires, 600 kilometers (370 miles), is the province and city of Cordoba. Here the country becomes a fertile paradise of temperate zone agriculture. But there's more to it than farms and cattle, for there are many delightful tourist and non–tourist towns where the people are friendly and the climate is superb.

The city of Cordoba boasts over 1 million inhabitants and is one of the most interesting metropolitan areas in South America. Clean, prosperous, modern––as you come to expect of Argentinian cities--Cordoba is the metropolitan center of a rich agricultural area. Yet the city isn't an overgrown farm town; it is distinctly European. Buildings at the city center are a mixture of Colonial and modern styles, reminding me of Barcelona or Toulouse.

The prosperity of the province is abundantly evident in both the suburbs and the city itself. In the very center of town, the streets turn into artistically designed pedestrian malls, with arbors of flowers that spread a lacy shade over walkways that were once the domain of autos. Shoppers wander through seemingly endless galleries of smart clothing boutiques, jewelry stores, and bookshops in pursuit of luxury goods of all descriptions. There appears to be an area of about 20 square blocks dedicated to pedestrian shopping. There is an unmistakable impression that everyone has plenty of money to spend, for the malls are always crowded.

The affluence of Cordoba is best seen in the edges of the city where residential areas are quite pleasant, with landscaped yards and gardens lush with colorful flowers. Here is good city living combined with a wonderful country atmosphere. As in most of the provinces, small town and large city alike, custom calls for a long lunch hour, from noon until 3 p.m. This is the time for rest, or perhaps leisurely strolls through the suddenly quiet streets of town.

A new, modern apartment in downtown Cordoba can be found for $200 or less and an older one for as low as $100. But because the outskirts of the city are so beautiful, I would be tempted to go for a house and pay a bit more. Check the local papers for listings, or one of the real estate agencies in the center of town.

THE "BLACK FOREST" COUNTRY OF CORDOBA

Early in World War II, the German battleship *Graf Spee*, after being chased into the South Atlantic, fought a final battle against three British warships. The German ship, outnumbered and out-fought by the enemy, took several direct hits, and crippled, withdrew to the estuary of the Rio de la Plata near Montevideo. Surrender seemed to be the only choice. Instead, the captain ordered his men ashore to nearby neutral Argentina, scuttled the ship and committed suicide.

The crew, about 900 sailors, was stranded for the duration. The seamen explored Argentina, discovered the country around Cordoba, and fell in love with it. Rich agriculturally and scenically, it reminded them of Germany, particularly the area known as the Black Forest. Many of them immediately began making plans for living here after the war was over. They bought land, started farms, and after the war, sent for their families and friends. Today, this is one of the most interesting and desirable places to live in Argentina. German–style hotels, chalets, and farmhouses dot the countryside. Although everyone speaks Spanish formally, you often hear German spoken. The center of this area is Villa General Belgrano, where a legendary Oktoberfest celebration draws people from all over the country, to listen to music, dance, drink beer and sample German foods.

There is, incidentally, a rivalry between British and German type beers in Argentina, with each side having its own aficionados. There are many excellent breweries, and instead of all of the beers tasting pretty much alike as is the case in the United States, each has an individual character. Fancying myself as an expert beer drinker, I have to come down on the side of *Quilmes* brewery, which is a British–type.

Throughout this part of the country you'll find charming little villages where peace and quiet are the rule, as well as bustling little towns where tourism thrives. Lakes are plentiful, with tree covered shores and flotillas of houseboats available for fishing or leisurely cruising. Peron, during his heyday as the champion of the working man, built a half–dozen or more huge resort complexes for the exclusive use of workers. Constructed in pine forest and lake settings, these resorts offer swimming, boating, horseback riding, and more, for about $2 a day for labor union members. It's my understanding that they're also open, space available, to the public. But it's possible that there is never space available at those low rates.

The nice thing about this part of the country is that, although it appears to be almost alpine in character, with pines, mountains and lakes, the climate is quite mild. Its distance from the equator is about that of Florida's, so winters are very mild, with no snow in the lower altitudes, rarely even frost. Summers can't be beat. For that reason, it's quite popular with Argentinians, but almost unknown around the North American tourist circuit.

Houses and chalets in the resort towns are not too easily found in the summer because of the tourist crush and the custom of reserving a year in advance. But by going a few kilometers away from the lake, to an ordinary village, you can find some real bargains. Since there aren't many Americans living here, this might be for those with Spanish skills (or those who are serious about sharpening them).

THE OTHER SIDE OF THE MOUNTAIN

West, across some low mountains from Cordoba, is a place known as *tras las montanas* (across the mountains). It has been highly recommended to me by a retiree friend who claims this is an even better place than Cordoba for year–round or summer living. He recommends the towns of Sierra Grande, Mina Clavero or Villa Dolores. There, during the high season, a fine two- or three–bedroom chalet can be rented for $500 to $800 a month. While this may seem high for Argentina, my friend assures me that it's well worth it, and that more modest accommodations may be found. By renting a place for the full year, the monthly costs come down to an affordable rate even for the budget traveler. Because of the abrupt rise of the high peaks mountains to the west of *tras las montanas,* the cold winds from the Andes are deflected up and over, giving the region a truly mild winter with resort temperatures year–around.

THEATER IN THE PROVINCES

Buenos Aires is quite fond of the theater and has a large selection of stage plays at all times. One would imagine that when the Portenos go on vacation, they would forget about the theater. Not so. One of the biggest vacation resorts is Villa Carlos Paz, a town of some 50,000, located on the steep banks of Lago San Roque, about 30 kilometers (18 miles) from Cordoba. During the off season the town supports about five theaters, but during the popular summer months, a cultural explosion occurs. An additional 20 theaters appear! In other resorts people come to waterski or fish, but in Villa Carlos Paz, they come to enjoy the theater.

Banners strung across the streets advertise different theater groups, amateur and professional, often with pictures of the actors swaying in the breeze to attract attention. Actors, playwrights, directors and audiences enjoy a virtual orgy of legitimate theater during these summer months.

Of course, there is the ubiquitous casino for those who manage to sneak away and place a few bets (all dressed up and full of dignity, as usual). Villa Carlos Paz is a dreamy place with an intellectual, yet fun atmosphere that goes well with the gorgeous lakeside setting. Housing here is scarce during the summer season, but like most resort towns, the bargains are either found in year–round leasing or in going to one of the surrounding villages, away from the lake.

This resort town is very popular with the British community in Argentina. They're fond of the fishing and boating on Lake San Roque, as well as much tennis and golf. Since the altitude is high here and there is usually snow in the winter, the British come here for the ski lifts in June, July and August.

PATAGONIA, THE TEXAS OF ARGENTINA

There are a couple of explanations for how Patagonia received its name. The most popular is that the early explorers thought that the Indians there sported unusually large feet and nicknamed them "patacones" (big feet). Some early travel writers claimed the natives had only one foot, a huge one, on which they bounced about like pogo sticks. The other explanation is that the word comes from the Greek *patagos*, which describes a roaring and gnashing of teeth. Considering how the Spaniards treated them, it's no wonder the natives roared and gnashed their teeth from time to time. The Indians here were very fierce, and weren't totally pacified until the "War of Extermination" in the late 1800s.

If you like west Texas––if you particularly admire flat, sagebrush–covered wastelands––then you'll adore southern Patagonia. Mile after mile of treeless emptiness drags into forever, broken only by a sudden rushing of a flock of rheas (Argentinian ostriches), or an occasional herd of delicate guanacos (the small Argentine llama–like animal). Once in a while you'll see an irrigated farm, because like west Texas, it's amazingly fertile when irrigated. You might go another hour or so until the next farm. The land can grow almost anything, and water for irrigation is only a few feet below the surface. Yet, few farmers bother to work the land. The reasons are twofold: There are so few people around, and, there is so much naturally–watered land in the Pampas that few bother with Patagonia. Like Texas, Patagonia has a lot of oil reserves, much of it barely touched. Also unexploited are coal and iron ore deposits, all of which could make Argentina one of the few fully self–sufficient countries in the world.

Sheep, who will eat anything, appear to make a good living in Patagonia. Years ago, these empty lands attracted Welsh settlers who were used to sheep–raising back home. They found the cool climate and sheep–rearing possibilities not too much different from coastal Wales. So during the late 1800s and early 1900s, Welsh settlers brought their customs, language, families, and of course, their sheep.

At first they kept the Welsh language as their primary language, using Spanish only to communicate with their neighbors, but each new generation learns less and less of that amazingly complex Celtic tongue. Very few still speak it.

I frankly doubt if many North Americans will find much to be enthusiastic about in southern Patagonia as far as long–term living goes. However, it's definitely worth a visit. Particularly interesting is the Valdez Peninsula, a wildlife preserve. There you can visit elephant seals, walk among them, watch them battle in the water while the ones on shore snarl at you and try to frighten you away. A few beaches away, you find "lobos," a seal that is somewhat larger than our common harbor seal, and more dangerous and aggressive. The largest penguin colony on the continent is found on an island off the peninsula. Guanacos, rheas, and of course, sheep are common here, and there is at least one *estancia*, or sheep ranch, where visitors are welcome and are served delicious *parrilladas* of chicken, beef and lamb.

THE LEGALITIES OF ARGENTINA

To enter Argentina, a U.S. or Canadian citizen needs a valid passport which is then presented to the nearest Argentinian Consulate for a visa. A travel agency can do this for you. The visa is good for four years of unlimited entry and exit privileges. Upon entering the country, you are given a tourist card good for 90 days (just the right time for a summer). Theoretically, you can get a 90–day extension, but the easiest way to handle this is to simply leave the country for a day or two, then re–enter on a new tourist card. (Crossing the river for a day at the beach, dinner and an evening on the town in Montevideo is what most do.)

Should you decide that Argentina is for you, that you wish to stay permanently, look for a job, start a business, whatever, then you will need a permanent resident visa. The Argentinian consulate advises me that the best way to do this is start the proceedings in the United States or Canada. Yes, it can be done in Argentina, but it can involve more red tape, because almost all of your documents must be notarized in the area where they are issued. Listed herewith are the latest rules issued by the Argentinian consulate in San Francisco:

To begin the application for residency the applicant must make an appointment to appear personally at the Argentine consulate with the following documents:

1. *Valid Passport*

2. *Medical certificate:* A special form required by the "Direccion Nacional de Migraciones" should be obtained from the consulate. It must be fully filled out by a physician and then legalized (notarized) by the local Health Department where the physician practices.

3. *Police Letter of Clearance:* (This is no longer required, but I'm listing the old requirement just in case they decide to reinstate this rule.) This must be obtained in the cities and towns where the applicant has resided for the last five years. It should be legalized by the Argentinian consulate whose jurisdiction covers the region where the cities or towns are located. (This wasn't required for children under 15 years.)

4. *Diploma or Documents Stating Career, Knowledge or Skills,* duly legalized (notarized) by competent authorities.

5. *Letters of Introduction* from two employers, institutions or societies with which the applicant has been affiliated.

6. *Four Photographs,* passport type, color or black and white. Once the visa is authorized, the applicant will be notified and must appear personally at the same consulate, presenting the following documents:

7. *Certified Copy of Birth Certificate:* This must be legalized by the Argentinian consulate for the jurisdiction where the birth certificate was issued.

8. *Certified Copy of the Marriage, Widowhood or Legal Separation Certificate:* This document must also be legalized by the Argentinian consulate of the jurisdiction *where the document was issued.* This means that you may wind up dealing with another Argentinian consulate if you were married, widowed or separated in some other far part of this country.

9. *Father's or Legal Guardian's Authorization* (if under 21). By Argentinian law anyone under the age of 21 cannot enter or leave Argentina without their *father's* (or legal guardian's) written authorization. This must be notarized and certified by the county clerk where you live and then legalized by the consulate where the travel

documents are applied for. It doesn't matter if it's okay with mama or not, it's *daddy's* permission that is required! They are quite serious about this.

All documents must be of recent date, showing the handwritten signature of the official authority, the typewritten signature and official seal of the office. The cost for applying is $4 and the final resident visa fee is another $8.

It sounds complicated, and like all dealings with foreign consulates, requires patience. But if you are considering working, buying a business, or just plain retiring for any length of time, it's worth the hassle. If you're just planning on a summer, remember that a 90–day stay is automatic on the regular visa (free) and you can enter and leave the country as often as you wish for four years. My advice would be to take advantage of the regular visa, leaving the country for a few days, even overnight, and getting another 90–day visa. You can prolong your living experiment, and then––when you're absolutely sure you want to stay––return to North America and get matters started through your local Argentinian consulate.

CHAPTER 7

Uruguay: Unexploited and Uncrowded

Uruguay is the second smallest country in South America (only Surinam is smaller), and one of the most comfortable for Americans, particularly for those who like Argentina. For the Uruguayan people are very much like Argentinians, although they tend to be somewhat more reserved. The country measures some 72,000 square miles; slightly larger than Missouri. But Uruguay's population of 2.8 million people is only about 60 percent that of Missouri's. The result is an underpopulated land. As in other South American countries, people prefer city life; more than half of all Uruguayans live in Montevideo, the capital, turning their backs on the countryside.

It's a rich countryside, too, with broad plains and low, rolling hills covered with tall grass, dotted with trees and crisscrossed by lazy streams--not much different from Illinois or Indiana in summer. While the world grows short of farmable land, Uruguay is land rich. About 90 percent of the land is suitable for agriculture, exceptionally productive agriculture. Yet only about 12 percent is actually used for crops. The rest is either dedicated to livestock or lies fallow. Remember, half the country (over 1.5 million people) live in Montevideo while another million live in other cities. That doesn't leave many to work the land. In fact, less than 19 percent of the Uruguayan people choose to live in the country and some of these are drawn away to the cities every year.

CLIMATE

Uruguay's location in the Southern Hemisphere gives it a climate comparable to Georgia and Florida in the Northern Hemisphere. This means pleasantly mild winters and warm summers, tempered by breezes from the Atlantic on the east and the huge estuary of the Rio de la Plata on the south. Most all crops do well in its potassium–rich soil, and Uruguayan beef is considered to be equal to, if not better than Argentinian beef. A couple of juicy steaks in a Montevideo restaurant will convince you of that.

Some more interesting statistics: The literacy rate is an incredible 97 percent. Education is both free and compulsory. Unlike most of the world, where population growth is out of control and is impoverishing countries, Uruguay has a very low birth rate, a modest 0.5 percent natural increase per year. Compare this with Mexico's alarming 2.8 percent, which is more than five times as high, or neighboring Brazil with an equally high growth rate. Uruguay is a country where a few more visitors or residents wouldn't make much difference at all.

HISTORY

To understand the ethnic makeup of the Uruguayan people, we need to look briefly at their historical background. When the Spanish began colonizing, it was the same old story: They were interested in gold and silver, not agriculture. Uruguay offered few mineral resources, and its Indians fought the intruders with a vengeance, so the country was mostly ignored as a place to settle. It was left alone for two centuries. But the Portuguese had their eye on Uruguay and insisted that it legally belonged to Brazil. To underscore their point they established a fort across the Rio de la Plata from what is now Buenos Aires. To counter this threat, the Spanish put a garrison at nearby Montevideo. For years the two rivals attacked each other's positions. Neither side scored any big victories, but in the long run the Spanish were finally able to nail down their claim to Uruguay.

In the meantime, some cattle managed to find their way into the rich grasslands and flourished without any help from man. This attracted the intrepid gauchos--the "cowboys" of Argentina--who followed the herds and killed them for meat and sold the hides. Things went along this way for years until Uruguay's independence from Spain in 1828. Suddenly, the gates swung open and settlers from Europe began arriving, attracted by abundant, rich land and the chance for a new start in a new world. Most of them came from Italy, and a lot of them from Spain. The result is a population that is almost exclusively southern European. Since Uruguayans never practiced slavery, you find no African influences other than a very few blacks who have come in from Brazil. In contrast with neighboring Argentina, there is little German or British cultural influence in Uruguay.

Politically, Uruguay has had a history of democracy and governments interested in social welfare. Many liberal laws were passed to benefit the poor and huge amounts of money were spent on schools, public works, public health and welfare. Because of the rich bounty of agricultural exports, the country could afford to indulge its citizens. Particularly during World War II, import money came pouring into Uruguay. The government had almost unlimited funds at its disposal. Then, when export demand slowed and money became scarce, the collective belt was tightened, and a period of social unrest followed. Unemployment, something unknown before, became rampant. Things started falling apart.

A terrorist, urban guerilla movement (known as the Tupamaros) began operations in Montevideo. Things went from bad to worse, and finally, the military seized the government, ostensibly to prevent the country from falling into utter chaos. Whether they were heroes or opportunists depends upon who you talk to. To their credit, they were not as brutal as some military usurpers in their repression of civil rights and dissent. They allowed most political refugees to leave the country, rather than execute them as was done in Argentina. To their discredit, they turned the names of the political exiles over to the Argentinian authorities, and many exiles found themselves in custody in Argentina.

After 11 years of military rule, the control of the government was finally returned to civilians in 1985.

WHERE DO NORTH AMERICANS PREFER TO LIVE?

With most of the country sparsely settled, the concentration of people is along the river and ocean coast. Here is where you find places best liked by most Americans. Prices, once high, have dropped to the point where Uruguay is at this time the cheapest of the "quality" countries in South America. Even Punta del Este, the luxury spot of the Southern Hemisphere, is an affordable place for Americans with dollars in their pockets. Incidentally, Uruguay is one country where you can trade your traveler's checks for dollars, where there is no "parallel market" in currency.

Since most people begin their exploration of Uruguay from Buenos Aires, let's start from there and cross the Rio de la Plata to Colonia del Sacramento, the old Portuguese fortress town. To get there, you go to the Onda bus ticket offices on Florida and Lavalle in Buenos Aires and purchase an advance ticket on the "Aliscafa" hydrofoil. It leaves about every hour starting at 7 a.m., from a riverside dock on Avenida Pedro Mendoza. Be sure you show the taxi driver your ticket, because there are other, slower ferries going to Colonia. For an extra few dollars you can sit in the first class seats on the top deck where you can better take in the view as the boat clips along at about 75 kilometers (45 miles) an hour. The slow ferry takes three hours for the crossing but carries automobiles as well as passengers.

Once aboard the hydrofoil, you gain an appreciation of the enormity of the Rio de la Plata. At 75 kilometers an hour, the boat takes an hour to cross the river! Although it is technically an estuary at this point, you know it is still a very powerful river even at that width, with a depth that easily accommodates the biggest of ocean ships. There is an obvious current, and the water is as coffee brown as the Mississippi, bearing muddy sediments from the network of rivers that join to form this monster stream. When it finally hits the ocean, some 300 kilometers (185 miles) farther on, the water is still brown and colors the ocean for some kilometers out from its mouth.

COLONIA DEL SACRAMENTO

Portuguese soldiers founded Colonia del Sacramento in 1680 as part of their effort to establish the border of Brazil at the banks of the Rio de la Plata. The Portuguese had more interest in agriculture than the Spanish and recognized the potential richness of the land. They laid out a fortified town on the river's edge, planted trees, left room for plazas and built substantial homes and government buildings. Despite frequent battles with the Spanish, the town thrived. Soon houses and small farms began springing up outside its walls. When the Spanish or Indians attacked, the villagers would rush into the safe confines of the heavily fortified town.

After a century and a half of Spanish and Portuguese battles for possession of the town, Uruguay suddenly gained its independence and became a buffer state between Brazil and Argentina. Colonia, no longer a bone of contention, lost its main reason for existence. Today it sits on the river's edge like a relic of centuries past, suspended in time. Homes and sturdy public buildings, some as much as 300 years old, stand as solidly and patiently as in the days when the Portuguese built them. Eerily quiet, with only a rare automobile to stir the silence and an occasional pedestrian to tread the cobblestone streets, the town is the most peaceful and relaxing I've ever seen. It invites you to stay, to shed your worries and let them slip into the wide river. The streets are shady, and park benches encourage you to sit and let your mind wander through the past. The town's few restaurants and hotels are tucked away unobtrusively, careful not to destroy any image of the colonial times.

At least 25 percent of the houses in the old section of town appear to be uninhabited, with many having "for sale" signs on them. Thick-walled, constructed to withstand the wear of centuries, many have wrought-iron balconies and windows. Some display woodwork on doors and shutters that must be hundreds of years old. These jewels are just begging for someone with taste and imagination to come along and refurbish them. Perhaps I wax too poetic about Colonia, but it's a place I'm keeping in the back of my mind for that day when I want to look for perfect peace, yet not be more than an hour away from the good restaurants and conveniences of Buenos Aires, my favorite big city.

Prices are shockingly low, with a marvelous dinner for two coming to about $6, including wine, dessert and coffee. Some of the more picturesque hotels charge for their uniqueness, but others, the newer ones away from the old section, are very reasonable, charging from $10 to $15 a day for two, some even less. Because many of the homes in the old section are owned by Argentinians and only used as weekend retreats, there aren't too many rentals available. However, a little asking about among storekeepers or people gossiping on street corners can usually turn up something. An interesting alternative might be to rent a room with a local family, giving you the opportunity to quickly become a part of the neighborhood. There are few native English speakers here, so this is a good place for forced immersion into Spanish in order to join in the gossiping. As in Argentina and other South American countries, most people study English in high school, but don't expect much fluency. It's up to you to learn *their* language.

Between Colonia and Montevideo there are several little towns, mostly farming communities. They look pretty much like farm towns in North America. My impression of them is that they would be equally stimulating, if farming is your interest. Otherwise, you would be interested in seeing the city and resort portions of Uruguay.

MONTEVIDEO

The metropolis and financial hub of Uruguay, Montevideo is the only truly big city in the country. It is an interesting mixture of old, new, modest and affluent. The main part of the city is like Buenos Aires, but on a smaller scale. Modernization hasn't intruded upon the older sections of town to the same extent as in Buenos Aires. Broad boulevards cross the city, cutting across narrow streets and intersecting tree-shaded parks and wide plazas. It's obvious that Montevideo has seen its lusher days, but it's still a thriving city. Strolling its grand avenues while savoring its distinctive character is a true delight. There are many hotels and bargain apartments available near the center city, but the most pleasant parts are along the ocean shore heading east, away from the city. The estuary side of town is *cafe au lait* water from the center of South America and no one swims there.

As you drive or walk along the metropolitan beachfront, you suddenly realize why Montevideo is famous as a resort town. The beaches are beautiful. The ones closest to the city center are not my favorites, although they are popular with the townspeople. But as you continue along the beachfront boulevard, you find each beach better than the last, the homes and apartments classier and snazzier.

At the eastern edge of town you come to Carrasco Beach and the Carrasco Casino, a must see for its ornate construction and elegant decorations. Here is where most Americans are tempted to stay. Despite the opulence of the area, many reasonably priced apartments and duplexes are available. The reason for this is the emergence of Punta del Este as *the* resort, *the* in place to spend vacations. Because many local and Argentinian sun-seekers keep on driving another couple of hours to Punta del Este, Montevideo is left forlorn and over-supplied with rentals. The Montevideo papers have many rentals listed in their classified sections. Inquiries at any of the restaurants or boutiques will turn up houses or apartments that never make it into the newspaper.

THE BEACH ROUTE

From Montevideo eastward you will find over 300 kilometers (185 miles) of some of the finest beaches you can imagine. There are endless stretches of sandy shore broken by small bays and coves bounded by tree–covered hills. My recommendation is not to take the toll road unless you are in a big hurry. Instead, drive along the coastal road and make detours into the several resort towns along the way. Exquisite villas and modest, comfortable–looking homes make the winding road an interesting trip in itself.

The little towns scattered along the coast are quiet and relaxing, with tree–shaded streets and old–fashioned hotels and bungalows. They somehow remind me of little Mississippi River towns where time has skipped over, leaving the pleasant past to be leisurely enjoyed. The first beach town, and one worth considering as a spot to tarry in during your second summer, is Atlantida, about 45 kilometers (28 miles) from Montevideo. Despite its closeness to the city and being a resort, Atlantida has the calmness and a quiet charm of a midwestern college town. With tall shade trees and large, older homes, Atlantida has an air of dignity that few beach towns can ever maintain. Nevertheless it boasts a country club and golf course in its dedication to tourism.

Farther along the highway you come to another little gem of a beach town, Floresta, smaller than Atlantida, but possessing the same charm. Housing may be more difficult to find here, as most chalets belong to absentee owners from Argentina who may be difficult to contact. If your Spanish is adequate, the best way to house–hunt is by inquiry at local stores and restaurants.

The next town is one of my favorites. With a gently curving bay lined with soft sandy beaches, Piriapolis is another town that time has passed by. Once *the* resort along the coast, throngs of holiday–seekers used to journey from Montevideo and Buenos Aires to enjoy the beaches and carnival–like atmosphere of Piriapolis. Luxury hotels with gourmet restaurants fronted the beaches. A truly impressive casino and spa lorded it over the town. Piriapolis represented seashore vacations at their best.

79

Then the "big money" interests discovered Punta del Este. A fantastic surge of building and development, fueled by an endless supply of dollars (borrowed from U.S. banks) began to attract the curious. Attracted by Punta del Este's glamour, vacationers abandoned Piriapolis and its slow and stately ways. Piriapolis found itself with fewer and fewer tourists and plenty of empty hotel rooms. Although tourists from Uruguay and Argentina still frequent the beaches of Piriapolis and still enjoy the great seafood restaurants, the crowds of yesteryear no longer stifle the town. There is plenty of room to stretch out on the sand.

The town is bordered by hills swathed in pine, acacia and eucalyptus trees, and is dominated by a tall geological formation known as *Cerro Pan de Azucar*, or "Sugar Loaf." Unlike Rio's Sugar Loaf, you'll have to walk up this one, because there isn't a cable car.

Between here and Punta del Este are numerous beaches, long and unspoiled, with expensive–looking chalets and an occasional tastefully designed hotel. It's without a doubt the most affluent–looking stretch of ocean front I've ever seen. Most of the homes are owned by foreigners--Argentinian, German, American or French--and are set on multi–acre grounds. There are, however, large stretches of land that haven't as yet been developed, places I'm keeping in the corner of my mind for that day when I suddenly win the lottery and decide to build my dream house.

PUNTA DEL ESTE

An easy two–hour drive from Montevideo, about 140 kilometers (87 miles), is the internationally famous mecca of luxury, Punta del Este. As you drive along the gorgeous ocean–front highway to Punta, you cannot help but be impressed by the skyline ahead, while impressive private homes that look like country clubs boast of wealth and high living. The towering buildings of Punta del Este are mostly apartments and condos; all appear to be sparkling new. Actually, they are, because until 10, or so, years ago there was very little of anything in Punta. It was a sleepy town, located on a narrow point of land sticking out into the Atlantic. Suddenly, Punta was shaken awake when Argentinian promoters started construction. They built the town largely with borrowed petrodollars that flowed so freely back then. No expense was spared to make this a beautiful city.

As you enter the point, tall condos gaze toward the oceanfront along wide boulevards lined with sidewalk cafes and restaurants. But as you reach the downtown, or actual point of the tiny peninsula, the buildings are restricted to no more than four stories. This makes for a pleasant, low–density kind of city center. The tip of the peninsula is reserved for single family homes for the super–rich. This is truly a place where millionaires can live without feeling uncomfortable, for there is absolutely no trace of anything remotely resembling poverty to make them feel guilt. Yet, there is nothing gaudy about the town–– everything is tastefully done and understated, if anything.

Surprisingly, despite its aura of classy opulence, Punta del Este is *not* expensive, at least not by American standards. A steak or sea-food dinner for two including cocktail, wine, dessert and tip in a nice restaurant, costs from $10 to $16. The same meal would cost $6 to $9 in a Montevideo restaurant, or $45 to $55 in a similar establish-ment in New Orleans.

The overwhelming majority of the thousands of apartments there belong to wealthy foreigners. Argentinians, mostly, although Europeans and Americans have their hands in as well. While some condominiums top $500,000, others go for as little as $18,000 to $20,000. That's the price at the time of publication; my guess is that they will begin edging upward as the Uruguayan economy improves. The reason for the low cost here is the same reason Buenos Aires real estate is so low. People have sacrificed real estate to have cash dollars in their hands. Real estate is a poor short–term investment during times of hyper–inflation because when tenants can't afford to pay high rents, real estate earns but a fraction of what cash would earn at interest.

Although you might look at super–plush Punta del Este and assume that you can't afford to rent there, look again. Rents are very reasonable. True, you can't think about living here on $400 a month, because your rent for a nice apartment, or a small house on the out-skirts of town will cost you that much, maybe from $500 to $600 a month during the summer season. Add $200 a month for food and another $150 for a maid–cook, entertainment and an occasional rental car, and you are looking at close to $1,000 a month. But you can be sure there is no place in North America where you could even dream of renting a house or apartment like one of these for less than $1,500 a month, and that's just for rent!

Another surprise about rentals is that during the off–season, there are so many vacancies that rents are almost free! Example: In

February 1986, we inquired about a three–bedroom house in a lovely residential area known as Paradas. We wanted it for the coming summer season of December, January and February, planning to split the rent with a friend and her family. The agent informed us the rent would be $3,000 for the season, including gardener care. That came to $1,000 a month, which, split two ways, didn't sound bad. My friend then wanted to know how much it would cost for a full year's lease, because she might want to stay on. "The whole year would be $4,000," the rental agent informed us. "Three thousand dollars for three months, and only $1,000 for the other nine?" I asked in astonishment. "That's correct," he replied. "We couldn't rent it anyway, and the owner would much prefer to have someone live there than have it sit vacant." At that rate, the average monthly rental would be about $333. A house in a similar area, like Palm Springs, would cost half a million dollars to build and considerably more than $333 a month to rent! With rental income like that, you can understand why property values are so depressed in Uruguay. But it's hard to say how long this condition will last.

Because there are so many apartments and condos in Punta, there is a surprising lack of hotels. It seems that most vacationers rent an apartment or condo and stay several weeks or the entire summer, rather than just a few days as they might at a similar beach resort in Florida or California. For the Argentinians, the custom is to take an apartment for the season and install the wife and kids in it while the husband works in Buenos Aires or Montevideo and commutes to Punta del Este for weekends. Therefore, there isn't as much demand for hotels as you might expect. Only a couple of "luxury" hotels are available, and few of the ordinary hotels are very large. They're expensive by South American standards, but are bargains to North Americans. Rooms range from $30 to $50 a day for a couple. Away from the center of town, more reasonable accommodations can be found, starting at $10 a day.

An attractive alternative to living in downtown Punta del Este would be to go to one of the "suburbs" such as Maldonado, or across the river to the Manantiales section. Maldonado is quite ordinary but comfortable, slow–paced and inexpensive. It's a typical Uruguayan small town with the traditional town square and old cathedral. Here the only concession to tourism is a couple of inexpensive hotels that catch the spill–over from nearby Punta. Single–family homes are the rule here, and probably not a great number are for rent at any given time. Rentals are usually handled through word of mouth around town. Inquire in stores, restaurants, the bank, or through rental agents who handle rentals in Punta del Este.

The other residential possibility, a bit more expensive (but worth it because it's on the beach) is found by driving along the ocean and crossing the interesting inverted "W" bridge that spans the Maldonado River.

From this point on, most houses are built on the sloping shore, with each enjoying a gorgeous view of beach and surf. Few structures are over two stories, most being single–story dwellings. As you drive farther along the beach you'll find fewer houses until vast stretches of unspoiled beaches are yours to enjoy as if you were Robinson Crusoe. Mile after mile of beach look as if they have never known human footprints.

The road continues along the beach for another 20 kilometers (13 miles), passing several villages and isolated beach homes. There's a break in Highway 10 where you must detour around Laguna Ignacio. Then on to another stretch of truly isolated beach. This would be a great place in which to get lost and shuck civilization for as long as you wish.

The interior of Uruguay is very rural, with lots of space between towns. Although there are some beautiful places, particularly around the low mountain ranges in the center of the country, there is little tourism. People living there would be astonished to see a gringo arrive and set up housekeeping. But you can bet that they would be friendly and accept you without hesitation.

VISAS AND IMMIGRATION RULES

Like neighboring Argentina, Uruguay issues 90–day tourist cards at no charge. However, a visa is not required, just a current passport. These tourist permits are issued when you enter customs, a matter of filling out a simple form. The permits may be renewed at: Direccion Nacional de Migracion, Misiones 1513, Montevideo. But to avoid red tape, it is just as easy to exit the country briefly and obtain a new 90–day permit upon your return. This might be a good time to visit Iguazu Falls, or to visit Porto Alegre, Brazil.

To apply for longer residence than 90 days, or to apply for pensioned status, you must start your application in Montevideo. You will need approximately the same documents as you need for a permanent visa in Argentina (see Chapter 6). There is a certain amount of fixed income necessary to become a permanent resident, and you aren't supposed to work for wages. At the wages paid in Uruguay, you probably wouldn't want to work anyway. The Uruguayan Embassy in Washington D.C. is of little help in emigration matters and they've closed most, if not all, local consulates as an economy measure. As in most Latin American countries, don't expect to get much accomplished by correspondence with a government entity. Plan on making application for long-term residence in person.

CHAPTER 8

Chile: Land of Temperate Extremes

The last country in my Euro–American triad is Chile. Like the other two countries, Argentina and Uruguay, Chile is also "under-populated." There is plenty of elbowroom there. In land area, Chile is one–third larger than France, but it's population of 11.1 million is only a fifth of France's, or about equal to that of Ohio. Long, narrow as a ribbon, and mountainous along its spine, Chile runs 2,700 miles north to south from the tropics down to sub–Antarctic. Yet its average width is only 110 miles. In the north, a practically rainless desert stretches some 800 miles before merging with the equally dry desert of southern Peru. In the extreme south, glaciers and fjords end at the Strait of Magellan and Cape Horn.

Because of the long Pacific coast and the narrow width of the land between shore and mountains, the cold waters of the Pacific Ocean moderate the climate and keep Chile free from temperature extremes. Snow and ice are almost unknown except in the mountains. But, even though temperatures are even, rainfall patterns are not. Chile boasts some of the wettest lands on earth and some of the driest deserts imaginable. However, between these extremes can be found some very pleasant living.

Chile is included in Euro–America because its people have so much in common with Argentina and Uruguay, both culturally and historically. Yet, although Chile's culture and architecture is European, you will notice a higher percentage of darker–skinned people here than in Argentina and Uruguay. Blond hair and blue eyes are also much in evidence, but a hint of mestizo tints the faces of many Chileans. Sometimes it is so faint that you aren't sure, but it's there.

In the matter of racial composition, the history of Chile diverges a bit from Argentina and Uruguay. European settlement in Chile began earlier than in the other two countries, and the settlers were initially of a higher social class: conquistadores. They quickly divided the country into huge estates and used the peaceful Indians in the north as serfs to work the land. They intermarried rather thoroughly to form a mestizo race, although they remained fully Spanish in culture. But the Indians south of the Rio Maule, where the best farmland lay (about 200 miles south of Santiago), were far from peaceful. Like their brothers on the other side of the Andes, they resisted the white man quite effectively, keeping European settlers out of their lands for over 300 years. The two cultures didn't mix.

With the best agricultural lands pretty much closed to newcomers, the other main attraction was copper mining. These were worked with native miners, so there was little to attract waves of immigration. The more lucrative gold and silver mines were in Peru. Since at that time Chile was part of Peru and prohibited from engaging in foreign trade, French smugglers became common in the seaports. Some settled there. Then, by the end of the 18th century, British, Irish and Germans began moving in, bringing modern European ideas and notions of democracy to Chile. When thoughts of independence began to grow, these newcomers stepped to the forefront of the action. Two heroes of the Chilean struggle for independence from Spain (which was at that time occupied by England's archenemy, Napoleon) were Bernardo O'Higgins at the head of the army and Lord Cochrane in charge of the navy. O'Higgins became the first Chilean head of state. Later, he was forced to resign when his liberal philosophy collided with the conservative power structure of the large landowners. This was to be a pattern of Chilean political conflict that continues to this day: land-rich conservatives against liberal reformists.

After independence, the Chileans undertook a campaign to wrest control of the southern part of the country from the Indians. The job took some time, but by the late 19th century they had almost wiped out the Indians and the land was then opened for settlement. About this same time, the high tide of emigrants from Europe to the New World began flowing into Chile, bringing German, French, Italian and Swiss farmers to settle its southern lands. Later migrations sent other Europeans to the north, around Santiago and Valparaiso. This sudden and massive influx of Europeans overwhelmed whatever traces remained of the mestizo cultural influence. The result is a Euro–American culture, a blend of Spain and Europe, different from Argentina, different from Uruguay, yet closer to both than either Indo–America or Afro–America.

In the south, particularly, German colonists who settled Valdivia, Puerto Montt, Puerto Varas, Orsorno and Chiloe, left a distinct mark on both the land and people. You see a lot of blond farmers tilling the fields, and German–style thatched roofs on farmhouses and barns.

Like the other countries of Euro–America, Chileans love the cities. Almost 80 percent live in one city or another, about half in the capital, Santiago. And like the other two countries, agriculture is all but neglected. Even though Chile has rich agricultural lands and is famous for its exports of fruit, it doesn't produce enough food to feed its people. One indication of this is that 25 percent of its total imports are food, food that could be easily grown domestically if it were not for the country's inefficient distribution of land and horse–and–wagon farming methods.

GOVERNMENT

Like Argentina and Uruguay, Chile fell under the rule of a military junta a few years ago, but unlike them, hasn't been able to achieve a democratic change. General Pinochet is in total control, and it doesn't look as if he is willing to step aside until March 1989. This may be a problem for many Americans, because they take political freedoms for granted, and feel concerned when they are suspended. However, it's best to keep your opinions to yourself until you know who you are speaking with. People in the street, cab drivers, and others are very reluctant to talk about the situation with strangers. But you can tell from some of the guarded things they say, that they are apprehensive about what may happen when things finally explode.

The political problem in Chile stems from the contrast between the working class, and the middle and upper classes. Where Argentinian workers traditionally have depended on labor unions to provide for their well–being, and where Uruguayans have depended upon their welfare state government, the Chilean workers put their hopes in political parties. For this reason, the communists have been active, and enjoy a substantial following. Although poverty and unemployment in Chile is nothing in comparison with most other South American countries, it is still a problem. When a worker is under–unemployed and without hope for an immediate change, anything looks better than the system he has.

Because of the possible instability of the government, and because of the potential for turmoil if the government falls, my recommendation for Chile as a residence is a cautious one. I certainly would feel very uneasy about investing money or buying real estate there. My choice would be to rent and always keep my eye on the political situation. There is a chance that a change from military to civilian rule can be accomplished peacefully, and that real progress can be made in improving conditions for workers. If that happens, Chile could be a real possibility as a long–term residence or retirement. In the meantime, it's great for an extra summer of interesting travel and relaxation.

At the moment, the government is issuing visas for no more than a year, which are renewable. The consulate I spoke with emphasized that this visa doesn't permit you to work, and the application has to be made from up here, not in Chile. You can obtain a 90–day tourist permit simply by showing your passport. This can be renewed inside the country. Unless you have some pressing need to stay in the country longer than three months at a time, the tourist permit is the best route to follow.

SANTIAGO

The fifth largest in South America, Santiago is one of the prettiest cities on the continent. Whoever laid out the town must have given a lot of thought to parks, for they are everywhere. Often, the center of a wide boulevard is beautifully landscaped, planted with graceful trees and beds of flowers. Several blocks of downtown have been turned into pedestrian malls, giving some sections of the city a park–like atmosphere. Modern for the most part, Santiago has only traces of its colonial past. It was founded in 1541 by Pedro de Valdivia, and grew slowly for centuries until the boom of last century. When that happened, the older buildings gave way to ornate 1890s architecture, which in turn is being replaced by steel and glass. Some of the older buildings of the 18th and 19th centuries are disappearing in favor of modern and, hopefully, seismic–proof construction.

Since Santiago is located about as far south of the Equator as Los Angeles is north, their climates are similar. My impression is, however, that Santiago winters are a bit warmer and probably dryer than those of Los Angeles. When people talk about an "eternal spring," I suspect that they have someplace like Santiago in mind.

One impressive feature about Santiago is the chain of mountains in the distance. Fringed with snow all year around, the Andes are quite high here, reaching up almost 23,000 feet, the highest in the Western Hemisphere. Even though they are about 60 miles from the city, they look as if they are just a few miles away. There are some excellent ski resorts here which attract plenty of enthusiasts and Olympic hopefuls for ski practice when it's summer in the rest of the world.

Chile probably has more ocean front land per square mile than any other country in the world. The Humboldt Current, which follows the coastline and controls the climate, also provides some of the best and varied seafood I have ever sampled. Don't miss going to a good seafood restaurant for a *curanto*. This is a dish piled high with every kind of shellfish imaginable, and some that are beyond imagination. One in particular, called a *picoroco*, which means *rock–beak* or something like that, is actually a giant barnacle, sometimes served attached to a broken piece of the rock on which it has grown. You pull the beak–like appendage that sticks out of the barnacle's shell and draw out a delicious chunk of meat that tastes like dungeness crab leg. Dip it in lemon butter and––oh, my!

A must to visit is the hill of Santa Lucia where views of the surrounding mountains compete for attention with the dramatic views of the city of Santiago below. The landscaping and historic monuments on this park–mountain make the climb to the top well worth while.

Santiago is a manufacturing center, and for this reason, plus what appears to be an inversion layer, a light smog sometimes covers the city. It usually isn't apparent until you climb one of the two peaks in the town, and look toward the mountains in the distance. As far as I know, smog isn't a serious problem. The amount I've noticed there would be called "haze" in many U.S. cities. Autos aren't too plentiful on the streets, so this keeps down air pollution. Public transport is heavily used. An excellent, sparkling clean subway, the Metro, takes you to the suburbs quickly and quietly.

Take the Metro north to find the pretty, affluent neighborhoods where most gringos choose to live. Here are substantial–look-

ing apartments and condominiums, as well as private residences rang-
ing from elegant to stunning. Yet rents are as reasonable as you could
expect to find anywhere in Latin America. The neighborhoods are
peaceful and sparkling clean. Along the main thoroughfares, shops,
restaurants and small businesses are comfortably interspersed among
single–family homes and small apartment buildings.

To the south of town you find working–class barrios and even
"shanty towns" where poor people live. The contrast in atmosphere
between neighborhoods is dramatic. Here is where police routinely
run searches for people opposed to the military government. Here is
a place Americans would be wise to avoid. The U.S. State Department lists 5,927 U.S. citizens living in Chile, most of them in Santiago. At one time an English–language newspaper brought news of
happenings to the expatriate colony, but now you must rely on the
Spanish–language daily, *El Mercurio*. Apartments for rent are listed
there. In renting a house or apartment, be fully aware of the political
situation and look for something in a middle–class neighborhood.
Unlike Argentina and Uruguay, the working class *barrios* are not
prosperous, and can be downright dangerous to live in. The upper-
class areas, however, are quite pleasant. It's as if the neighborhoods
were in totally different countries.

For skiing, you need only go 90 minutes to Farellones. The
months of June to September offer some really great slope adventure.
Then at Portillo, just a few kilometers farther, you'll find some of the
best snow conditions possible. Because of the altitude, there are no
trees, and the ski runs charge downhill to gently level out on the
frozen lake that covers the valley. Farellones is reached by daily
trains from Santiago. Several other resorts are within easy commute
from the capital.

Like the ocean? Vina del Mar is undoubtably the most popular
ocean resort in Chile. It's an easy 9–kilometer electric train ride from
Valparaiso. Rents in Vina del Mar are inflated somewhat, and many
choose to stay in Valparaiso and catch the train whenever the beach
mood settles in. Valparaiso, incidentally, is also on the ocean, but
doesn't have Vina's resort atmosphere.

SOUTH OF CHILE

If the northern part of Chile is one of the driest places in the
world, the southern parts make up for it by being the wettest. An

electric railway runs south as far as Puerto Montt, affording some of the prettiest scenery and richest farming countries to be found anywhere. The snowcapped Andes are always towering to the east and an ocean breeze (often bringing rains) blows from the west. Vineyards climb the foothill slopes, drinking run–off from snows and yielding lush harvests to produce the famous Chilean wines.

The social problems and politics of the city are soon forgotten in the south of Chile. "Nothing ever happens here," said a taxi driver one day. "All of the politics happen in Santiago." There are many large, prosperous farms, but also many more small, family farms that use oxen and mules instead of tractors. In the far south, you see farmhouses with thatched roofs, legacies of the German immigrants who settled here in the early part of the century. Their descendants comprise a good percentage of the population in this region and have considerable influence even today.

As you go farther south, the rainfall becomes greater, until at last, on the island of Chiloe you find an incredibly heavy annual precipitation table. The countryside is perpetually green, and when covered with wildflowers, is gorgeous. The people here seem to be serious and quiet. You can easily tell when Americans or Argentinians are present because of the typically loud talking, opposed to the soft–spoken, understated Chileans.

Puerto Montt is the last of mainland Chile with any appreciable population. A town of a little over 100,000, it presents a dreary face to the visitor at first, due to the unpainted, shingled wood buildings that make up most of the town. The reason for this type of construction, according to local residents, is that buildings of masonry soak up moisture and never dry out, whereas wooden buildings give up the water when the sun comes out, and in the long run they are dryer inside. But after while, the natural charm of the town comes through, and the buildings don't look quite so drab.

By the way, the seafood here and in neighboring Angelmo is probably the best in the whole world. Something about the cold ocean at this point produces shrimp, crab, oyster, clams and fish that are so superb that words cannot describe them. It's worth any amount of inconvenient traveling just to spend a few days filling up on the fruits of the sea in Puerto Montt. At the wharf in Angelmo, there is an old wooden building where fishermen bring in their catch. Inside the building and outside under canvas there are a couple of dozen small stands where they cook and serve fresh octopus, squid, tuna, oysters and shellfish of all descriptions. Abalone, steamed and drenched with butter--$1 for five of them. I defy any two hungry people to finish a *curanto* of seabass, oyster, mussel, picoroco, shrimp and crab that is, for some reason, topped off with a plump sausage. You sit on an orange crate in front of a wood–plank table and dig in! It might cost as much as $2.50. I wouldn't trade an afternoon here for the most expensive, white–tablecloth restaurant in the world.

From Puerto Montt south, you must take a ferry to the island of Chiloe. Along the coast you'll find scattered farms with patches of wheat and potatoes, and the inevitable flocks of sheep. Some of the farms edge on the ocean and some of them continue on by cultivating oysters in the shallows. Inland there are almost impenetrable beech woods and cold rain forest. The island is large, over 9,000 square miles, but with only two towns and very few people living in the country. Like the mainland, Chiloe has a rugged coastline of fjords and glacier–carved inlets. This is almost the last of human inhabitation in the Southern Hemisphere.

I have mixed feelings about recommending this part of the world as a place to spend more than a couple of weeks of sightseeing. Were it not for the bonanza of seafood, I probably wouldn't return. I am a man for the tropics. Yet, I met a couple of Americans (one from Los Angeles) who positively adore this part of South America. One of them has his own discovery even farther south of Chiloe, a tiny village on an inlet which leads to a freshwater lake. After hearing his description of the salmon fishing in the inlet and his warm relationship with the villagers, I came to understand his enthusiasm. Like many other parts of the world, it takes a special kind of person to find his own special adventures in a place others might not like at all.

CONCLUSION

Chile is my third choice among the three Euro–American countries. I personally prefer the more outgoing Argentinians or the friendly Uruguayans, but these are purely subjective impressions. I've met people who disagree vigorously with my analysis of the Chileans and the political situation there. These are decisions each must make individually, with as few preconceptions as possible. My suggestion is to go to Chile and see for yourself. Certainly, it's a very pleasant place for a vacation, an extra summer, or at the least, a dish of *curanto*.

CHAPTER 9

Indo-America: Struggling Societies

To truly understand why Indo–American countries are fundamentally different from the Euro–American nations, we must journey into the past. If we understand *who* settled there, *why* they came and *when* they arrived, we will have some insight as to why these countries are so different. The who and when and why are keys to explaining why most Latin American countries differ in economics, politics and philosophy from North America and the Euro–American countries. By understanding these factors, you will realize why things change so drastically when you cross the border from one country to another, why Mexico is so different from the United States, why Argentina is so different from Bolivia.

Almost 500 years ago, a tiny fleet of Spanish ships set sail to search for a shortcut to India. After several weeks, they ran into a problem. An unsuspected continent blocked their way.

Spain and Portugal soon bubbled over with news of Columbus' discoveries of rich land within easy sailing distance, and immediately dispatched expeditions to report back on possible wealth. Stories of abundant gold and silver trickled back to tantalize the adventurous. The largest gold rush in history was on. First Mexico, then Peru, along with what would later become Bolivia and Ecuador, fell under the scrutiny and superior arms of Spanish prospectors and miners. These nations, in particular, quickly became accustomed to their new masters, since they already had long traditions of bowing to authoritarian political bosses who told them what to do. The conquering newcomers, mostly men, quickly intermarried with the local belles,

Indo-America

and founded the large mestizo race seen today in the Indo–American countries.

Colombia was tougher to conquer than Peru, but soon its mineral wealth was being gleaned from the earth to enrich Spanish coffers. Venezuela also contained gold, and was quickly overrun by the gold–hungry Spaniards. Other countries, such as Argentina, Uruguay and Chile weren't very valuable, at least in the eyes of gold hunters. Besides, the Indians here weren't used to "civilization" like the Incas and Aztecs, and fought fiercely to maintain their freedom. This prevented quick settlement and division of lands as happened in Indo–America.

Spain, at the time of New World discoveries, had just finished defeating the Moors after centuries of systematic warfare, and was in the process of consolidating several kingdoms into a nation. A class of aristocratic warriors, the *hidalgos*, had evolved over the years of fighting. Now that the nation was finally unified, there was nothing for them to do but settle down and become landed nobles. How much more exciting was the prospect of conquest and riches of a new world! At the same time, the rulers of Spain saw the opportunity to rid the country of a potentially dangerous class of warrior–aristocrats who knew of nothing but conflict and excitement. Royal grants were handed out freely, giving the hidalgos and others of minor nobility huge tracts of land in the New World. Immense sighs of relief must have sounded through the royal chambers in Castille when the dangerous ones departed.

When the new tenants arrived to take possession of their lands, they happily discovered a civilized population of *indios*, hard–working and accustomed to taking orders from their masters, much as the serfs in Spain were used to tilling fields for the feudal nobility. To work with one's own hands was not a habit of the nobility. That's what serfs and slaves were for. The notion that the elite does not do manual labor has carried down to the present time, almost 500 years later. A Latin American gentleman today seldom calluses his hands at work, it's considered almost degrading. Farming is typically done "plantation" style, with large estates often worked with inefficient methods and minimum–wage workers. When the land isn't rich enough for this kind of farming, landowners institute a system of "sharecropping" with absentee owners taking a percentage of the harvest. This is the same feudal system their ancestors brought with them from Spain or Portugal centuries ago. Much land lies fallow because the wealthy landowners don't need additional income.

Principles of industrialism are almost foreign to this class, because the Industrial Revolution exploded in Europe *after* Indo–America was already settled and "civilized." Today, modern equipment isn't much admired or understood by absentee owners. Machinery is often not maintained properly, and inefficient manufacturing methods are common. Poverty and low standards of living characterize the lower classes, while the upper classes live in luxury, often residing in Europe and running their business by mail.

This is all in high contrast with Euro–America and North America, which were largely settled by workers and farmers displaced during the Industrial Revolution and its aftermath. England, Italy, Germany, France and other European countries went through great upheavals. Their emigrants were the poor, the unsuccessful, workers who had lost their jobs, small farmers who no longer had land to work with their plows. All they knew was working with their hands, utilizing whatever tools and whatever land they could find. Work was not an embarrassing disgrace. Since they understood tools and machinery, they also understood the need for maintenance and repair.

To recap: three factors were at work in the developing colonies. One was the time frame in which the countries were settled: Either before or after the Industrial Revolution and either before or after independence from Spain. The second was the attitude of Spain toward its colonies as a source of extractable, not cultivated, wealth, and as a place to send surplus nobility. The third was the social classes of the emigrants: factory workers, farmers or aristocrats. The interplay among these factors accounts for today's differences between Indo–America and Euro–America. They help explain the philosophical differences among Latin countries, the spread between rich and poor, the dichotomy between notions of superiority and equality.

The story of Paraguay, the fifth country included in Indo–America is different. Instead of being conquered by the hidalgos, the Indians of Paraguay were contacted by Jesuit missionaries, and peacefully introduced to European civilization. The missionaries encouraged the Indians to leave the jungles and adopt the ways of European civilization in what amounted to a socialistic–paternalistic society. They built towns and learned skills as builders, artists, and craftsmen of all kinds. The missions they set up were splendidly self-sufficient, and even became manufacturers and exporters. Because few settlers from Spain entered Paraguay at that time, outside influence on the Indian race was and still is minimal. To this day, almost all Paraguayans speak their original language, Guarani, in addition to Spanish. Apparently, Paraguay was on its way to becoming an advanced nation when the Jesuits were suddenly expelled by the King of Spain in 1767. Economic and political pressures on the Indians caused the social system to collapse, and Paraguay never managed to recover. It's history has been one dictatorial ruler after another, with thoughts of freedom and democracy strictly suppressed.

CIVIL STRIFE

For centuries, civil unrest stirred by the unequal balance between rich and poor has agonized Indo–America. The wealthy oligarchy is understandably reluctant to surrender its position of power and affluence, while the peasants and workers are often attracted to drastic reform movements that lean toward violence and dynamite as political statements. Efforts toward compromise, agrarian change and economic betterment for the peasant classes are underway, more in some countries, none in others. But these underdeveloped countries have a long way to go. For these reasons I would hesitate recommending retirement or long–term residency in any of the Indo–American countries.

Some are continually on the verge of a popular revolution. Others are problematical. Since change has been contained for so long, a successful revolution could spell disaster for foreign interests. Colombia, for example, has been fighting civil wars for so long that guerrilla combat and violence has become almost institutionalized. While there are a number of U.S. citizens living there (12,912 in Bogota, 5,611 in Barranquilla, according to the Foreign Service Institute), my guess is that most of them are there as employees of international corporations or in business for themselves. Few North Americans have the courage or patience to put up with constant threats of violent crime. An acquaintance of mine was robbed at knifepoint in Bogota one night a couple of years back. When he reported the crime to the police, they seem to feel that it was his own fault because he wasn't carrying a gun to protect himself.

While crime in Peru, Ecuador and Bolivia isn't as violent as in Colombia, it is appallingly common in the form of pickpocketing, burglaries and petty theft. I love to visit these countries, and encourage others to enjoy their scenic and archaeological treasures. But after a while I become weary of continually clinging to my camera and hiding my wallet. I feel relieved to return to Argentina or Uruguay where things feel safe. Americans who live in Peru or Bolivia, and who enjoy living there, tell me that after a while, all of this becomes second nature and it doesn't bother them at all. There are 2,380 Americans living in La Paz and almost 10,000 in Lima. The ones I've met seem to love it, so what can I say?

The problem here is economic, with petty crime an attractive alternative to toiling for shockingly poor wages. The only solution would seem to be a dramatic economic change, with jobs and financial security substituting for crime.

Venezuela is another story. It has a fairly high standard of living and seems to be politically stable. Much of this is due to its enviable position as a petroleum exporter. But the cost of living is high there, as well. Wages are higher, for many jobs, than even in the United States, and rents and food are also expensive. Caracas is a great place for a visit, but my budget takes a shredding after a couple of days, and I can't help but think of how much better off I would be spending my money in Mexico or Costa Rica.

The final country in our survey of Indo–America is Paraguay. This is a peaceful country, because General Alfred Stroessner, its strong–fisted president crushes all opposition. If his critics look as if they *might* not be peaceful, they tend to disappear. I must admit that I've never visited Paraguay, but I believe I am being fair in not recommending it as a safe place for North Americans. The people I've interviewed, including some U.S. citizens who work there, tell me that it isn't a particularly pleasant place to be under any circumstances.

None of this is meant to discourage tourism in Indo–America. The inconvenience of having to be careful for a few weeks is nothing compared to the glorious adventures awaiting you in these countries. From dense jungles to panoramic desert scenery, city and primitive village, Indo–America is a sightseer's delight. The seafood restaurants in Peru and Ecuador rival any in the world. Coffee farms in Colombia, tin mines in Bolivia, archaeological treasures such as Machu Picchu, Lake Titicaca, Nasca, and other amazing sites are mandatory sightseeing if you are to really know South America. It's just these places are not my idea of a place for permanent or semi-permanent living.

CHAPTER 10

Afro-America: Brazil and the Guianas

The last four countries in South America comprise Afro–America. These are Brazil and the three Guianas: Guyana, Surinam, and French Guiana. Actually, French Guiana, or Guyane, is still part of France and not properly an independent country.

The Guianas are tiny places, while Brazil is enormous. Almost as large as the United States, Brazil takes up nearly half of all of South America. Its population, about 130 million, is rather sparse for the amount of land, and is crowded into a long coastal strip along the Atlantic Ocean. The interior of Brazil is among the least settled places on earth. One third of the country is a rain forest famous for its isolation and wild Indian tribes: the Amazon Basin. Jungle, forest, swamp and mountain separated Brazil from its neighbors and helped it form a distinct Brazilian culture, isolated from Spanish influences.

Portugal jumped into the New World settlement race early. As a seafaring nation, the idea of overseas colonization wasn't new to it. Successive Portuguese kings had colonized areas as far away as the coasts of India and China. Columbus was well aware of this, so when seeking funds for his ambitious westward voyage of discovery, he came to the king of Portugal first. Although the king gave Columbus the brush–off, he watched the expedition with keen interest. As soon as word about Columbus' discoveries slipped out, the king began outfitting his own ships. Eight years after Columbus' blundering mistake, Portugal planted a permanent colony on the north coast of Brazil at Salvador da Bahia.

Afro-America

GUIANAS

BRAZIL

Rio de Janiero •

Sao Paulo •

The type of settlers from Portugal were similar to the ones Spain sent: aristocrats who often became absentee landlords once their huge estates were functioning properly. The earliest developers were rich settlers from the north of Portugal and they brought with them traditions of large feudal estates. The big attraction was the chance to turn enormous profits without working too hard in the process. Brazil is tropical, just right for sugar cane, a crop that could lead to instant riches in those days. The new settlers intermingled with the natives, creating the forerunner of today's mestizo population. Large numbers of Indians fell under the onslaughts of white man's diseases and plagues. Others fled into the jungles to escape their demanding new masters. This caused a labor shortage, which the Portuguese solved by importing slaves from Africa. To supply the demand, the Portuguese (along with the British and Dutch) developed the infamous slave trade, ravaging Africa for humans to be sold and worked like machines.

The aristocratic landowners felt little attachment to the land; their interests were in reaping whatever harvest they could, mineral or agricultural, and moving on. This "frontier spirit" is evident today in modern Brazil. In a way, it's perfectly understandable since there seems to be unlimited land for exploitation. But many are growing concerned about the wanton destruction of irreplaceable rain forests and their delicate ecology. Ironically, a great deal of Brazil which could be economically farmed remains relatively unexploited.

The bulk of the rain forests are sparsely inhabited by primitive tribes. Over the centuries they have evolved a workable culture which enables them to survive in this hostile environment. When whites start cutting trees and trying to do traditional, European-type farming, it usually turns out to be a disaster. Once the trees are gone, heavy rains leach nutrients from the shallow soil, turning it into muddy goop in the wet season, and brick-hard pavement in the dry season. Once the trees are gone, little can grow in this ruined soil, and it takes centuries for the trees to make a comeback, if at all.

For many years Brazil rolled along easily, with little conflict, either with neighbors or with the mother country. Then in the early 1800s, when Napoleon invaded the Iberian Peninsula, Brazil joined the other countries of South America in demanding independence. It's an interesting aside to note that few colonies wanted independence from Spain (or Portugal) so much as they refused to be governed by France. Napoleon had invaded the Iberian Peninsula, placed his cousin on the Spanish throne and tossed the king of Spain into prison. The king of Portugal fled to Brazil. The unusual thing about Brazil's independence was that it was the king of Portugal himself, King Joao VI, who declared Brazil to be independent from Portugal.

Until the middle 1800s, whites were by far the minority group. blacks and mestizos formed the bulk of the population, with blacks the majority. Then from 1842 on, one crisis after another in Europe stimulated emigration to South America. The same kinds of displaced people who descended on Argentina, Uruguay and Chile (as well as the United States, Costa Rica and Canada), came pouring into Brazil. Of the millions of immigrants from Europe between 1800 and 1955, 30 percent were Portuguese, 32 percent were Italian. Germans, Poles and Slavs also came in appreciable numbers. With all this immigration, the balance between whites and Africans changed until today 60 percent of Brazil's coastal population is Caucasian, or mostly so. About 36 percent is black, mulatto or mestizo. The percentages in the southern part of Brazil, from Rio de Janeiro south, show a much higher white population. In the north, especially around Bahia, blacks are in the majority.

While racial discrimination is officially illegal, there seems to be much de facto discrimination in that most of the best jobs and professions accrue to the whites. It's in the *favelas*, or slums, where the high percentage of blacks make their presence known. Literacy is much lower in Brazil than in the Euro–American countries, with only 60 percent of the people staying in school long enough to become literate.

Things are changing, although very slowly. For example the average life expectancy has risen from 39 years before World War II to 58 years today. Lower by far than Argentina or Uruguay, but a dramatic improvement, nonetheless.

RIO, THE EPITOME OF JET SPLENDOR

According to government statistics, there are 37,000 U.S. citizens living in Brazil. The overwhelming majority are in either the Rio de Janeiro or Sao Paulo areas. Most are employed in Brazil's burgeoning manufacturing industry. But a large number of North Americans also seem to prefer Brazil as either a full or part–time living experience. Most choose Rio de Janeiro–13,800, according to the Foreign Service Institute.

The beauty of the scenery here is almost beyond description. Travel books and magazines lavish flowery descriptions on Sugar Loaf, Corcovado, the mountains, the bay, the ocean, but few of them are good enough to capture the pure beauty of Rio.

One of the plushest cities I've ever seen, Rio is more than just a collection of tall apartment buildings and classy restaurants. It seems to have a certain beat about it as though *Carnaval* is a year–around state of mind. The tempo is fast, and people walk along the streets to the beat of a city on the move. Samba music sounds from music stores by day and from discos and outdoor restaurants by night. The stereotypical languor and laid–back living of the tropics is just not the way it's done in Rio.

In Rio's posh Ipanema and Copacabana neighborhoods, you find numerous expatriates renting or owning apartments within walking distance of the beaches. Some stay all year around (the winter seldom becomes so chilly that you can't enjoy the beach). Most, however, are "snowbirds," flying south at the first taste of dreaded snow and ice of the northern winters, then returning to enjoy spring and summer at home.

Rentals in Rio are quite reasonable, even in Ipanema and Copacabana. The exception is any time close to the famous Carnaval. It pays to rent a place for the year around and let it sit vacant for half the year rather than try to rent something during that rush season. A two–bedroom apartment that rents for $150–$300 a month all year–round can command $100 a day during Carnaval.

Food, both in restaurants and in supermarkets, is as low–priced as any I've seen in South America, less than in most places. In Ipanema, on one of the main squares, one day a week is set aside as market day. It is worth visiting if only to see what kinds of foods are available. Individual booths and stands line the square, tempting buyers with luscious displays of vegetables, tropical fruits, freshly caught fish, meats and foodstuffs of all descriptions.

Recently, the government instituted currency reforms together with price and wage controls, much the same as Argentina did six months earlier. It remains to be seen whether the effort will be effective or not.

The one drawback to choosing Rio as a residence is the high rate of crime. This is another place where you must be continually aware of what is going on around you. You must hold onto your camera at all times, keep your wallet hidden and not carry a purse if you don't have to. The police urge motorists not to stop for traffic lights at night; just make sure no one is coming and drive on through. In some rough neighborhoods, thieves have been known to rob motorists who are out late at night. I don't know why the police urge the motorists to ignore the signals at night; they seldom observe them in daylight! Traffic laws there don't seem to be taken seriously. The drivers are some of the wildest I've seen this side of a destruction derby.

An interesting thing about traffic in Brazil is the lack of exhaust fumes and odor. Since 1983, all new autos sold must burn alcohol instead of gasoline. When alcohol burns, its emissions are water vapor and odorless carbon dioxide. Traveling through one of the long tunnels that bore through the mountains to get from one side of Rio to the other places you in the middle of four lanes of traffic almost bumper to bumper. Yet the air smells as fresh as that outside the tunnel! It's a strange feeling to expect exhaust fumes and smell fresh air instead.

As much as I love the excitement and the low cost of living in Rio, I would hesitate to recommend it as a long–term residence. The reason is what would have to become your continual preoccupation with the petty crime of the city. This is pretty much how I feel about most of the cities in Brazil. But as a winter escape, or even a summer sojourn, it can be a memorable adventure in foreign living. Affordable, too.

Should you decide to try a winter there, my suggestion would be to look for an apartment in the Ipanema or Leblon sections. These stretch along the beach and are separated only by a canal. Leblon is more expensive than Ipanema, but perhaps a little less touristy, and with fewer pickpockets working. If you travel farther along the coast you come to a more peaceful section called Barra (pronounced *bah ha* by the Brazilians). This is on the edge of Rio, where the city starts to meld into country. While it isn't exactly rural, it is quieter and the pace is slower. You can find small houses for rent here, and the beaches are far less crowded.

The best place to watch for rental ads is the newspaper classified sections. Also, many hotel clerks can steer you to a reasonable apartment, because they keep a list of places where they can steer guests to when their hotels are full. To find an apartment in Copacabana, all you have to do is walk along one of the main streets with a suitcase in your hand––you'll have half a dozen people offering to show you one. Apartment rentals are a big business there. You can rent by the day, the week, the month or the year.

SAO PAULO

Another exciting city with lots happening, Sao Paulo is said to be the fastest growing city in the world. A hundred years ago it was little more than a grubby collection of shacks, yet today it spreads out over 1,500 square kilometers (700 square miles). Its population (10 million+) surpasses that of Rio by far, and could be even larger than Buenos Aires, making it the largest city in South America. Yet it has managed to avoid the jumbled appearance of most boomtowns. With ample parks and well–lit streets, its skyscrapers seem to have a certain grace and urbanity. Its subway is superior to Rio's and its automobile drivers are perhaps a bit more ferocious. Sao Paulo is the second most popular spot in Brazil for Americans. Statistics show 12,364 U.S. citizens living there. Of course, most work for a living, but many simply like Sao Paulo.

Here, as in Rio, you feel an intensity of purpose in the air. Factories, manufacturing, sales—everything seems to be booming. New people arrive at the rate of 150,000–a–year to seek their fortunes. The frontier mentality of the Brazilians is as prominent here as anywhere in the country. This area turns out over 75 percent of the automobiles manufactured in the country, and 90 percent of Brazil's textiles, chemicals and pharmaceuticals. In addition, it is in the center of an extremely rich agricultural area. The demand for electronics technicians and engineers is one of the drawing cards for savvy Americans, who recognize Sao Paulo as the new land of unlimited opportunity.

Sao Paulo is the most European of Brazilian cities, and probably the most cosmopolitan. Here you'll find a considerable sprinkling of Japanese technologists and businessmen, as well as industrial representatives from all over the world. This is a city for those who love big cities. My understanding is that crime here is less ubiquitous than in Rio, yet like most cities in Brazil, it's there. This might be the choice of someone who wants to work for a living or start a new career.

ROMANTIC BAHIA

A thousand miles north of Rio is another popular place for American tourists, the state of Bahia. A few, about 800, stay year around in the capital, Salvador. More use the entire state of Bahia as temporary winter quarters. Bahia attracts hundreds of thousands of tourists every winter, particularly for the world-famous Carnaval in Salvador. People there want to do the Carnaval celebration right, so they start warming up in November to make sure they have it down pat by February. If you like parties, you'll love Bahia.

With 35 or 40 miles of great beaches lining the coast, Bahia is a beachcomber's paradise. Because it's closer to the equator, the winter temperatures are higher than Rio's and the water is warmer. Here is where many Brazilians and Argentinians love to spend the months of June, July and August, to escape their winter season and seek *their* "second summer." April and May are the rainiest months and things can get rather muggy.

In Bahia you definitely know that you are in "Afro-America" because of the dark faces you see around you, and hints of *candomble* you feel in the air. Candomble is the local version of voodoo. Bahian cuisine, distinctive and delicious, traces its roots to Africa. You'll find dishes in which fish, shrimp, crabs, nuts and coconut milk are cooked together, or chicken is cooked in a stew of its own blood. Not as bad as it sounds, actually.

This was the first part of Brazil to be settled by the Portuguese, and it's here that you can find plentiful examples of early colonial architecture. Unfortunately, much of it has fallen into disrepair, as if the people were more interested in the modern sections of town with tall buildings.

Unfortunately, despite all of its charm, Bahia, like the other cities in Brazil has fallen under the curse of crime. It's probably even worse than Rio or Sao Paulo. People who live there claim all of this started six to seven years ago, and has steadily become worse. Who knows, maybe things will turn around someday.

To enter Brazil as a tourist, you must obtain a visa from a Brazilian consulate *before* entering the country. You then are entitled to 90 days, multiple entry. On this visa you cannot work. If you are going to work, the visa is issued for one year and routinely renewed once. Then another application must be made. For retirement, you must prove a monthly income of $500. To start a business, a minimum amount of money must be deposited in a Brazilian bank. The consul I spoke with advised people to "visit Brazil for at least 90 days before deciding to apply for a resident's visa." But the paperwork must be started at a Brazilian consulate in the United States or Canada.

Brazil is a fascinating country, one where I hope to spend many winter months of my life. The people are friendly, the cost of living affordable, and there are many, many interesting places to visit. My main reservation about Brazil as a choice for long–term residency or retirement is the annoying petty–crime that's so common in the cities. For that reason, I hesitate to recommend the country for other than vacations or an occasional escape from northern winters. Many Americans will disagree with me on this, particularly those who live there permanently. This is another one of those individual situations which may suit one person and not the other. By all means, give it a try if you think that Brazil might be your Shangri–la.

THE GUIANAS

These three little pieces of land nestle in the uppermost corner of the continent. The only colonies in South America settled by European countries other than Spain or Portugal, they never attracted many European settlers. It isn't surprising. The interiors are all but uninhabitable, and the climate is hot and steamy. Most people live in narrow strips of land along the ocean. Many people, including the people living in the Guianas do not consider the residents there as Latin Americans. Since they speak neither Spanish nor Portuguese, they fall outside the bounds of our definition of *Latin* America, but because they are physically located in Latin America, they are included in this book. The cultural differences and isolation from the rest of South America, and the fact that they were colonies of Europe long after the rest of Latin America gained independence makes them very different from the rest of the countries discussed here.

Columbus explored the coast here in 1498, but found nothing worth looking into further. Later Spanish and Portuguese colonists thought the Guiana coast uninhabitable and didn't bother to land. But the British, French and Dutch were quite anxious to establish a foothold in South America. They tried several places, but were rebuffed by the Spanish and Portuguese, so they settled for the unwanted Guianas. Today, the countries are still almost uninhabited, hot, muggy and isolated. It looks as if the early Spanish and Portuguese explorers were correct in their analysis.

The three countries which comprise the Guianas are: Guyana, which until 1966 was a part of the British Empire; Surinam, which received its independence from the Dutch in 1975; and French Guiana, which remains an Overseas Department of France.

SURINAM

It's interesting to note that Surinam was originally settled by the British, who in a diplomatic bargain, traded it to the Dutch in return for title to an island the Dutch had colonized in North America. The island, then called *Nieuw Amsterdam*, would later be known as Manhattan. The swap must have looked like a good deal to the Dutch back then, because they had only paid $24 worth of beads and trinkets for the 23-square-mile island. Somehow I feel the Dutch got the worst of the deal. Of course, it could have been worse, they might have accepted Pittsburgh in trade.

While other countries in South America are gaining in population, Surinam is losing citizens as they emigrate to the Netherlands as quickly as they can. The political and economic situations are not happy in Surinam. Dutch in the official language, but the large black population speaks "pidgin" English, and standard English is quite common. The racial makeup of Surinam is an interesting mixture of African-Europeans, East Indians, Chinese and "Bush Blacks" (descendants of escaped slaves who live remarkably as their ancestors in West Africa). Only 2 percent of the population is pure European.

In the 1600s, about 1,000 British colonists began farming in Surinam, planting tobacco and importing many slaves. Later, when slavery was finally outlawed, the planters began bringing in indentured Chinese as replacements. These Chinese and blacks formed the nucleus of the present-day population. Further immigration from Java and India completed the mixture which today is Surinam. Holland granted independence in 1975, but in 1980 a military coup toppled the government. What followed is typical of situations like this: Press censorship, and a "temporary" state of emergency was declared.

GUYANA

Formerly British Guyana, Surinam's neighbor to the west, is in a similar position as far as politics and economics is concerned. The racial makeup is similar. From both countries come reports of hostility toward the white population, which comprises less than one percent of the total. Guyana is equally unlivable from my perspective, and equally unsuitable for consideration as a residence.

Although the country has over 80,000 square miles and is almost the size of Britain, only 0.5 percent of the land is cultivated. The first colonists from England and Holland imported over 100,000 slaves, and later, when slavery was abolished, brought in Chinese and East Indian workers. Today the racial balance is less than 1 percent European, 61 percent East Indian and about 30% African.

Some travel books warn about criminal activities such as purse snatchings, muggings and robberies. There are also warnings about racial tension and anti–white prejudices. Food shortages, expensive accommodations and political unrest all combine to discourage all but the most intrepid traveler. If you can put up with these inconveniences, there is said to be some interesting country to be seen inland, some spectacular waterfalls, for example. But for long–term living or retirement––hardly.

GUYANE

The most easternmost country, Guyane, may have a hope for the future, since it still belongs to France and the French government has been talking about development and massive aid. But like its neighbors, Guyane suffers from hot, muggy climate and heavy rainfall. Not a place many would want to visit, much less live. I'm afraid that's my opinion of all of the Guyanas. But then again, they really can't be considered part of Latin America, since the language, the culture and the people have very little in common with Latin America.

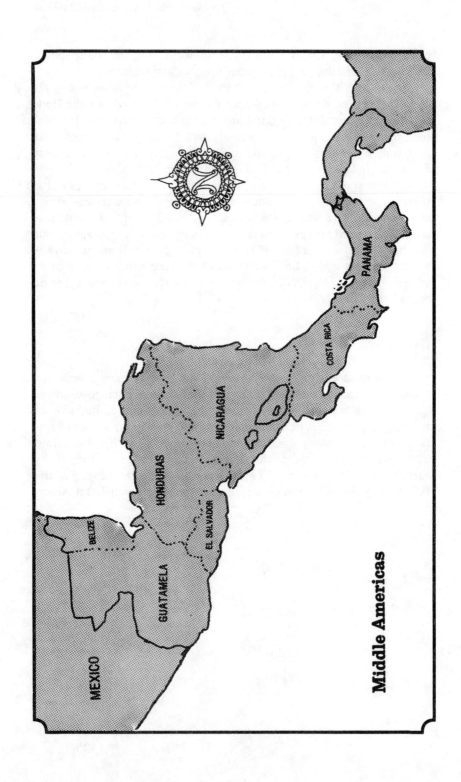

Middle Americas

CHAPTER 11

Why the Middle Americas?

By Middle Americas, I mean that stretch of land between the United States and South America. Geographically, Mexico is part of the North American Continent, yet its culture, temperament, and language are so closely connected with Central America that I feel it should be grouped with the Central American countries. So Middle America, in this book, takes in Mexico, Guatemala, Belize, Honduras, El Salvador, Nicaragua, Costa Rica and Panama. Each country is different in many ways from the others, but there are enough common links to justify treating them as a unit.

We hear mostly about Mexico and the Central American countries in terms of inflation, drugs, revolutions, wars, mercenaries and terrorists. Why would anyone in his right mind want to travel, live or retire there?

First of all, the news media reports from Central America are highly exaggerated. Events that are confined to small, often inaccessible areas tend to be applied to the whole. You might be interested to know that people down there receive the same kinds of messages about the United States. They learn through TV programs (with Spanish subtitles) that sex, crime, violence, drugs and sadistic behavior are the way of life in the United States. They believe we live in constant fear of being struck by stray bullets or having criminals burst into our homes. According to the media, these are everyday happenings in North America. (Nobody on my block has been hit by a stray bullet in weeks.) Most news stories about the United States deal with serial killers, rapists, Mafia capers and drug busts. Sure, these things occur here, they can anywhere, but unless you live in a far different neighborhood than mine, it's highly unlikely you've ever seen these things happen except on TV.

It's interesting to think about why U.S. newspapers run banner headlines when an American is robbed or killed in Mexico or other parts of Middle America. When an undercover narcotics agent was killed in Mexico, it made great news copy—even the President of the United States held a news conference to denounce it. But had the agent been blown away in Miami by Cubans, or in Chicago by U.S. mobsters, the event wouldn't even make front page headlines in the local newspapers.

It's the old story of what makes news: when a dog bites a man, it's not news, but when a man bites a dog, that's different. Murders in Mexico and Middle America are rare. Murders and drug killings are so common in the United States that if the front pages were to cover every one, there wouldn't be room for anything else, and the paper would be boring.

It's my firm opinion that tourists and residents are safer by far in most parts of Middle America than in some places "back home." Far safer. This opinion doesn't come from the top of my head, it comes from years of first-hand experience. I've lived and traveled in Mexico and Central America since I was a boy. I've traveled by train, air and bus. I've driven more miles in Mexico than any North American I've ever met, and more than 95 percent of the Mexican citizens I've ever met. Two years ago, I put 12,000 miles on my pickup in just one five-month trip. Never in all my years have I been hassled (other than with deserved speeding tickets). Never have I ever talked with anyone who has been molested. Occasionally I've listened patiently while someone tells me the story about a brother-in-law who has a friend who claims he has been mistreated. Until the day I run into that brother-in-law's friend and hear the details from him, I'm dubious.

True, there are bad things happening in some Middle American areas, some countries where you would be advised not to consider anything more than a short vacation. But these trouble spots aren't places you would want to live even under the best of circumstances. Before we go any further, let's clear up some common misunderstandings about other aspects of life in Middle America.

REVOLUTIONS, WARS, POLITICS

Contrary to popular belief, there have been few genuine revolutions in the Middle Americas during its entire history. We must distinguish between a *coup d'etat* and a revolution. A *coup d'etat* is simply a small group of military officers taking control at gunpoint and kicking out the previous group of military officers. A coup rarely means change, other than deciding which clique gets to enjoy the spoils of graft and corruption. But in a revolution, the people rise up against the government to install a completely new government. A revolution is the ultimate expression of the people when there is no democratic mechanism for changing the government through elections. A revolution cannot succeed unless civilian disgust with the government is so strong that it is able to overwhelm the armed forces of that government.

Unfortunately, the United States, through the CIA and other organizations, has been instrumental in several ill-advised adventures that have resulted in repressive governments in Middle America. Perhaps the alternatives to dictatorships might have been worse under the circumstances, but the point is, these changes in government weren't revolutions, they were military takeovers. Happily today, presumably with the blessing and encouragement of the United States, changes are taking place in all of Latin America. Country after country has been getting rid of the military governments and testing the waters of democracy once again.

Guatemala is only now, after 40 years of military mismanagement attempting a return to democratic rule. Nicaragua, after suffering more than 50 years of the Somoza family (who were installed by U.S. Marines) finally threw off the stranglehold of the Somoza family, only to fall under a Marxist dictatorship. Whether the people can regain control remains to be seen. El Salvador has felt the yoke of militarism since the 1930s, and is fighting a civil war that pits rebels against an oligarchic–military regime. The sad thing is that no matter who wins, it is extremely unlikely that conditions will improve in El Salvador. About 26 wealthy families own almost everything there, but if you were to take all their wealth and distribute it among the peasants, they would still be desperately poor. Under the best of conditions, neither El Salvador nor Nicaragua would be countries where you would want to spend much time anyway, for climatic and esthetic reasons, never mind the politics and fighting going on.

The only other revolution that has taken place in Middle America since independence from Spain is the Mexican revolution of 1910–1920. So, what the newspapers love to refer to as revolutions are simply "palace coups", in–fighting among military cliques. Seldom are civilians ever injured or inconvenienced in these coups. The deposed president usually goes back into his general's uniform, or takes a job as ambassador to Holland or someplace safe and out of the way.

I mention these circumstances only to give you an idea of what is happening. Never would I advise long–term living or retirement in Nicaragua or El Salvador. Nor would I recommend Panama or Honduras. Yes, there are North Americans living in all of those countries, but each that I've talked to either have special reasons for living there—job or a business—or they are into adventure and exotic living. That isn't to say that short–term travel isn't interesting in these areas. I've driven in Central America recently and have talked to several people who've driven cars, even a motor home as far as Panama, with never a problem. Of course they were careful to detour around the trouble spots.

Clearly, traveling in the wrong parts of El Salvador or Nicaragua these days could be highly exciting, and occasionally dangerous. I know Americans who have vacationed right through the war areas anyway and reject my suggestion that they aren't playing with a full deck. The worst thing about travel in Nicaragua (away from the jungles where the skirmishing is happening) is rationing of gasoline, plus the unrealistic money exchange rate the bureaucratic government places on tourists. My recommendation is: If you must travel through these countries, do as I do, stick to the main highways and don't tarry. You wouldn't want to anyway, even if things were peaceful.

What about wars? Aren't you liable to be caught in the middle if one country invades another? No. Except for the outside–financed mercenaries who raid Nicaragua from Honduras, the question of war between these little republics is all but ludicrous. The only incident in this century was the "Soccer War" between Honduras and El Salvador in 1969. It started at a soccer game between the two countries, when boisterous fans got out of hand and began to riot. The El Salvador police, who were keeping order, started shooting the Honduran fans. Honduras, infuriated, declared war and invaded El Salvador. There were several weeks of fighting, resulting in several hundred deaths. After a few weeks, a cease–fire was agreed to and Honduran troops withdrew.

This war is the exception to peaceful co–existence among Middle–American countries. It was confined to mountainous areas where few if any North Americans were living. Still, even if countries like Nicaragua, Panama, Belize, El Salvador and Honduras were models of international peace and cooperation, not many gringos would choose to pay them more than a passing visit. The principal reason is not danger of war or revolution. These countries are uncomfortably poor, have high crime rates, and more importantly, suffer from climates that are unbearably hot and humid.

GUATEMALA

That leaves us with Guatemala, Mexico and Costa Rica. Guatemala too, has had a succession of military governments, mostly extremely corrupt. However, things are changing, with a free election in 1985 and a hope for a return to democracy. The country seems ready to support a peaceful change. Perhaps with the military government out of the picture, the reason for the current insurgency might be removed.

But Guatemala is so beautiful and the conflicts so far removed from where Americans would care to live, that many do live there. There are 6,600 U.S. citizens there, mostly in Guatemala City, but with many scattered around the countryside.

Guatemala has a special type of internal conflict, the kind that appears to have no solution. It's a racial–cultural problem, between Indian and white. There are many tribes of indigenous peoples, descendents of the Mayas, who are living pretty much as their ancestors did before the Spanish came almost half a thousand years ago. They have never assimilated the European culture the conquistadores brought with them. A large percentage of the Indian population has never even learned Spanish. The conflict arises between factions of the whites over what to do with the Indians.

One side maintains that the Indians are poor, deprived, oppressed, and should be allowed to enter the 20th century. They feel that the Indian has been deprived of many of the benefits of civilization and deserves a better life than a harsh, primitive existence. They accuse their opposites of being cruel, cynical and unfeeling over the fate of the Indian.

The other side of the argument is that the Indian has developed his way of life over the centuries, and that he is happy and at peace with the environment. The maintain that it would be cruel and unfeeling to force the Indians to become wage slaves, and to give up their culture. They accuse their opposites of wanting to exploit the Indians for cheap labor in factories, and to move them off the land for selfish motives.

Both sides sound reasonable. There seems to be no middle ground. Unfortunately, partly because the Indians don't speak Spanish, no one bothers to ask what *they* want. The end result has been a war of attrition against the Indian, with thousands of them being slaughtered by some of the past military governments. Hopefully, this is a thing of the past. Again, most of this fighting has taken place way out in the jungle, where few, if any, North Americans ever venture. I made an archaeological trip there—about four years ago—in the middle of the Peten jungle, where soldiers and guerrillas were hunting each other. We were pretty sure that both sides knew we were there, but we were ignored.

I could urge a cautious look at Guatemala as a possible living location, at least for part of a year. Particularly if the unrest in the countryside is resolved by the new government. If and when this happens, there will be a rush to return there. With 6,600 U.S. citizens living there, it can't be too bad.

The biggest drawback to long–term living or retirement plans in Guatemala is the high cost of living caused by the artificial money exchange rate. Some people who live there say I'm wrong about this, that costs are very reasonable. But I remember paying $3.50 for a gallon of gasoline and $5 for a meal that would cost half that in Mexico. Certainly wages are low, and probably if one lives there as a resident, and knows where and how to buy, it's different. Anyway, I'm hoping that the movement towards calmness in the countryside continues. If this happens, Guatemala could be one of the great retirement spots as it once was. For now, let's just say that it bears watching and consideration.

MEXICO

Mexico is a great retirement option. Don Merwin and I covered Mexico in great detail in our recent book CHOOSE MEXICO. The big advantage to Mexico is its proximity to the United States and Canada, allowing you to drive your auto there and try it out without making any drastic moves. Mexico is certainly a priority candidate for retirement living. More than a quarter of million Americans must think so, because that's how many live there. The political climate is very stable, the dollar goes a long way, and the people like Americans.

But what about the prophecies of revolution and communist take–overs in Mexico? Will this be our next Nicaragua? The answer to that is *no*. An analysis of the Mexicans' political setup will show why. It's often claimed that they have a one–party system. While it's true that the same party wins election year after year, the fact is that there are countless political parties, all running hard, campaigning freely, pulling no punches. From the extreme left to the extreme right, each party puts forth a platform of action and reforms, and each campaigns vigorously. But the ruling party, the PRI, sits back and shrewdly counts the votes that each party gathers. Then, in the next election, PRI simply incorporates the vote–getting issues into *its* platform, thus taking the steam and initiative away from the opposition groups.

The result of all of this is that the changes that voters think important are implemented. The voter's candidates may lose, but his demands and needs are met, anyway. He really doesn't mind, because he wasn't voting for the person, he was voting for the platform the person espoused. There is a very important principle involved here: As long as the voters control a government, and can make needed changes, even in a backhanded way, there can never be support for a revolution. For a revolution to have a chance, the overwhelming majority has to be behind it, enough to crush the military.

But what about a military takeover? Again unlikely, because the military has never been powerful under the Mexican system of government. It is under control of the civilian government, which is in turn controlled by the ruling political party. The army in Mexico is a nonpolitical, professional organization, the same as the military in the United States and Canada.

COSTA RICA

Finally we come to Costa Rica, one of my favorite countries. A large North American population is already there, and more are making their plans. Like Mexico, the Costa Rican government goes way out of its way to encourage pensioners. Tax breaks, duty–free goods and other special considerations are offered as enticements to pensioners. But even if it weren't for that, it would still be a good deal. The country is absolutely gorgeous, with one breathtaking view after another, leaving the newcomer somewhat numb from all of the beauty.

But perhaps the country's richest resource is its people. Friendly, affluent, and fiercely proud of their pure democratic system, the people are open and exuberant. Their personalities are very much like those of Americans. That's probably why we feel comfortable and welcome there.

In 1948, Costa Rica freed itself from a military government, and decided the only way to prevent itself from being taken over again by the military would be to abolish the military. Today, it has no army. Costa Ricans spend what would otherwise be a military budget on schools, roads and public works. But, as a tiny country without an army, isn't it a sitting duck for a hostile government like Nicaragua? Or a communist takeover?

The function of the typical Central American army is not like ours, that is, to defend the country from aggression or to prepare to invade another country. The Central American army's job is to protect the government from the people, not to protect the country from outsiders. Even during Somoza's heyday, when he once talked roughly to Costa Rica over a personal matter, he didn't consider military action. His army had enough trouble controlling its own people without fighting a real war against people who might shoot back.

Since Somoza was deposed, the Sandinista government has never threatened Costa Rica. It has, on occasion, chased the "Contras" back across the border and tried to destroy their camps. But this was understandable, since the mercenaries were killing and raiding, then hiding out on the Costa Rican side of the border. The Contras are in Costa Rica illegally, by the way, without approval of the Costa Ricans

What about a communist insurgency? Again, the answer is no. If the communists wanted to "take over" Costa Rica, it would be a not-so-simple matter of convincing the people that the Communist party should be voted into office. All political parties are legal in Costa Rica, and the communists campaign as hard or harder than all of the other parties. But they've found that it isn't so simple to convince the voters, because they usually capture around 2 percent of the votes. With only 2 percent of the country behind them, there would be no way to rule a nation, no matter how they got into government.

In view of all of this, and because of the fantastic beauty of Costa Rica, I can wholeheartedly endorse retirement there. Costs are a bit higher than in most of Latin America, but still much less than in the United States A couple can still make it on $400 a month here, but it would take some strict budgeting. Even if it were as expensive as the United States, it would still be a great place to live.

CHAPTER 12

Costa Rica: Democracy's Tropical Bloom

Costa Rica is a marvelous choice as a long–term living or retirement country. Per capita, more Americans live there than in any other Latin American country and, as far as I can tell, more than in any other foreign country in the world. According to the latest figures available from the U.S. Foreign Service, there are 20,000 U.S. citizens in Costa Rica. Since the population of the entire country is only 2.4 million, you can see that the North Americans figure prominently. In restaurants, one constantly hears "American" English spoken as expatriates sit around planning their next business or real estate venture. There are two "American" grammar and high schools for their children, plus a junior college program. An excellent English language newspaper, the *Tico Times*, keeps the American community well–informed about local and Central American developments. There is even an English–language TV channel and video cassettes of the latest sports events and movies are flown in from Miami regularly. American businesses, farms and ranches are spread throughout the country. Most importantly, the government welcomes North American immigrants and retirees, and encourages our participation in their commercial and cultural world.

THE COSTA RICAN PEOPLE

What is it about Costa Rica that singles it out as such a popular place for long–term living and retirement? If I had to isolate one factor, it would have to be the people of Costa Rica. They are so much like North Americans that we feel very comfortable there. Open, friendly and fiercely democratic, the Costa Ricans have a sense of equality that is very different from any of their neighbors. Instead of being shy, family–oriented and reluctant to make friends outside of their family (as is the case with many Latin Americans), the Costa Rican is extraordinarily outgoing and is likely to attack you with friendliness. Several times, while traveling on a bus or train, the person sitting next to me struck up a conversation, and by the end of the trip I had a dinner invitation at the home of a Costa Rican family. That would seldom happen in other Middle–American countries. If it did, you might suspect some kind of scam in the wind. Costa Rica is friendly.

The second attraction––first in the minds of many––is the incredible beauty of Costa Rica. Often called the "Switzerland of the Americas," this little country is a gem of scenic beauty. High mountains, swathed year–round with lush green vegetation, surround a central valley where coffee and sugar cane thrive. About two–thirds of the country's people live in this broad valley. The climate, at 4,000–feet altitude, is tropically superb. San Jose, the capital and largest city, enjoys spring–like temperatures year around. Flowers bloom everywhere and glow with color in the crystal–clean air. When you cross over the mountains you drop down to the tropical lowlands where many North Americans work plantations of coffee, bananas, macadamia nuts, black pepper and other exotic crops for export. The country is so fertile that wooden fence posts invariably sprout and soon become trees. Costa Rica is an agriculturist's dream.

It's a small country in size; only El Salvador is smaller in Middle America. It's small in population, too; only Panama has fewer people. Costa Rica isn't crowded.

One thing in particular makes Costa Rica's people distinct from others in Middle America: their racial composition. The citizens there are predominantly white European stock, particularly in the highlands and on the Pacific coast. On the Atlantic coast, you'll find a sizeable minority of blacks who speak both Spanish and English with a delightful Jamaican lilt. You rarely see any of the few surviving Native Americans; they prefer to live in isolation in the jungles. Most of them died off early from European diseases like smallpox and diptheria.

The reason for the heavy European influence is that Costa Rica's history and settlement patterns parallel those of Argentina and

Uruguay. That is, with little obvious gold or silver resources to recommend it, early Spanish settlers largely ignored Costa Rica. Until the late 1800s and early 1900s, the country was practically empty. Suddenly, displaced emigrants from Europe began searching for a place to begin a new life in the "new world." Those who knew farming looked for a destination that had rich soil, abundant crops, inexpensive land, and an atmosphere where they could prosper and feel free. Costa Rica was their land of opportunity. These newcomers weren't strangers to hard work, and soon established a tradition of small, family–owned farms and businesses which characterize the Costa Rican economy of today. Few people there are either very rich or very poor. This is, I am convinced, one of the keystones of the democratic, egalitarian way of life enjoyed by the Costa Ricans.

Settlers streamed in from Italy, Spain, Germany and other parts of the Continent. Italian immigration was particularly heavy. World War II brought further immigration, and now a new wave of North Americans is discovering the delights of Costa Rica. By and large, the heaviest influences are from Spain and Italy, but you can feel a current from all Europe throughout the country. But with the present trend of immigration, American influence grows stronger year by year.

The original settlers of Costa Rica didn't have slaves, so the black people along the Caribbean coast are also newcomers. Starting in the middle 1800s, many Jamaicans came to build the railroad from Limon to San Jose or to work as laborers for United Fruit Company in the developing banana plantations. Because of epidemic yellow fever along the coast, movement of people between the lowlands and the rest of the country was severely restricted. Therefore, the blacks living along the coast developed independently from the whites in the highlands. They managed to preserve much of their Jamaican culture and way of speaking. Most speak English with "British" pronunciation, although many use a Jamaican "pidgin English" for informal occasions. Yet they also speak excellent Spanish. Their bilingual abilities makes them desired employees, frequently in executive positions, for businesses that deal with tourism or with overseas customers.

WHAT IT'S LIKE IN COSTA RICA

To the east is the Caribbean Sea (the locals insist on calling it the Atlantic) and on the west the Pacific Ocean. If you wanted to, you could easily drive from one ocean to the other in a single day. On the north is Nicaragua, on the south, Panama. With so many people choosing to live in the large central valley, this leaves the rest of the country open and relatively unpopulated. The first impression visitors receive is that there is plenty of room in Costa Rica, even in the cities. Open land, forests, rolling plains and green–clad mountains abound. You're never far from nature.

Another reassuring thing about this country is the government's awareness of the need to protect its natural beauty and wildlife. Until just a few decades ago, many of the forested parts were uninhabited and unspoiled. Fortunately, before immigration became too heavy, people became aware of the worldwide destruction of rain forests. Conservationists worried particularly about the unique cloud forests of Costa Rica. A progressive and enlightened government made some admirable moves in protecting this environment and today we see one of the finest national park systems to be enjoyed anywhere. A visit to some of these parks offers you the opportunity to observe a bewildering array of flora and wildlife. The last of the quetzal birds can be seen here as well as 900 other species of birds (in all of North America there are only 600 species). You'll see butterflies by the millions, monkeys, armadillos, anteaters, coatimundis, deer, wild pigs, and occasionally an odd–looking tapir. Ocean conservation also ranks high on the priority list, with one of the best programs for sea turtle protection in the world. Look in the *Tico Times* and you'll likely see advertisements for "turtle nesting safaris" offering to take you on a nocturnal adventure to watch the half–ton leatherbacks lumber ashore to bury their eggs high on the beach.

DEMOCRACY IN ACTION

Costa Rica is a model of democracy, a model admired and envied by citizens of neighboring countries, and, hopefully, a model that will be emulated by all of them some day. The people there are intensely aware and proud of their democratic heritage. Any threat of infringement of their rights is the surest way to stir up the *Ticos*, they see their neighbors suffer from totalitarian injustices and are determined never to let this happen to Costa Rica.

I happened to be in Nicaragua at the inception of their revolution and had the opportunity of talking with some student activists, or *Sandinistas*. It wasn't a Marxist movement at that point, rather a coalition of all sectors of the economy, determined to get rid of the Somoza dictatorship, and hoping for a democracy like Costa Rica's. When the Sandinistas learned that I was a writer who spoke Spanish, they were anxious to talk to me. They said: "People in your country wonder what we want down here in Nicaragua. The answer is that we want to be rich and free, just like your country is rich and free. Don't say it can't be done. Just look at Costa Rica; it is rich, it has democracy, its people have freedom. That's precisely what we want." Unfortunately it didn't work out that way––partly because of the way the United States bungled the situation––but that is another story.

Costa Rica's brand of democracy is one that hasn't been seen in the United States since post–revolutionary days. This is possible because Costa Rica is such a small country––the entire population is only twice that of the county in which I live. Because of this smallness, a kind of "town–hall" government by consensus is possible. When the question of pornography came up, for example, instead of fighting it out through the courts with a tiny group of lawyers and judges arguing the question, it was put to a vote, with every citizen getting the chance to express his or her opinion. The people voted to keep pornography out of the country; that was the will of the people, not just that of a handful of lawyers and judges. The country is so small that one's opinion and vote carries a great deal more weight than in an enormous country like the United States And, because of its size, government institutions can afford to be open to the people to a much greater extent than is possible in a larger country. Thus it is perfectly feasible to take any argument you like to the supreme court if you don't like a lower court's decision. The court system tries harder to be scrupulously fair than in any country I know.

However, the Tico system of government suffers some of the ailments inherent in democracy: Bureaucratic red tape and inefficiency. The Costa Ricans' Latin temperament somehow exaggerates these ailments, making them particularly frustrating at times. You can't have everything.

The country is so small that the politicians are not far removed from the people. You are likely to see a senator, or the president, or their wives pushing shopping carts in the supermarket or having dinner at the next table in the restaurant. During my last trip there, I was absent-mindedly crossing the street against the red light one day, when suddenly, an aging black Cadillac squealed to a stop to avoid hitting me. Sheepishly, I looked up to give a shrug of apology for my absent-mindedness. To my surprise, there sat the president of the republic, gripping the steering wheel, trying hard not to look angry. He forced a smile and waved me across the street even though he had the right of way. (I might have been a voter, you see.) By the time I made it across safely, he had missed his green light and had to wait until the next one. Now, when was the last time a president or prime minister stopped his car so you could cross against the red light? When was the last time a president drove his own car? Or went anywhere without an escort of police motorcycles and secret service men?

FRONTIER VITALITY

One feels a dynamic sense of progress in the air in Costa Rica. This is the country of the entrepreneur. This is a country of wide-open opportunity, cheap land, dependable labor, honest government. Modern-day Costa Rica is much the way it was back in the frontier days of North America. "Put your brains and brawn where your mouth is," says one very successful gringo, "and you can't help but make money." Costa Rica is full of success stories about Americans who've opted to "start all over again." Most haven't become rich in a financial sense, but their peace of mind and sense of accomplishment means more to them than millions of ulcer-supported dollars.

I have to confess that I've always been able to control my enthusiasm for the traditional free-enterprise ethic of work and accumulating money just for the sake of having money. I've never been the least interested in becoming a millionaire; I simply want to *live* like a millionaire. Now you can understand why I love Costa Rica. I feel like a millionaire there, and I live like a millionaire. I have access to some of the most beautiful beaches in the world. The best restaurants aren't out of my price range—I habitually order without looking at the menu prices. There isn't a thing that a millionaire can do or enjoy that I can't do on my budget if I liked. Climate and beautiful surroundings are free; scenery isn't for sale.

Don't misunderstand, Costa Rica isn't the cheapest place
Latin America to live. For years, the government has been holding ─
currency, the *colón*, at high exchange rates against the dollar, which
keeps prices artificially high. And with higher prices for coffee, things
could go even higher. There are other places in Latin America much
less expensive to live, but few as pleasant. Still, if it isn't the cheapest, Costa Rica is certainly affordable. It's a place where an American can live in dignity and comfort on an amount that would put him
close to the poverty level in the United States or Canada. More importantly, it's a place where an American can feel welcome.

SURVIVALISTS AND REAL ESTATE SALESMEN

Costa Rica attracts more than its share of real estate speculators
and survivalists. It seems like every gringo who buys a piece of property eventually goes into real estate business for himself, selling lots,
farms and houses to the next batch of tourists off the plane. This is
one country where you needn't be a citizen or go through all kinds of
legal gymnastics in order to own property. Just as in the United
States, buying real estate is a simple matter of making a choice, arriving at a price and making sure the title is clear.

Survivalists adore Costa Rica. You find them buying farms
either in the temperate highlands or in the tropical lowlands with the
express goal of establishing a self–sufficient retreat in the event of a
nuclear war. With year–round growing seasons and near perfect climate, they can produce all their own vegetables, raise their own
chickens, have a cow and a pig, all on a few acres. The ideal survivalist ranch will also have a stream running through it for turning the
electric generators necessary for their refrigerators and VCRs. The
same water supplies brook trout and freshwater lobster for the table.
For cash crops, they rely on coffee, macadamia nuts, black pepper,
or citrus. If you talk to one of these enthusiasts, he'll cheerfully point
out that in the event of a nuclear conflagration, radioactive fallout
will circle the *northern* part of the globe, and that Costa Rica will
escape damage. Sometimes I get the impression that they wish something would happen so they can test their self–sufficient hideaways.

I'm not a survivalist, but I was once tempted to buy an almost–
self–sufficient coffee farm near San Jose. It was about 16 acres of
coffee plus a couple of acres of truck farm. The property was listed at
$18,000 and included a small house for the owner and a larger house

for the caretaker's family. The caretaker assured me that if I bought the property and kept him on, that "we can make enough from the coffee that you will never have to work, and we can raise enough vegetables and meat that you will never have to buy food from the store." He and his family farmed and maintained the property for minimum wage, free rent and the right to sell the surplus vegetables. At that time the minimum wage was less than $80 a month. I'm convinced that living there would have really made me feel like a millionaire! (Today's prices would be considerably more for a farm like that one, but still not out of reason.)

With all the real estate salesmen around, you can be sure that no available piece of property escapes being listed. An advantage of buying property in a small, democratic country is that transactions can be monitored rather easily. If you are careful and deal with a competent, long–established firm and escrow company, the chances of your being taken in a real estate deal are small. You can easily go to the National Registry, where all records are public, and see if there is any encumberance on the deed or if the seller actually owns the property. If the deed is clear when you change it to your name, there is no way that someone later can try to pull any surprises on you. Another good thing about the country being small is that the law can keep a close eye on the real estate people and promoters. It takes a very dim view of any shady dealings. However, you will be well advised to ask a reputable lawyer to oversee your transaction. That is good advice for any foreign country.

HOW STABLE IS COSTA RICA?

As mentioned earlier in the book, Central America has been drawing a lot of unjustified smears from the news media. Costa Rica in particular has been depicted as a country about to be overwhelmed by conflict, turmoil and communism. This is absolute nonsense. Newsmen and U.S. officials who should know better make all sorts of gloom and doom statements about Costa Rica's stability, about the possibility or probability of one of Costa Rica's neighbors attacking this little peace–loving country. You'll read dire warnings that the communists have their eyes on Costa Rica and are going to subvert the country or invade from Nicaragua. Even though this has been covered earlier in the book, let's analyze this once more, in a bit more detail.

First, let's remember some facts about Central America and Costa Rica. Fact number one: Central American countries do not attack or invade one another.

The exception in this century was the "Soccer War" in 1969 between the military dictatorships of El Salvador and Honduras. Some might say, "Well, just because it hasn't happened, doesn't mean it won't." True. And just because Canada has never attacked the United States, doesn't mean it won't. But it's highly unlikely. The only other inter-country fighting that I'm aware of in this century came when U.S. troops invaded and occupied Nicaragua in the 1920s and 1930s, or when General Pershing went into Mexico after Pancho Villa in 1916 and the Marines occupied Veracruz about the same time. Today's "freedom fighters" in Nicaragua are simply mercenaries. They are financed and supplied by the United States. These mercenaries will probably disappear the moment their paychecks are cut off.

Fact number two: The only two instances of communism being successful in the Western Hemisphere have occurred when a military dictatorship was overthrown by an overwhelming uprising of the people--extremely poor, desperate people--who would accept any government as better than the one they had. And in both of these instances, Cuba and Nicaragua, the communists were in the minority at first, and were able to maneuver themselves into power during the transition period from military to civilian rule. Costa Rica is *not* poor, its citizens control their government and are optimistic about the future. Their standard of living is the envy of most of Latin America. Should they grow dissatisfied with anything their government is doing, they simply vote to send it in a new direction. A most crucial point, too often overlooked, is that revolutions are the last resort of people who *cannot change their government any other way.*

Fact number three: The biggest threat to democracy in Central America has always been the military. Time after time, just when democracy looks as if it is going to break through in one of these countries, a bunch of military goons take over to control and loot the country. This can't happen in Costa Rica. Why? Because years ago, its citizens voted to abolish the army. They don't need it. The military budget has been diverted to education, highways, conservation and health care, all adding to the high standard of living. One problem here is that the United States has been encouraging. Costa Rica to form an army so that we might sell it arms and military equipment. So far the citizens have resisted that idea fiercely, because they recognize the danger in having a military. In February 1986, they over-whelmingly elected a presidential candidate who vowed not to allow the United States to place troops in Costa Rica.

Fact number four: Three Latin American countries have iron-clad treaties to defend Costa Rica. These allies are Panama, Colombia and Venezuela. Should any country attack Costa Rica, the full weight of these countries' land and air forces would fall heavily on the aggressor. That alone would clearly deter any adventurism on the part of Nicaragua, which is Costa Rica's only neighbor to the north. In addition, could anyone believe the United States wouldn't imme-diately send its military might to smash an aggressive action against this little jewel of a country? Say what you like about the neighboring Sandinista government, it is neither stupid nor suicidal.

Fact number five: Costa Rica's political parties enjoy complete freedom. The communist parties there are very active, and very legal. They try their best to convince people that their economic system would be best, but they never are able to convince more than about 2 percent of the voters. There is always the possibility that the people might, at some future time, be convinced to *vote* communism into their country. But that is about as likely to happen in Costa Rica as it is in the United States. As far as I know, no free, democratic country in the world has ever voted to go communist, and I can't imagine that happening in Costa Rica either.*

The fact that there is no military in Costa Rica comes as a shock to many Americans who are used to enormous military ex-penditures supported by monstrous taxes. This deserves a little expla-nation. There never was much of a military presence in Costa Rica, because of its isolation, its predominance of small farmers and its social moderation. Instead of an army to drain off tax money, Costa Rica has a sort of national police force, the *Guardia Civil*. It has the appearance of an army, with khaki uniforms and all, but is under strict control of the civilian government. This organization corre-sponds roughly to our concept of state highway police in the United States except that its emphasis is more on law enforcement and

---

*Now, please don't write to point out that Chile voted to go communist, because it didn't. Salvador Allende was elected on a technicality—the majority voted against him. More to the point, electing one man who happens to be a communist doesn't necessarily turn an entire country communist. Suppose we discover that Margaret Thatcher was secretly a member of the Communist Party? Would that mean that Great Britain was therefore a communist country? Of course not. In Chile, Allende hoped to be the first in history to establish a demo-cratic communist state—a contradiction in terms— but the military quickly put an end to that experiment before it got started.

peace–keeping rather than traffic control. Like state highway patrols up here, this police force is non–political. And, unlike police in some Latin American countries, the Guardia Civil isn't supported by *mordidas* or bribes from the citizenry. (*Don't* offer them money to get you out of trouble.) Instead of spending money on tanks and war-planes to intimidate its own citizens, Costa Rica devotes 27 percent of its national budget to education and culture.

If examination of these facts don't convince you that Costa Rica is virtually disasterproof, then you must go there to see for your-self. Talk to Costa Ricans, and ask them if they fear invasion from either of their neighbors, Panama or Nicaragua. The response will usually be an amused smile. Most citizens of Costa Rica were de-lighted to see the Somoza dictatorship fall. Many actively helped the Sandinistas, and some even carried weapons against the Somoza family's regime. You might be surprised to know that Eden Pastora––the famous "Comandante Zero" who led the battle against the Nica-raguan dictatorship––was a Costa Rican citizen, not a Nicaraguan! Today, the majority of Costa Ricans disapprove of Nicaragua's Marx-ist government, and are disappointed that democracy lost its feeble toehold there. But most have hopes that eventually, Nicaragua will be able to become a democracy like Costa Rica. Maybe it will, but from my viewpoint, it won't happen until Nicaragua can get rid of its mili-tary.

WHAT'S THE CLIMATE LIKE?

In the tropics, climate is controlled by altitude, with a one–de-gree–Fahrenheit drop in temperature for every 100 meters (328 ft.) of elevation. For this reason, the plateau in the center of Costa Rica enjoys one of the most delightful climates anywhere in the world. A continual breeze from the Pacific ocean courses up over the central plateau and then down across the lowlands to the Caribbean coast. This breeze, cleaned and tempered by the ocean, is refreshingly spring–like. The pure air makes the profusion of flowers seem to glow with phosphorescent brilliance. In summer the breezes bring rain showers, but there are very few days that the sun doesn't shine for a majority of the daylight hours. Winter is the "dry" season, but even then occasional rains keep things green and lush.

An excellent way to get a flavor of the contrast between tem-perate highlands and tropical lowlands is to board one of the narrow-gauge trains that wind through the incredibly scenic mountains down to either the Atlantic or the Pacific coast. You will start in the mild-temperature highlands, and wind upward through the mountains, past luxurious coffee farms. Then, after cresting the cool summit, you will start down through banana and sugar cane country where the temperature can make you sweat a bit. But because of the proximity of the oceans, the tropical sections of Costa Rica seldom become unbearable, as happens in other Central American lowlands. Many Americans have elected to live by the shore and enjoy the soft sea breezes and tropical evenings. I know one couple who have a gorgeous place at Punta Cahuita on the Caribbean coast, a thatched-roof cabin set among 10 acres of coconuts and fruit trees. The surf washes at their front door, spilling into a small depression of smooth black rocks where their children play as if in their own private swimming pool. They ask, "Why would we ever consider living anywhere else?" I can't think of an answer.

The Pacific coast is a bit dryer than the Atlantic or Caribbean coast, and has less rainfall. At some places on the Atlantic side they record as much as 300 days of rain a year! (Rarely does it rain all day, but there is usually some precipitation in those areas). For some reason the Pacific coast seems to be hotter in the summer than the jungled east coast. Still, it has more North Americans living there than on the other side. Many small towns and villages dot the west coast where Americans have beach-front cottages and imaginatively designed houses. The *Tico Times* is full of ads for fishing lodges and hotels and resorts owned or operated by Americans on the Pacific coast.

Farther south, around Golfito, the country becomes very tropical, with heavy jungle crowding the shore, and gold seekers prospecting the streams for their fortunes. I don't know how successful the adventurers are, but again, in the *Tico Times* you will find plenty of ads asking for partners in the search.

The Pacific littoral, to the north, is great cattle country where the beasts graze to perfection on lush grass. Americans who have been served corn-fed beef all their lives are in for a treat when they taste a grass-fattened filet mignon. Nothing like it; it's easily the match of the best Argentinian steak. As you might guess, many of the ranches here are owned by recent immigrants from Iowa or Ontario.

FISHING

Both sides of Costa Rica are world famous for fishing, and there are plenty of facilities to make it easy for the fisherman. On the west coast, the sailfish are probably more plentiful than anywhere in the world. In a recent tournament near Puntarenas, the contestants caught and released an average of 1.5 sailfish per person per day! Also plentiful are tuna, blue marlin, roosterfish, dorado, and on and on. You'll find many sportsfishing lodges all along the coast, many operated by North Americans. The east coast is said to be even better for fishing, if that's possible. One of the popular fish there is tarpon, which is caught in jungle rivers and lagoons. While waiting for exciting action, you are treated to sights of monkeys frolicking in the trees, parrots, toucans, and sometimes an alligator or crocodile lurking along the shoreline. Check the San Jose paper for tarpon and snook lodges where boats, guides and everything are provided.

LEARNING THE LANGUAGE

San Jose is famous for its language schools. Several foreign governments routinely send their embassy personnel to San Jose for a course of intensive Spanish study before assigning them to Latin American posts. Intensive courses mean complete immersion in the language, with eight hours a day in classrooms and living in a home with a Costa Rican family where no English is ever spoken. I strongly recommend this as not only a beginning or brush-up on your Spanish, but also as an introduction to Costa Rican culture. You find out first hand whether you will like living there. This is covered in Chapter 20, but it's worth repeating here: You can live in Costa Rica-- go to school, live with a Costa Rican family, receive all meals and even have your laundry done--for as little as $600 a month. Complete!

A further benefit is the network of friends and social contacts you make through school. You not only meet other Americans who are in the same position as you, but by living with a local family, you have the chance to make friends in the Costa Rican community. It can't be emphasized too strongly that building a network of friends and acquaintances is very important in any retirement or long-term living in a foreign country. Because of the small population, you will be surprised how quickly your circle of friends expands and how quickly you find that you have friends and acquaintances in common with other foreign residents you meet. Even if you plan on becoming a hermit on one of Costa Rica's isolated beaches, there will come times when you need some help, or maybe just someone to chat with.

My favorite school is Centro Linguistico Conversa—Calle 38 a 1-3 No. 342 N of Central Colon, telephone 21-76-49. Conversa offers any level of Spanish needed, and has a classroom setting on a beautiful farm high above Santa Ana, a suburb of San Jose. The school arranges for your stay with a Costa Rican family. The entire package, including meals with the family is only $1,080 per month. A real bargain, even if you just want to enjoy a cultural experience. Other schools offer classes for as low as $600 a month, room, board and laundry included.

An important bonus to being a student is that you will be in a different status than a tourist. The school has no problem arranging for you to stay past the limit of a 30-day tourist visa. So, you can combine your schooling with a two or three month investigation of Costa Rica. You can try it before buying it. While you are there you can do much of the groundwork for later applying for immigration papers. See the section in Chapter 13 for the regulations.

Three other schools with good reputations are: Instituto Idioma Internacional—75 meters south of the Automercado in Los Yoses, San Jose; telephone 25-01-35.

Instituto de la Lengua Espanola—Calles 29-33, San Francisco de Dos Rios; telephone 29-92-22.

Intensa—Calle 33, a 507, Barrio Escalante, Apdo. 8110, San Jose; telephone 25-60-09. There are several other schools, and a look through the *Tico Times* ads will list most of them. Ask around for others' opinions as to which school is best.

CHAPTER 13

Where Americans Live in Costa Rica

Costa Rica is a beautiful country, one of the prettiest anywhere, yet it is underpopulated. Its low population density is one of its natural resources, for there is land aplenty for expansion. The entire population is only 2.4 million. That's about the same number of people as live in Harris County (Houston), Texas. Its capital, San Jose, is the largest city in the country with a population, including suburbs, of 850,000--just a little larger than its California namesake on San Francisco Bay (although it looks to me as if it is about one fourth that size). There are only a handful of other towns in the country with populations over 20,000.

Two thirds of the people live in the 4,000-foot-high Central Valley where San Jose is located, 40 percent of them in or near the city itself.

There are three basic climatic zones in Costa Rica. Your choices are: the temperate-to-cool Central Valley (including the sometimes chilly mountain slopes); the tropical wet Atlantic coast; and the tropical dry Pacific coast. Most people, both American and Costa Rican, live in the pleasant environs of the Central Valley, either in San Jose or one of its small satellite towns scattered around the valley. Others--the more adventurous--choose to live in more picturesque locations, in rain forests, jungles or on beaches, to fulfill a fantasy of adventure, perhaps to create a business in exotic agriculture, or simply for pleasant, relaxed living. Since most live in the more temperate parts of Costa Rica, let's start there.

SAN JOSE

San Jose itself is a rather modern city, very clean, with excellent public transportation. One needn't bother with an auto there, although you can always rent one for special occasions or for sightseeing tours through the countryside. Housing is reasonable, with a two-bedroom apartment renting from $200 a month and up, and a nice two- or three-bedroom house going from $300-a-month to as much as you'd like to pay. Since San Jose is a very middle-class city, almost any neighborhood is suitable for residence. You'll find Americans scattered throughout the city, with a higher concentration in the Escazu and Santa Ana areas, which are a 20-minute bus ride from downtown. Here, the neighborhood is more than comfortable. Some of the homes are downright luxurious, set in gorgeous landscaping that only a year-round, balmy climate can support. There are few sections of the city that would be uncomfortable to live in, and none that I could properly call slums.

San Jose has an interesting mixture of modern buildings with a hodge-podge of architectural styles, some European, some uniquely Costa Rican. Around the city, mountains rise gently for another thousand feet or so. There, picturesque, family operated farms grow the world-famous Costa Rican coffee.

Even though San Jose is a fairly large city, it still thinks like a small town in many ways. An example is the street numbering system: There isn't any. Well, yes, many of the buildings and houses now have numbers, but few people use them. How do you find an address? That is a fascinating question. The streets usually have names (not always), and an address is given by reference to a known landmark, directing you so many meters or *varas* (paces) in one direction or another. For example, to find an address you might be told: "From the Caballo Blanco, 200 meters north and 50 varas east." This translates "two blocks north of the store called 'Caballo Blanco' and 50 paces, or half a block to the east." My favorite address is on a business card of a real estate agency. It reads, "150 meters south of where the Mas Por Menos Market used to be." It's hard to explain just why the San Joseans stubbornly cling to this ancient system. It's even harder to explain how the mailmen ever find the right house to deliver the mail. Apparently, they have no problem.

To compound the situation they have a street system that defies written explanation. You have to be there with a map in your hand to completely understand it. The streets (*calles*) and avenues (*avenidas*) run at 90 degrees to each other and are numbered, but with even numbers on one side of town and odd on the next. Therefore, after you cross Second Street, the next is Fourth, and the next is Sixth. Sometimes the streets have signs on the corners of the buildings, sometimes not. I can't imagine how even the natives ever get used to this system.

The cultural center of the country, San Jose boasts a symphony orchestra that plays in the famous National Theater along with many visiting orchestra and opera troupes, plays, and cultural events of all descriptions.

Even though San Jose has a relatively large population, you get the feeling that you are always in a small town, because the houses are mostly single–family dwellings or small apartment buildings. Highrises are few and far between. Once you leave the city limits in any direction, you suddenly find yourself in the country, with breathtaking views on all sides. Then with a few kilometers of driving, some of the other towns of the Central Valley begin cropping up.

ALAJUELA

The third largest town in Costa Rica is Alajuela, population 28,700. Even though it's only 20 kilometers from San Jose, Alajuela is warmer because it has 200 meters (660 feet) less altitude. Here sugar cane thrives, and going up the slopes, the crops change to coffee, which likes altitude and cooler weather. The town is renowned for the profusion of flowers growing around the town and for its market days. The town plaza is one of the most peaceful I've ever seen, with enormous mango trees casting shade over trimmed lawns, and park benches that invite quiet meditation. Like all of the towns on the plateau, it is scrupulously neat and prosperous looking. Like all of the suburbs, it enjoys regular bus service to downtown San Jose.

One of the attractions of Alajuela is the Ojo de Agua swimming pool, where a large spring of crystal clear water bubbles up from the earth, spilling into an olympic–sized pool and an artificial lake. This is a very popular weekend spot for people from San Jose and the surrounding valley. A pleasant restaurant and picnic facilities are included on the grounds.

Alajuela is popular among North Americans because of its warmer climate and because of the many small farms in the area.

Access to shopping in San Jose is easy by bus, and the roads are in fine shape for commuting.

HEREDIA

With a population of 23,000, Heredia is about halfway between San Jose and Alajuela. The 10-kilometer bus ride is pleasant and the service is frequent. Because it's so close to San Jose many Americans choose to live here. As with all of the suburbs, there are numerous small farms just minutes away from the central town square. Almost every issue of the *Tico Times* will list homes and farms for sale in the surrounding towns.

CARTAGO

On the rail line that goes to the Pacific port of Limon, Cartago is the first "large city" stop on the way at 22 kilometers. Although quite important in the region it has a population of only 25,000. Its altitude of 1,440 meters puts it a bit higher than San Jose and makes it ostensibly cooler, although during the daytime it certainly gets its share of warm weather. This is a popular destination for day excursions from the capital, with frequent bus service as well as the daily trains to there. The countryside between here and Turrialba has some great coffee farms. Coffee, incidentally, is a crop that is ideally suited to small, family-operated units. A good way to get into the business is to hire a family to live on your coffee farm and work for shares.

Here is the starting point to visit the country's only active volcano, the peak of Irazu. From 1963 until 1965 the volcano poured millions of tons of black ash to cover an area of almost 450 square miles of fertile land. Dire predictions of ruin and disaster accompanied the build-up of ash. But, apparently this has always been a natural phenomenon, contributing to the astounding fertility of the Costa Rican soil. Today, the ash has been converted into rich, black earth, porous and moisture-retaining, perfect for plant roots.

Like most of Costa Rica, Cartago is subject to earthquakes, but possibly the proximity to the volcano enhances the seismic activity. As a result, almost all of the local buildings are of one-story, earthquake-resistant construction. A very interesting stop here is to visit the old parish church which was destroyed in a particularly nasty earthquake in 1910. Instead of being rebuilt, it was left in ruins, with lovely gardens planted around it. Fish ponds, flowers and shrubbery make the ruins a pleasant retreat.

Costa Rica is a very Catholic country, with one of the highest percentages of churchgoers in Latin America. The Basilica of Nuestra Senora de Los Angeles, the patron saint of Costa Rica, draws pilgrims from all over the area who visit its shrine for the healing powers attributed to the bubbling spring there. Although the country is Catholic, there seems to be little religious intolerance, because other denominations operate with no interference.

THE CARIBBEAN COAST

The second largest city in Costa Rica is Puerto Limon, at the end of the narrow–gauge railroad that starts in San Jose and winds its way through the picturesque countryside. The rail trip in itself is a reason for visiting Limon. With old–fashioned wooden cars and wooden seats, and windows that either don't close or are missing, the little train chugs along like something out of the past century. Because of the steep grades and sharp curves, the train seldom achieves a speed of more than a fast walk. I've seen butterflies fly lazily into a window, inspect the passengers and then flutter on out the other side of the car while the train struggles up a grade.

As the train approaches Limon, the countryside changes from tropical mountains into lowlands—-tangled jungle, sugar cane fields, and the inevitable banana plantations. The racial composition of the people also changes from predominantly European white to African black. Masonry and adobe construction give way to wooden structures built on stilts, sometimes with thatch roofs that wouldn't look out of place in Nigeria. Blacks comprise 33 percent of the population in the province of Limon, and indigenous Indians about 3 percent. Here is where most of the estimated 5,000 Indians live, the survivors of European conquest. Most of the blacks speak Jamaican English, heavily laced with pidgin, and most also speak excellent Spanish. Oddly enough, in a country with an exceptionally high literacy rate, the blacks here have only a 15 percent rate, one of the lowest in all of Latin America. I'm at a loss to explain this.

The city of Limon is comparatively large, with a population of almost 50,000, the overwhelming majority of them black. Here was where Columbus landed on his last voyage to the New World, and if

I'm not mistaken, was the only place where he actually set foot on the North American mainland. The town is the main port for the east coast; it's major export is, as you might expect, bananas. There are several interesting things to see there, such as the promenade in Vargas Park, where tropical trees grow with vines clinging to them, flowers grow at their bases and sloths move so slowly in the treetops that it takes concentration and a lot of time to spot them.

But very few North Americans live in the city of Puerto Limon. To tell the truth, there isn't much there for them. By and large, the city doesn't look like a typical Costa Rican town. It has neither the modernity of the plateau nor the charm of the small beach villages. It's a rather plain–looking place. There are a number of agricultural projects inland from Limon where a few gringos raise black pepper, macadamia nuts, and tropical curiosities. How they fare in these enterprises is a matter of who you talk to. Some claim great success. But many of the projects are operated by managers, allowing absentee North American owners to enjoy the more temperate climate of San Jose or its suburbs.

To the south of Limon there are some very interesting villages along the Caribbean beaches. My favorite is Cahuita. Outside of a beautifully isolated beach–and–jungle setting, Cahuita has absolutely nothing to offer except charm and atmosphere. Except for a handful of North Americans and Europeans, the inhabitants are all black. The village looks more like something out of Africa than Latin America.

Noisy parrots quarrel in the treetops, and back in the jungle, white–face monkeys and howler monkeys add to the tropical din. Butterflies, birds and other wildlife are everywhere. Once I found an enormous beetle, about the size of a clenched fist, toddling along the dirt main street of town. Thinking I had made an astounding discovery, I picked it up by the turtle–like shell and went running into a store to show it to the people gathered there. They looked at the beetle with bored expressions and one man said, "Oh, yes, those little ones are the females." Apparently the male rhinoceros beetle is twice as big as his lady friends.

There is only one hotel in town. It looks like a setting out of a Garcia Marquez novel, but there are rooms for rent with some local families. This is a cultural adventure you won't soon forget. I saw absolutely no evidence of racial animosity; the people are very friendly. I enjoy Cahuita very much, but the temperature can be sultry, particularly in the summer. And in the winter, it's usually nice, but it can vary between stifling hot to chilly, depending on whether the winds are coming out of the north or the south.

Cahuita and the other coastal villages (such as Puerto Viejo, a bit farther south) are great places to spend a U.S. winter, and to enter into a cultural adventure that would be impossible in other settings. But, except for a special kind of adventurous gringo, or those interested in tropical agriculture, or perhaps someone looking for a place to "drop out," the Atlantic coast isn't practical as a year–round living choice.

To the north, the coast is sparsely populated. About the only people who live there are those hopelessly addicted fishermen or naturists who love the wildlife of the area. Tortuguero National Park attracts those who are fascinated with the huge sea turtles that come in to nest here. The Costa Rican government has one of the most enlightened and effective conservation programs anywhere when it comes to protecting this endangered species. The only way north is by boat or to fly into one of the fishing camps.

WEST COAST COSTA RICA

Because the west coast is dryer, you find many more Americans living here. For those who are familiar with the coast around Acapulco, the Costa Rican beaches will strike a responsive chord. People who have traveled the world over have assured me that Playa Manuel Antonio cannot be surpassed in beauty, wherever you might roam. The beach is a national park, with camping and motel facilities near the entrance. The park boasts an unspoiled jungle environment, complete with monkeys, sloths and toucans, and is one of Costa Rica's national treasures. Between Quepos, the nearest town, and Manuel Antonio, there are many homes and beach cottages owned by gringos. Most are seasonal residents, however, since summers can be warm here. Unlike Acapulco, where daily rains cool things in the summer, nothing seems to help here. Personally, I don't mind this, because I love dry, hot weather. If you're the kind of person who likes Phoenix summers, you might like it in Quepos, the nearest town, and Manuel Antonio.

The racial mixture on this side of the country is completely different from the eastern coast. Whites and mestizos account for 98 percent of the population here. The largest town here is Puntarenas, with 30,820 people. Very popular with tourists from the San Jose area, Puntarenas is reached by an electric railway (about a four–hour trip), or by automobile (only about 90 minutes). Drawbacks to Puntarenas as a long–term living place are the warm summers and the muddy–looking beaches. The sand is colored with black volcanic ash which makes it look dirty, although it really isn't. There are numerous family–operated hotels along the beach, some of them owned by gringos.

Where most of the North Americans find their dream locations on the west coast is north of Puntarenas, on the Nicoya Peninsula and farther on up the Guanacaste coast. There are numerous small bays, coves and beaches with villages, or sometimes, just clusters of homes. Access is usually by graded roads branching off from the Pan American highway that heads north and disappears into Nicaragua. Even as isolated as they are, most have regular bus service. A couple of the more popular places are Playa del Coco, and Tamarindo Beach. At Playa Naranjo you could be treated to the sight of as many as 60,000 Ridley sea turtles coming ashore to deposit their eggs in a single day.

World–famous is the park and settlement of Monteverde. Here you will find one of the few remaining "cloud forests" in the world. It's cool and wet here, and rubber boots are in order for hiking the trails, but the scenery and view make any inconvenience worthwhile. The farms and village here were started by American Quakers, who, back in the 1950s, recognized the land around here as perfect for dairy cattle. They produce some excellent cheeses.

COSTA RICAN FOOD

It would be difficult to point at any particular menu and say, "that is a typical Costa Rican dish," because the cuisine is so varied that almost nothing is exclusively "Costa Rican." An exception might be the rice–and–black bean dish called *gallo pinto*. Very simple and easy to prepare, gallo pinto is served with eggs in the morning, with lunch and often even at supper. The black beans color the rice purple and after a while, you discover that eggs don't taste right unless there is a side of gallo pinto on the plate. Black beans are also served as a soup, with a poached egg floating in it, and garnished with sprinkles of chopped scallions. Delicious! As you would expect, tropical veggies such as fried plantain and yucca bread are common.

There are both supermarkets and open-air markets for grocery shopping, as well as *pulperias*, or small neighborhood stores. Coffee should be purchased at one of the shops where it is being roasted and ground before your very eyes. The odor is so tantalizing that you find yourself inhaling deeply to the point of hyperventilation.

Shopping is a pleasure in Costa Rica because of the bewildering assortment of fresh tropical fruits and vegetables. Besides beautiful corn, tomatoes, squash, pineapple and other fresh offerings, you find such odd but tasty items as zapote, guanabana, chayote, breadfruit and papaya. Locally grown apples and grapes are available, but they don't do well in a climate that doesn't have freezing winters, so you might be disappointed with these old standbys. Instead try substituting passion fruit, pomegranates or any of the amazing assortment of tropical delicacies.

Since Costa Rica is a cattle-growing country, the steaks and roasts are as good as you might expect, and inexpensive. But you might be surprised to discover pork and chicken are high priced and sometimes scarce. The reason for this is that pigs and chickens require high amounts of protein in their diets, which isn't available in bananas or other cheap tropical foods. The required protein supplements in their feed boost the prices. The quality of pork and chicken is very good. Costa Rican eggs are delicious, having a brighter colored yolk and a better flavor than our mass-produced eggs.

With ocean on both sides, Costa Rica has a great selection of seafood. And since the shipping distances from either ocean are only a matter of hours, the seafood is fresh. Almost any kind of fish and shellfish you can imagine is available, plus some you can't imagine. You might want to try some of the clams and conch which are found exclusively on Costa Rican shores.

Imported foods are very expensive. Partly because of shipping costs and partly because of foreign exchange problems, most American and European products are prohibitive, but available in most supermarkets. Costa Rican products are often as good, and certainly, fresh foods are much better than canned or packaged anyway. The one imported item that can't be readily substituted for Costa Rican products is wine. There is some local vintage available, but not of the best quality. So unless you can train your palate to enjoy beer or mineral water as a substitute, you'd better plan on spending a lot for French or California vintages.

DOMESTIC HELP

If you are affluent to the point where you can afford a maid to do some of your cooking, you are in for a treat, for you will have someone who knows how to fix some of the tropical specialties. Actually, servants aren't that expensive, with the going rate about $100 per month, and well worth it. But hiring a maid–cook or a gardener isn't quite the simple procedure you find at home where you merely come to a salary arrangement and that's that. There are some strictly enforced labor laws in Costa Rica. All employees are entitled to certain benefits by law, and it is foolhardy to try and evade giving them. A new employee must be registered with the Department of Inspections, and the employer has to present his passport and residency papers for inspection. Monthly social security payments must be made for the employee, amounting to 9 percent of the wages, and this must be paid either in person or by sending a messenger to wait in the lines. Part of a democracy is the bureaucracy, right?

Other rules are that live–in help cannot work more than 12 hours a day and must have a half day off every week. Hourly employees can work no more than eight hours a day. Female employees are entitled to maternity leave of 90 days at half pay—–social security pays the other half. And a 15–day vacation is due plus an *aguinaldo*, or Christmas bonus, of two weeks pay to any employee who has worked a year or more. Most people pay a month's bonus for Christmas. When an employee is dismissed, the employee is entitled to a proportion of the accrued vacation and bonus pay. All of this sounds like a lot of trouble, but the laws are there to protect the workers from exploitation, and you must realize that the actual pay is very low. The best part about Costa Rican workers is their attitude towards work. They have a reputation for being naturally neat and maintenance–minded, something lacking in many other Latin American cultures.

MEDICAL CARE

On my last trip to Costa Rica, I ended up in the hospital—–so I think I can speak with some authority about Costa Rican medical care. Actually, my problem was a bad case of flu and my fear that it was turning into pneumonia. I went to a doctor, who recommended that I spend a few days in the hospital for a checkup and some bed rest. During my stay at Clinica Catolica, a modern hospital in San

Jose, I underwent extensive tests, including an electrocardiogram, X-rays, and blood tests of every type. The bill for the room and three excellent meals was $30 a day. The tests were $50, including an appointment with a doctor who went through them, explaining what each meant. Not only that, I was given the X-rays as my personal property—something not done up north, even though you've paid for them!

On the same floor where I was staying was a lady from New York who had come to Costa Rica for a face lift (the country is famous for skilled and inexpensive facial surgeons), and when she discovered that a place in a four-bed ward was only $10 a day, including meals, she decided to stay for a month. She couldn't even afford a cheap hotel room for that kind of money. Since the hospital wasn't crowded, she had the four-bed room to herself.

The people we queried as to medical expenses reported that an average doctor's visit was $15; hospital $30 per day; an appendectomy about $250; a complete face lift $1,300; dental cleaning and x-ray, $20; capping a tooth, $150. Compare these prices at home, and you can see why many retirees don't feel that the lack of Medicare coverage outside of the United States is very much of a problem. If a serious problem came up, one which could involve thousands of dollars, the respondents all indicated they would probably return home to take advantage of government insurance. But for minor ailments or surgery, Costa Rica has more than adequate facilities and reasonable costs.

WANT ADS

A great way to get to know something about a country is to study the classified ads, the "want ads." Here are some ads taken at random from issues of the *Tico Times* in May 1986.

$19,500 buys 2 br. home, also 1 br. house. 10 acres, plenty water, electric, mountain view. 35 minutes from San Jose.

Limon—private island 4–12 kilometers of beach, 568 acres, asking $476,000.

Cashew Nut Farm—60 acres: 10 planted, 37 ready to plant, 13 wooded, ocean and mountain views, year round river, well, electric, peon house, nursery, $1,900 acre.

---

25 acres on Pacific beach. Dock your yacht in front of your property. Has 2 cabins and many fruit trees, $35,000.

House, 3 bdr., 2 ba., ample living and dining. 1 acre lot, $41,500.

Mediterranean–style house and coffee farm, 7 acres, 4 bdrm., beautiful view $150,000.

Escazu house, 4 bdrm., 2 bath, $24,000.

Americans selling nice 4 bdr. home with pool. Private, quiet 1/2 acre, 30 fruit trees, beautiful view of valley. $35,000.

Furn. 3 bdrm. mountain cabin on 2 acres, view, 30 min. to city, phone & caretaker, Rent $299.

---

12 room house, 6 bdrms, 4 acres, 220 fruit trees & 750 coffee plants, beautiful view. $175,000 or $1,500 monthly.

$150 monthly. Nice fully furn. 2 bdr. house, 10 acre farm, TV, linens. radio, utilities, 35 min. from S.J.

Hotel apartments, from $400 per month, cable TV, swimming pool, 2 tennis courts, maid service, live music every night.

Modern apartment, 1 bdrm., liv–dining, small garden, $175.

Small house, 1 bdrm, telephone, gardener, night guard included, $300.

---

2 bdr. house with spectacular valley view. Furn., fireplace, washer & dryer, incl. linen, etc. 12 min. to S.J. $360.

Family rents furnished room, breakfast, laundry, TV, $8 day.

GETTING STARTED

Visit Costa Rica and spend a few months there before you decide anything. This advice should go without saying, but many people--after seeing a couple of weeks of the country at its best--are often tempted to buy a piece of land and rush back to quit their jobs and join the fun. By extending your visit past the ordinary 30 days, you will have the opportunity to test the bureaucracy and red tape involved, and thus discover whether you have the stamina and patience to wade through the involved task of obtaining *pensionado* or *rentista* status. It isn't granted automatically; you must qualify.

Because of Costa Rica's desirability as a place to live, The procedures of entering and exiting Costa Rica are tougher than in most nations. The government wants to avoid having adventurers entering legally, and then conveniently forgetting to exit.

The first place you should stop, if you are at all interested in staying for any length of time as a resident or pensionado, is at the offices of the Asociacion de Pensionados y Rentistas. This is an association of foreign residents (mostly Americans) that has been given office space in the Costa Rican Institute of Tourism building (2nd floor, ask for: Asociacion Centro de Informacion). They also feature newcomers' seminars, free of charge, where the featured speaker is Edwin Salas, chief of the Tourist Institute's pensionado department. You will hear from doctors, lawyers and influential locals who are there to answer questions.

To enter the country, as a U.S. citizen, you need a tourist card from the airline or from a consulate, which costs $2. You need a passport to apply for the card. Canadians get a break, because their entry is for six months instead of the one month allowed U.S. citizens. Believe me, immigration officials are serious about their 30–day limit. To extend your stay, you must request an extension from the Departamento de Migracion (which is across from Parque Nacional). You need two passport pictures, plus a ticket out of the country and proof of enough money to last you for the 30–to–90 day extension. Cash won't do; for some reason, the money must be in either traveler's checks or on deposit with a local bank.

By the way, your passport and tourist card are very important in Costa Rica. They should be carried on your person at all times. Because of the problem of illegal aliens, the police do a lot of checking. If they see the same face around for a few weeks or months, they will one day demand to see if you are legally in the country. If you are uneasy about carrying a passport, the next best thing to do is to carry a photocopy of your documents, which will prove you actually have them. This could save you a trip to the police station.

LEGAL STUFF

Should you investigate Costa Rica and decide that it's definitely your style, your next step is to go for *Pensionado* or *Rentista* status. It is more complicated than in some countries, perhaps, but many of the detailed requirements are similar. Because I have a copy of the latest rules, and because they are concise and clear, it might be worthwhile to discuss them here. Edwin Salas, the chief of the Departamento de Pensionados kindly provided the following, up–to–date information on the various ways to obtain residency.

First of all there is the *Resident Rentista Status*. You can apply for this if you are retired and already receiving a pension from a qualified plan, or if you are receiving Social Security. This income must be at least $7,200 per year ($600 per month) and you must be able to prove it. You do this by furnishing an income statement from the qualified pension company or organization, or from the Social Security Administration, stating: 1) the amount of monthly income; 2) that this income is for life; and 3) the monthly amount that will be paid to you *in Costa Rica*.

If the income comes from a company not less than three years old, a statement of incorporation and economic solvency must be submitted, which has to be certified by a certified public accountant

148

(or equivalent, in the United States) or a charted public accountant (in Canada) from the state or province where the company is incorporated. This must be authenticated by a Costa Rican consul and attached to the income statement. In addition, two references from banks dealing with the company must be supplied.

Next is *Resident Rentista Status*. This is a little tougher, I suppose because they want to be sure you aren't going to come there and not have a steady income and become a burden on the state or be tempted to take a job illegally. There are two ways to obtain the Resident Rentista Status.

The first way to qualify is to prove a monthly income of at least $600 generated by interest. To do this you have to invest enough dollars in a certificate of deposit with a Costa Rican bank to generate the minimum $7,200 per year income. This will take about $75,000, and the Certificate will be locked–in for five years. This C.D. has to be renewed every five years for as long as you maintain this status.

The second way of qualifying for Rentista status is to prove a monthly income of $1,000 ($12,000 per year) coming from investments outside of Costa Rica. The proof necessary is a letter from a bank or recognized investment company which states the following: 1) The amount of monthly income, 2) that this sum is irrevocable, 3) that this sum will continue for at least five years. Again, if the income comes from a company not less than three years old, you need a statement of incorporation, economic solvency and existence of the investment, notarized and authenticated by a Costa Rican consul. Bank references are also required.

Understand, you have to do more than come up with some statements. You also have to prove you are getting all that money by showing deposit receipts from a Costa Rican bank.

I hear that some people have gone through the formalities of getting their pensionado papers themselves, but the best advice you can take tells you to go to a specialist, usually an attorney, and let him walk you through the red tape. By giving him/her a power of attorney, the process will go faster.

Here's what you will need:

1. a. An application with name, marital status, nationality and passport number, plus names of dependents, and their nationality and passport numbers.

    b. Proposed or actual date of entering Costa Rica and a temporary or permanent address there and a telephone number.

    c. A statement that you don't have, nor have previously requested a Costa Rican I.D. card or "cedula."

2. Income statement, as described earlier.
3. Two copies of your valid passport, and one copy for each dependent.
4. Birth certificates, marriage certificate, and naturalization certificate, if applicable.
5. A police report from the place you lived for the six months before entering Costa Rica. You also need one for all dependents over 18. Since a police report is only good for six months, I suggest this be the last document you obtain, just in case things are delayed.
6. The name and address of the person having your special power of attorney, who is is acting on your behalf.
7. A "Declaracion Jurada--Sworn Statement," which must be authenticated by a Costa Rican consul, and to which some $40 worth of legal document stamps will be affixed.

RIGHTS AND OBLIGATIONS

Once you are granted pensionado or rentista status, you have some benefits, and some obligations. Naturally your first obligation is to be a law–abiding citizen. Part of this is presenting annual evidence that you are complying with the financial requirements. You do this by changing U.S. dollars into Costa Rican *colones* in a Costa Rican bank and presenting the receipts to the ICT (Institute of Tourism). You must live in Costa Rica for at least four months out of each year, and you are not allowed to work for wages. While you can't work, you can own and manage a business. This is what many American residents do, and many quite successfully.

Many American residents attest that even were there no special breaks for pensionados or rentistas, they would still choose Costa Rica as their residency overseas. But there are some benefits that cannot be overlooked. These are in the form of duty–free imports. You are entitled to import unlimited household goods, and some of the local products aren't top quality. For most items, this is a one–time only deal, so you should be sure to bring new things. After three years, these items may be sold on the local market. You can bring in an automobile, motorcycle or airplane, and replace it every five years. Here is another big saving.

But the biggest benefit of all is having the opportunity to live with friendly people in a beautiful country.

CHAPTER 14

Mexico: Still American's Favorite

Of all the Latin American nations, Mexico is most chosen as a foreign living or retirement spot. Some reasons are evident: Mexico is convenient and inexpensive to reach by auto or public transportation, it has friendly people and a low cost of living, and it offers a chance to try foreign living or retirement without making a large commitment. You can immerse yourself in your adventure with short steps, then pull back quickly if you decide foreign living isn't for you.

There are so many Americans living in Mexico and so many different places to retire there that it would take an entire book to do it justice. It happens there's one available. It's called CHOOSE MEXICO (Howells and Merwin, Gateway Books, San Francisco, 1985).

PICK YOUR CLIMATE--TROPICS, ANYONE?

One of the attractive things about Mexico is the variety of climates available. From tropical coastal villages to cosmopolitan highland cities, Mexico has something to fit just about anyone's specifications. Many people love the "eternal spring" climate around Guadalajara and Lake Chapala, while others prefer the brisk mountain air of San Miguel de Allende or Guanajuato. Some can't stand it unless they have the ocean at their doorstep, and opt for Mazatlan, Acapulco or points between. And of course, the Caribbean coast of the Yucatan is just being "discovered" by Americans. Baja California and the north of Mexico has the convenience of being close to home, only one or two day's drive away from occasional visits with friends or grandkids "back home."

The southern parts of Mexico vary from steamy lowland jungles to cool agricultural highlands. You can be in San Cristobal de las Casas, where streets may be icy in the morning, then within a few hours drive that same day you can enjoy a rain forest where parrots and monkeys frolic about the treetops, snacking on luscious tropical fruits.

No matter what kind of climate you are looking for, you are sure to find it in Mexico.

BUT IS MEXICO A SAFE PLACE TO LIVE?

We who live in the larger cities of the United States are not strangers to crime and urban violence. In fact, this is often a motive for leaving the city, for moving to Mexico. When doing our research for CHOOSE MEXICO, Don Merwin and I asked hundreds of retirees how secure they felt in Mexico. Almost unanimously they agreed that they were very comfortable and felt secure living there. Don't misunderstand, there is crime in Mexico just as there is crime in Ontario or Utah. But muggings and violent crimes, so common in some places up north are rare in Mexico and in much of Latin America. In some places there, they are all but unheard of. The most common crimes are pickpocketing and burglarizing unattended houses. It so happens that these are the easiest crimes to prevent, simply by taking precautions as discussed elsewhere in this book. When a mugging or rape occurs in Mexico, it makes headlines in the newspapers. Such crimes wouldn't even make the back pages in most U.S. city papers.

Why are crime rates in Mexico and other parts of Latin America different? It's a matter of custom, strong family orientation, and very importantly, their different philosophy of law and order. Our philosophy of law is based on English common law, that is where each case is influenced by previous court decisions, where the accused is presumed innocent until proven guilty, and where circumstantial evidence is often disregarded.

But Mexico, like most non–common law countries of the world employs what's commonly known as the Napoleonic Code. Instead of referring to past decisions of other courts to decide guilt and punishment, all crimes are codified, with procedures and punishments clearly spelled out. From this comes the principle that it isn't the burden of the state to prove the accused guilty, rather, it's the accused's job to prove he's *not* guilty. As a result, few criminals get away to repeat their crimes again and again. With this kind of court system, the people in Mexico tend to be circumspect in their dealings with each other, making sure their behavior is always above reproach and suspicion. Criminals are removed from society (probation and parole isn't a normal component of their system), and repeaters receive mandatory 20–year sentences for what in the United States would be a 90–day jail sentence. Crime doesn't pay in Mexico.

Because of harsh treatment of criminals, and because of Mexico's community and family orientation, the streets are generally calm and safe, even late at night. Juvenile delinquency is almost unknown, particularly in smaller towns. You don't see graffiti or youth gangs, because this is not approved behavior.

MANY MEXICOS

Mexico is a country broken into many physical segments by geography and history. Several high mountain chains run north–south, which are in turn sliced across by deep east–west canyons. Few highways or railroads cross these mountains, so there has always been difficulty of communication across the mountain ranges. Each of these sections, over thousands of years of settlement, has developed its own variants of culture, food, housing and language. Today, despite radio, TV and modern communications, these differences, although diminished, still persist. They are a source of local pride. Anywhere you travel in Mexico, you will hear people boasting that their particular section of the republic is universally recognized as the very best place to live in the whole world.

Much of Mexico was "civilized" when the Spanish conquistadores entered the scene. The Aztecs, Mayas, Zapotecs, and other tribes contributed their words, beliefs, customs, food—all kinds of cultural artifacts—to the newly dominant Spanish culture. When the various peoples merged into one mestizo race, these artifacts were interwoven to form a rich tapestry of culture that is neither Indian nor European, but purely Mexican.

While there are many Mexicos, depending on the section of the country you visit, two important Mexicos everywhere exist simultane-

153

ously: (1) The Mexico for residents; and (2) the Mexico for tourists. It's up to you which Mexico you prefer. If you are a resident, however, you will rarely waste money on the Mexico of the naive tourist.

The tourist can easily find hotels in Mexico that cost over $100 a day. Any travel agent will gladly locate one—*prefers* to find you an expensive one—since he works on commission. Well, if you're only going to be there for a two–week vacation, and can afford the extra luxuries provided by the $100-a-day hotel, go right ahead. But residents in Mexico can rarely afford this. They know that a $5–a–day hotel is perfectly adequate, and that a $15 room is often as luxurious as the expensive one. Many have discovered that an apartment hotel is an even better bargain, where an efficiency, complete with kitchen and pleasant balcony for dining, rents for the same or a bit more than a conventional hotel room. The bonus is that the maid will even do the dishes if you leave a modest tip. You rarely find these apartments in a luxury hotel.

A friend of mine recently returned from a two–week vacation in Cancun. He shook his head, saying he couldn't understand how anyone could live inexpensively in Mexico. He and his wife and another couple shared a condo, for $175 a day. They ate most of their meals out, in tourist restaurants. Expensive without a doubt! I shrugged, and explained that the hotel I choose there isn't on the beach, yet it's air conditioned, clean, and only costs $9 a day—for two people. So I take a bus to get to his beach; the sand and surf is the same for me as for them. What he and his wife spend for rent every day would cover all my expenses there for a week, maybe two.

In addition, I never eat in "tourist" restaurants because of my firm conviction that if local people won't eat there, the food is over-priced, or not worth eating, or both. I never have understood people who travel to a foreign country, then insist on "steak and lobster" restaurants like the ones "back home." They dine on New York cuts and french fries, while I enjoy *jaibali* (wild peccary) or venison in sour cream, *cochinito pibil* (suckling pig baked in an earthen oven), or *huachinango al mojo de ajo* (red snapper grilled with butter–garlic sauce). All of these delicacies are commonly prepared in the kitchens of the many Mexicos, at a price that seems like a gift in comparison.

Before you make any firm decisions about where you might care to live in Mexico, it would be worth your while to investigate the various sections of Mexico to see which section, if any, appeals to you and fits your particular needs. You'll find the climate, the culture and the neighbors you desire if you look around. As with any experiment in foreign residence, my strongest advice is to try it for a few months first before you make a decision whether to stay or not.

CAN YOU DRINK THE WATER?

This question is often asked. The answer, with rare exceptions, is no, do not drink the water. Even in areas where the water is perfectly safe to drink, the locals tend to use bottled water for cooking or drinking. It becomes something taken for granted, something so natural that seldom does anyone question why they're using bottled water. Don't listen to anyone who tells you that you can get used to drinking tap water in Mexico. You cannot develop immunities to the organisms that cause dysentery. For simple "tourist trots," perhaps your stomach can develop a tolerance for some strange bacteria, but not for the real thing. Mexicans get sick if they forget. The point is, they are so used to drinking bottled water that they would no more consider drinking from a tap than you would consider drinking from horse trough. A horse trough could be safer.

Fortunately, some common sense behavior will avoid problems here. Particularly safe is eating at home, where you can make sure that the water is either bottled or boiled. The best restaurants are locally–patronized, family–operated affairs. These are good not only in terms of menu and tasty meals, but cleanliness as well. The cooking usually is done by family members, using the same hygienic practices as in their home. They are most anxious that customers enjoy the food and come back for more. But too often a restaurant—tastefully decorated, with white table cloths and black–tied waiters—is overly concerned with attracting tourists, whom they overcharge, and who aren't likely to return. Conditions in the kitchen can be very different from those in the dining room. If the help is low–paid and doesn't care, you could get into trouble.

THE ECONOMICS OF LIVING IN MEXICO

Back in 1948, when my parents moved to Mexico and set up housekeeping, prices were incredibly cheap. We had a maid who worked all month long for the equivalent of an average day's wages in the United States. Gasoline was inexpensive, food was cheap, and real estate cost a fraction of a similar property north of the border.

After a few years, prices began creeping upward, ever upward, as the peso gained strength against the dollar. A good part of this change was the growing economy of Mexico and the overall increase in the standard of living. The growth of the middle class since the end of World War II has been both dramatic and gratifying.

With the advent of increased Mexican petroleum exports, the relationship between peso and dollar began to change. The peso was pegged at an arbitrary value that had no real relation to its real worth. Dollars became cheap. Prices of domestic goods increased until the United States became a "cheap" place for Mexicans to shop and visit. Then came a period of manipulation, when pesos were converted to cheap dollars and then invested in U.S. real estate or deposited in Swiss bank accounts. Panic buying and currency trading hit. The President of Mexico at that time, Lopez Portillo, pledged to his people that he would "defend the peso like a dog." As one political columnist put it, Lopez Portillo finally retired to Spain with suitcases full of dollars, without even a murmur of apology to the dogs. It appears he had been playing the peso game along with everyone else.

Suddenly, the peso collapsed, slipping from 20 to the dollar to over 750 at one point. I can't see how it could go any lower (however, that's what I said when it hit 200 pesos). What did this mean in terms of purchasing power for those with dollars in their pockets? Simply that the relative cost of goods and services against the dollar were more realistic. The immediate drop was drastic. But once prices hit a level, they kept pace with inflation. This means that a meal, for example, that cost 600 pesos when the dollar was worth 200 pesos, now costs 2,100 pesos at 700 to the dollar. But in each instance, the cost to you is the same: $3. For the past several years, this condition has held, and it's my opinion (and that of more competent economists than I) that low prices will remain for a long time to come. Today's values are normal; those of the '70s were abnormal and artificial.

With the recent drastic devaluation of the peso, Mexico has suddenly become as cheap as it was years ago. A maid or cook is a possibility, gasoline is cheap and rents affordable. People are rediscovering a Mexico that is once again a bargain.

Because of the history of the peso, I would not advise anyone to keep more than a minimum checking account in Mexico. The interest rates look good, yes, and in the past many made good returns investing in pesos. Over 50 percent–per–year interest was common, and 10 percent–per–month not unusual. But when the bottom fell out a few years ago, many lost all the profits they'd made, and then some. Stunned, they converted their pesos to dollar accounts, thinking they would be safe. Wrong. Lopez Portillo's government decided that dollar accounts should be illegal and summarily changed them into pesos at an even lower, devalued rate. Unfortunate passbook holders lost another 40 percent, or more, of their savings.

In view of all this, I feel that the risks of high–interest accounts aren't worth it. Keep your money in safe investments at home and make arrangements to have money sent to you as you need it. With a small amount in your Mexican bank, you can't lose much.

LEGALITIES OF RESIDENCE

First of all, you can never at any time endanger your U.S or Canadian citizenship by taking temporary or permanent residence in Mexico. There are several options available, from tourist status through *inmigrado* papers which give foreign residents all the rights of citizenship except for voting. As a tourist, you are prohibited from working for pay, and are entitled to stay in the country up to six months. The inmigrado status is the highest and gives you the right to work or own a business. You also, with certain restrictions, may buy and sell property in your own name. To be eligible for this status, you must prove that you have a certain guaranteed income. The last I heard it was $950 a month for a couple or $750 for an individual. Of course you don't have to spend that much, but you must prove you have that much income per month over the five years it takes to qualify as an inmigrado.

If you expect to own a business or earn money in Mexico, this income requirement is probably not excessive. However, there are other options that don't have such stringent conditions. If your goal is simply rest, retirement, or to write a book or paint––anything that doesn't involve earning money *in Mexico*––then the easiest route is the tourist card. There are no income requirements, and the card can be renewed every six months simply by going out of the country, for even a day, and reentering on a new card. I know of one couple, who have lived in Mexico for 17 years, who go to Guatemala for a pleasant overnight stay every six months. Others take a jaunt to El Paso or Tucson for a shopping spree twice a year. Tourist papers can be obtained from any consulate, and travel agents usually have them.

You need a passport or birth certificate, anything that proves your citizenship status.

The next option is *visitante rentista*, or non–immigrant pensioner. Like tourists, the visitante rentista cannot work or own a business. It's necessary to renew the permit every six months for a period of two years. Then you must leave the country, re–enter and start all over. The income requirement is only half that of an inmigrado applicant.

The most popular status is *inmigrante rentista* or retired immigrant. With this, you may leave and re–enter Mexico without restriction, and the status exempts your household goods and auto from import and export taxes. You cannot work and you must meet the income requirements, but you can own a residence.

It's important to understand that the prohibition of working doesn't apply to creative work such as writing, photography or painting which will be sold outside the country. The rules against working are common–sense ones that protect citizens from unfair job competition from foreigners.

The Mexican government prefers that you have either of the inmigrante documents for living in Mexico rather than just a tourist card, which requires that you leave the country every six months. But the tourist card lets you experiment with living there without the expense and bother of the more permanent documents. Whichever way you choose to go, the government of Mexico welcomes American immigrants and tourists warmly. There are absolutely no indications, economic, political or otherwise that it will ever change its welcome.

Since the rules tend to change from time to time, you are well advised to consult a reputable attorney in Mexico before you make any firm decisions about your status.

HOUSING

Prices of real estate in Mexico don't seem to have any relationship to the value of the property. A lot depends on how much money the buyer has, and how badly he or she wants the property. This is particularly true when it comes to Americans. Since the seller knows you are dying to remodel that cute colonial house, and that you have plenty of cash with which to buy and repair, the price will be high. The seller is stubborn, partly because he knows if you don't buy it, the next gringo will. But the local Mexican views that house with a much different eye: it's nothing but an old, run–down house with worn–out plumbing and termites in the ceiling beams. He wouldn't pay more than $10,000 for a house you think is a steal at $50,000.

While $50,000, plus another $20,000 for remodeling, might be cheap in the United States for an historic old mansion like this, you have to keep in mind the absolute value of your investment. I looked at many homes like this when Don Merwin and I were writing CHOOSE MEXICO. There were some lovely places with three bed-rooms, pool, gardens, a maid's room, and a pleasant patio, selling in the $80,000 to $100,000 range. But when I asked what kind of rent they bring in, should the owner decide to spend part of the year up north, the answer was, "from $300 to $400 a month."

So, you can see that receiving only $300 monthly on an $80,000 investment isn't the greatest return in the world.

Furthermore, in Mexico, as in any country where there is a problem with inflation, most sellers insist on cash. That $80,000 you withdraw from your stock account could easily be returning $600 a month if invested in a safe utility stock. With that $600, you could rent that gorgeous house and have money left over for living ex-penses. You would also have your $80,000 principal safely tucked away.

However, if you really feel the need to own your own home, or if you have an irrepressible desire to remodel something, then see if you can't persuade a Mexican friend to scout around for you. Some-one who is familiar with the local economy can tell you if you are getting a good buy or not. He can tell you if the wages and materials necessary to reconstruct a house would be worth it.

There are problems and restrictions in owning and buying prop-erty that you ought to be aware of. It isn't a simple matter of putting up your money and moving in. The government's policy is to discour-age foreigners from coming in and buying up property. Too many Yankee dollars gobbling up land would soon make it impossible for a Mexican to afford to own anything. So, it is illegal for a foreigner to own any property within 100 kilometers (62 miles) of the ocean, or 50 kilometers (31 miles) of the border. Some get around it, granted, but with some fancy legal maneuvers and some risk. It's also illegal for a foreigner to own land anywhere until he has taken out his immi-gration papers, and agreed to abide by the rules governing foreigners in the country. There are special considerations for retirees over 55 years old who plan to use their property as retirement homes.

Still, plenty of foreigners own property in Mexico. How do they do it? One way is to buy the property through a bank, with the deed in the bank's name and you holding the mortgage. You lease the property from the bank for a period of 30 years, and can assign the lease or the mortgage. So, effectively, *you* are the owner, although on paper it's the bank. If that's the route you wish to travel, make sure you have a *reliable* lawyer watching over things. People have been burned by being too trusting.

Going into partnership with a Mexican citizen is another way of buying a property or business, but this has always seemed risky to me. Of course, marrying a Mexican citizen automatically entitles you to full economic rights in the country. However, just as in this country, a person too often loses all economic rights in the household when the new spouse takes over! That's marriage. Maybe you'd better go with the bank or the retirement provision.

There's no question but that a lot of gringos manage to bend the rules on owning houses and businesses, but you'd better understand the system thoroughly before you try. The Mexican government is quite serious about these matters.

There are special rules for investors. By investing a certain amount of money in a business, you are entitled to the economic rights of a citizen, such as buying housing. The amounts needed for investment change from time to time, and the amounts vary depending on where in Mexico you want to invest. Check this out with the Mexican government for the latest regulations.

MYTHS AND FACTS--MEXICO AND THE LAW

An often-told tale is the one about the tourist who encounters a crooked cop while driving through Mexico. He's stopped for speeding or going through a stop sign, and the cop demands money. Something like that can take the edge off an otherwise pleasant trip, not because of the small amount of money involved--usually $3 to $10--but because of the bitter taste of corruption in an otherwise sweet country. Yet the Mexican citizen sees absolutely nothing wrong with this system. It doesn't look like corruption to him!

The problem here is an interesting one of conflicting philosophies of law and order. While the gringo is horrified at the thought of a cop taking money, the Mexican taxpayer would be equally horrified at the suggestion that traffic cops be paid a living wage. He looks upon government officials or policemen as public servants. They perform certain duties and are expected to be tipped for their troubles much as a waiter is tipped for bringing you a meal. When the cop catches the Mexican citizen speeding, the driver considers that the cop is doing him a favor by accepting the fine, instead of making him go all the way to the police station to pay it. There is absolutely nothing crooked about this, in the eyes of the Mexican taxpayer, it's part of the wage system. If you don't agree that you've violated the law, the solution is simple. Accept the ticket and pay downtown, and the cop gets nothing for his trouble.

However, don't get the idea that you can buy your way out of anything. The Mexicans are quite serious about their laws, particularly those dealing with interpersonal relationships. For example, if you have a lease or contract of some sort, the law frowns severely on anyone violating that agreement. There are certain labor laws you must follow when dealing with your servants or employees. If you knowingly circumvent these laws, you are taking a big chance.

MYTH OF MEXICO AND THE CHURCH

Another common myth is that the Catholic church is all–powerful in Mexico, that it controls people's morals and behavior, and influences government decisions. Nothing could possibly be further from the truth. The Catholic church in Mexico is one of the weakest of any nation's.

"Wait a minute," you sputter, "there are churches everywhere! Full of gold altars and silver chandeliers. And, most all Mexicans are Catholic, right?"

True. But who owns the churches? The government! The Catholic church isn't permitted to own property. The gold and silver are, for the most part, government property, as well. Are the people Catholic? Well, nominally, but not in the sense that people in Ireland are Catholic or that churchgoers in France or the U.S.A. are Catholic. There are many churches, but attendance at mass is generally limited to the very old, and not too many of those. Since church weddings aren't legal (only civil ceremonies are recognized), many couples don't bother going through the religious service as well as the official one. Divorce is easy to obtain and the rate of divorce is as high as in countries where Catholicism is absent. Birth control and abortion clinics are government operated, free, and advertised exten-

161

sively. Religious education and training—seminaries, convents and such—are strictly prohibited. They're criminal activities, as a matter of fact. Until recently, it was a crime to wear religious habits in public and it's still a crime to broadcast a religious service over the airways. Of course, there are no parochial schools, and religious training for children is done on an informal, at-home basis, if at all.

All of this started in the last century, during the time of Benito Juarez. The Catholic church owned much land at that time and was exceedingly rich. But the Reform Laws of that time stripped the church of a lot of these riches. Then, after the Mexican Revolution (1910–1920), the church tried to regain its position by rallying the people behind it in the name of religion. The government retaliated, and strongly. Priests and nuns were expelled from the country. Some of those who stayed were thrown in jail. All church property was confiscated, and even the teaching of catechism was made a criminal offense. (Read Graham Green's novel, *The Power and the Glory* for a description of that era.) Organized religion never recovered from those days. Today, the separation of church and state is so complete that some government officials feel it is improper for them to enter a church for any reason.

Although you see many, many churches in Mexico, most are relics of the past centuries, government museums with neither congregations nor priests. None of this means that Catholicism or religiosity isn't important to the average Mexican. But God is more personal to most Catholics in Mexico than in other parts of the world, and they don't feel that it's necessary to have priests or nuns telling them about God in order to be a religious person. But, are the people Catholic? If you ask, the answer is usually, "Yes," and then they will add, "in my own way."

CHAPTER 15

Many Mexicos

One advantage to Mexico as a place for North Americans to live is the fact that there are so many of their countrymen living there. It's easy to find a community of English–speaking expatriates where you can make a network of friends and enjoy a full social life. Yet, in a way, this can be a disadvantage. It encourages people to stick with their own kind, never learning the language of their host country, seldom making friends with their Mexican neighbors. The ideal is a situation where you will be forced to learn Spanish, yet have access to English–speaking friends.

Fortunately, because of the diversity of Mexico, there is a wide selection of potential living places. Depending on your nature and personality, you can choose from places where almost no one speaks English, to communities of gringos who've lived there for years and haven't learned a word of Spanish. (This suits some people fine.) An interesting thing about Americans living in a foreign environment is that they make friends easily with other English–speaking foreigners. People who would never speak to each other in the States find themselves becoming close friends on foreign turf. It's as if each subconsciously recognizes the necessity of "networking."

Listed in this chapter are places in Mexico foreign residents and retirees most prefer. These are locations where you may begin your experiment in foreign living without too much dislocation in your lives. Each town is analyzed from the perspective of residence or retirement possibilities, not necessarily tourism. Space doesn't per-

163

mit a description of sightseeing and tourist attractions, restaurants or hotels. There are many excellent travel guides available that can do this much more efficiently, and in more detail than this book.

Once you decide you enjoy Mexico, you can then find the exact spot that suits all your needs. Generally speaking there are seven main sections of Mexico. These are the West Coast, the Central Plateau, Guadalajara–Michoacan, the Yucatan, the East Coast, and the northern and southern border areas. Each section is further divided into regions which are known for their own cultural flavor and climatic differences. Since each person is a little different, there may be conditions that one might desire that would be of no consequence to someone else. My best advice is to try a few sections for yourself before deciding where to live.

TRAILERS AND MOTOR–HOMES

An important question: Many people have written asking about the advisability of taking motor homes, trailers and mobile homes to use as residences. Many do, although to my way of thinking, it's not very practical. For one thing, some of the roads are narrow, sometimes pot–holed, often with poor or non–existent shoulders. This alone would make me nervous. Another consideration is that the streets in some of the smaller towns were designed for horse and carriage. Your wide motor home would feel uncomfortable in tight corners, or tooling around in traffic. And finally, housing is so inexpensive that it seems foolish to drag your own home around with you. I find that I can rent an acceptable hotel or motel double room for less than $20 a night (I've found great rooms for as low as $5), and I don't have to worry about towing my room behind me in the morning when I leave. Furthermore, for what a nice motor home or mobile home would cost, I could purchase a two bedroom home or an apartment with a view.

Compound all of this with the fact that RV facilities in Mexico are all but nonexistent in some areas, and you can see why I don't recommend the trailer or motor–home method of travel. If you plan on living for any length of time, you would be forced to stay in one of the few RV parks, which may not be in the side of town where you otherwise might choose to live. You've lost flexibility. People do travel that way, however. I've seen caravans of them as far south as the Yucatan. They have a great time. I know hardy souls who've driven them to Panama and back and had the time of their lives. But for long–term living, I would sell the mobile home and use the money to rent a nice house with a private patio and a hot tub.

BEACH RESORTS, ARE THEY PRACTICAL?

A common misconception about the coastal "resort" towns is that they are expensive. That is not necessarily true. Of course they *can* be expensive. Anywhere can if you want it to be. But if you plan on living in a resort, you must avoid the high–price tourist facilities. You'll find many resorts to be as reasonable as anywhere else in Mexico. The reason is, there has been such an overbuilding of apartments, hotels and houses that rents are at a bargain level. It's possible to rent a great two–bedroom apartment with a view of the ocean for $200 a month or less in Acapulco, for example. More modest accommodations are proportionately less. Some resorts like Zihuantanejo and Cancun, which are still growing, haven't reached this point as yet, and some people prefer to buy or build their own places there.

The advantages of living by the ocean are obvious to those who love the beaches and picturesque villages. If you enjoy warm weather and don't mind it when it gets a bit muggy in the summertime, then by all means keep the resorts in mind. They are affordable. One drawback for long–term living here is that the North American population seems to always be in a state of flux, with newcomers moving in as others return to the States. This makes it harder to maintain a circle of close friends in a resort than in a more permanent atmosphere.

If you're the kind of person who doesn't need a group of English–speaking acquaintances around you, you'll find many small "undiscovered" villages along the ocean where few North Americans even visit, much less live, and the people haven't yet grown bored with tourists. These can be great opportunities, both financially and esthetically, where a rustic beach cottage can be your base for an exciting, affordable adventure. In addition, a small village can be an adventure in cultural exposure. By being one of the few gringos in the village, you will be an overnight sensation, and have the opportunity to make friends with the villagers and participate in their lives in a way that would be impossible in a large resort community.

165

On the Gulf of Mexico from Tampico down around to Campeche, you find very few retired Americans, even though it would seem to be an ideal place. The problem here is the extremely hot summers, which tend to be even much for me, a person who loves hot weather. But there are places all along here where a pleasant, interesting winter can be yours for less than anywhere else in Mexico. A particularly delightful place is Campeche, with its ancient defense works against pirates, and its great seafood restaurants.

Once you turn the peninsula of the Yucatan, Caribbean breezes temper the summers, and although hot, are tolerable. Here the local people are pure Mayan. They live in unusual round houses with thatch roofs, and cling to their Mayan language, although almost all of them speak Spanish as well. They don't consider themselves Mexicans, referring to themselves as Yucatecans. To them the term *Mexican* refers to people from other parts of the republic. Their food and culture are adventures in themselves, and like Mexicans from other parts of the country, they are polite, gentle and friendly. The Yucatan will be covered later in this chapter. For now, let's start with the western part of Mexico, the most traveled of all.

WEST COAST "RIVIERA"

Easily accessible to the western part of the United States and Canada, Mexico's west coast is a popular location that draws thousands of residents and retirees, plus hundreds of thousands of tourists each year. Here we find the "Mexican Riviera," the famous beach resorts of Mazatlan, Acapulco, and Puerto Vallarta. Even though these places are posh, they don't have to be prohibitively expensive for ordinary, everyday living. They can be, if you go the tourist route. But, as a resident, you will be renting or owning a house and paying no more than a native pays. You will be shopping for groceries at the same places the local people shop, so your food bill needn't be any higher. You won't be shopping for clothing and other needs in tourist boutiques, where prices are adjusted accordingly. Some things in resort towns are higher, true. Taxis, for example, don't have to be competitive in a town where the tourist saturation is heavy. They boost their rates so high that the local people don't use them, and rely on public transportation instead. So you ride buses the same as the other residents. Rents along the beach will naturally be higher as landlords are besieged with tourists bidding up the going price. You can do as the locals do and walk a few blocks inland and find reasonable accommodations.

From the U.S. border down to the tropic of Cancer, the west coast of Mexico is pretty much desert. There are areas where irrigation turns the arid lands green with vegetables and row crops, but few places in the north are really suitable for foreign residence. The summers are unbearably hot and the winters can be chilly when a north wind blows south out of Canada. Fairly deep snows in the north of Mexico aren't uncommon. There are some towns that might be worth investigating as living or retirement places, but most are primarily agricultural in orientation, with little to offer in the way of recreation or cultural stimulation.

ALAMOS

An exception to the above descriptions is Alamos. Nestled in the foothills of the Sierra Madre, 80 kilometers (50 miles) east of Hermosillo, Alamos is just a day's drive from the Arizona border, making it quite accessible. Gold and silver attracted a large population back in the 1700s, but when the mines played out, Alamos became a ghost town. The Mexican government later recognized its colonial beauty and placed restrictions on building in order to preserve the town from modernization. Its development is due largely to retirees and artists who "discovered" Alamos and began restoring the picturesque old buildings.

Close to fishing and duck hunting, Alamos enjoys a great winter climate, dry and sunny. The summers can be hot, since the altitude isn't very high.

MAZATLAN

Mazatlan is the second largest port on the coast, with a population of 175,000. Besides its miles of sunny beaches it also boasts superb sports fishing. It bills itself as the "shrimp capital of the world," with justification, for the town's shrimping fleet daily brings home tons of the tasty delicacies. Modern, clean and full of tourists, Mazatlan stretches along the beach with wide boulevards, more appropriate to Florida than Mexico. Winters are pleasant, and summers livable.

Even though plentiful tourist dollars are pushing prices up, things are still affordable enough to keep Mazatlan on our list of places where it's possible to live on a minimal budget. Taxis tend to be expensive, so the local residents prefer to use the frequent buses. Because of tourists and large number of American retirees, plenty of English is spoken here, perhaps more than the other resort towns. This lack of "foreignness" is a plus for older and less adventurous retirees. Residents report that there are several good English–speaking doctors and dentists, and an excellent hospital there.

Condominiums, golf courses, housing developments abound, all directed at long–term American vacationers. An advantage here is the large English–speaking community, and the possibility of joining a network of friends with similar interests. A disadvantage would be the transitory nature of many foreigners as they come and go, depending on the season. Another disadvantage is higher prices than in some coastal towns.

SAN BLAS

About 150 kilometers (93 miles) south of Mazatlan, a side road turns off for San Blas, a reputed pirate's port of the 16th and 17th centuries. The road winds through picturesque jungles, crosses a few meandering streams and ends at the village of San Blas. It's as if time completely passed by the little town, with it's quiet town square and odd–looking church. Legend has it that it was a pirate's town, and today's village looks a bit like a movie set for some pirate movie. Many houses have thatched roofs, and an occasional sow may be seen herding a litter of piglets along the sandy streets. Although pirates no doubt visited from time to time, the port was actually a Spanish naval base, with gunships stationed there to chase the buccaneers who loved to prey on Spanish galleons coming back from China and the Philippines. Some hotels along the main street date back a couple of centuries. The beach is long, protected by a natural bay, and uncrowded.

Several Americans live there year round, but most come during the winter months to escape the cold and the higher expenses of nearby Puerto Vallarta and Mazatlan. Attempts have been made at turning San Blas into another primo resort, but all have failed. The major reason for the failure is a summer problem with mosquitos and gnats, a condition that's unknown in either Puerto Vallarta or Mazatlan. Winters are fine though, and summers are okay if you remember to use insect repellent. San Blas would be a great place to spend a few months catching up on your Spanish, enjoying shellfish and beachcombing, all without a tourist crush. Several families there take in boarders, an excellent situation in which to learn the language. Regular bus service from Mazatlan and Guadalajara makes San Blas accessible.

Farther south along the coast are some delightful beach communities that scarcely know the tread of tourist feet. San Francisquito and Rincon are just a couple. Some so small they don't make it on the maps. These are best reached by automobile, although I imagine that, like most remote parts of Mexico, regularly scheduled buses make their way into the villages. Land is inexpensive here, and labor costs low, so you might be tempted to choose this place to build that dream home. Always bear in mind that land ownership and titles are tricky anywhere on the coast. Be sure and check carefully with other Americans to see exactly how they managed it, because it's technically against the law. Check, and check again.

PUERTO VALLARTA

Another popular resort town, Puerto Vallarta is suffering growing pains. A few years ago it was a sleepy little village, all but inaccessible by automobile. But a new highway and airport changed all that. Like many resort towns, there has been an overbuilding of apartments, so some bargains can be found here. The secret is to look in the older sections of town, away from the beach. By renting in the summertime, which is the off–season, you can make a better deal through the winter season. If you lease for the entire year, costs come down considerably.

Because the town is located on a narrow strip of land a few blocks wide, between the ocean and some abrupt mountains, Puerto Vallarta can only expand north and south. Therefore it can't very well become metropolitan. With cobblestone streets and lots of small, adobe buildings Puerto Vallarta (or PV, as American devotees call it) manages to retain some of its village atmosphere. The highrises and luxury hotels are sprouting farther and farther from the old–fashioned city center. Unfortunately, these developments are gobbling up much of the pristine beaches that used to be the attraction here. The good news is that according to law, everyone has access to any beach, so you can still swim and surf on the beaches despite the hotels and condominiums.

There are plenty of full–time American residents, with a number of writers and artists living there. As you might guess, the flood of tourists has pushed prices higher than in most other parts of Mexico, making wages for servants out of the question for budget travelers. But by avoiding the tourist traps, Puerto Vallarta isn't any more expensive than other popular spots. There's a bulletin board on the town square where you'll find offerings of apartments and houses for sale or rent.

Several dozen kilometers south is the village of Boca de Tomatlan, which clings to the side of the canyon where the Tomatlan River empties into the Pacific. The banks of the shallow river are thick with tropical vegetation, in which you'll see a sprinkling of small houses. There always seems to be a couple for sale or rent. Several Americans live there now, and it's my guess that development will inevitably spill over into that delightful little village. Movie director John Houston built a house on a cove down the coast a little way, and reaches his property by boat from Boca.

From here, the highway climbs into the mountains, making Boca de Tomatlan the last of the beach locations for a while. As you head south you'll find a half dozen beach towns where Americans have residences. Any of these villages would make pleasant living choices. Barra de Navidad is the largest and most developed until you reach Manzanillo.

MANZANILLO

Manzanillo itself is an active commercial port, and as such is not as touristy as the other resort towns. The center of town is actually a bit dreary. Here, the better beaches are northwest, with many houses and apartments strewn along the highway. Many Americans love it here, forming little enclaves within compounds of small apartment complexes. I suspect that the social relationships among themselves accounts for a lot of the enthusiasm. Since it's a relatively short trip to Guadalajara and Lake Chapala, it draws heavily on the huge American communities there, particularly in the winter months. In the summer, when temperatures hit the eighties and humidity creeps up a bit, the sun–seekers return to the coolness of the Central Plateau, just a few hours away.

Often called the "sailfish capital of the world," Manzanillo attracts avid fishermen in search of that prize for the fireplace mantel. The temperature can get sticky in the summer, but look at it this way: Its winters are warmer than Miami's and its summers are cooler. Not too bad, eh?

ZIHUATANEJO–IXTAPA

A fairly new highway continues south of Manzanillo through some gorgeous country, with some spectacular views of the ocean. You pass a couple of small beach towns, the largest being Playa Azul. This is an interesting town, but the long beach here is open to waves rolling in 6,000 miles from China, making it rather dangerous for swimming. There is not much else to do in Playa Azul but lie around the beach. I'm not aware of any year–around North American residents here. The next important town is Zihuatanejo, about halfway between Manzanillo and Acapulco.

Zihuatanejo and its newer sister town of Ixtapa are recent entries into the resort competition. A few years ago the only way to reach here was by dirt road from Acapulco or on scary DC–3s using an unreliable landing strip. But with the new road and the government's development of the luxury resort of Ixtapa, the area has been booming.

A favorite with Americans, "Zihua" has been expanding into the surrounding hills along the harbor and around the bay to the great beaches as far as Playa la Ropa. Coconuts trees are plentiful and a feeling of old tropical Acapulco pervades the town. The sleepy little village of the past is gone as ever more tourists and residents crowd into town. But the "big spenders," the tourists with two weeks vacation and plenty of dollars to live it up, prefer glamorous Ixtapa. This keeps Zihuatanejo's prices from climbing out of sight. Ixtapa is pure tourist highrise and very expensive. I love the beach there for body surfing, so I simply make a 15–minute drive in the morning then return to Zihua for my accommodations.

Because of Zihuatanejo's steady population growth, apartments can be difficult to find. Houses are the alternative, but they can be scarce in the winter season, too. This may be the place to consider building something, possibly with a couple of rental units as an investment. Small mountains surround the bay and the town, so it's "up there," where the views are picture perfect, that the best building sites can be found. The usual cautions on legal niceties go here, as with anywhere in Mexico. Be particularly cautious with property near the ocean.

The harbor is popular with the yachting bunch, with crews stopping in on their way between California and Acapulco. The bars by the yacht berths seem to be forever full of yachtsmen swapping experiences of life under sail.

ACAPULCO

One of the original "Jet Set" towns, Acapulco became a synonym for glamour and elegant living. A generation of movie stars, millionaires and celebrities maintained winter homes in Acapulco, and many do to this day. The beaches are some of the best in the world, and the luxury hotels that ring Acapulco Bay are some of the most costly in all of Mexico.

Despite all of this, Acapulco can be one of the most affordable living places of all! The basic reason for this is that from the very beginning of its tourist boom, Acapulco's building outdistanced its population. New hotels and apartment buildings are rushed to completion, and before they can begin booking tenants, another hotel or apartment building sprouts up next door. Competition between rentals is fierce, with price cutting a way of life. None of this affects the tourist who makes his reservation through a travel agent, because the agent is interested in the commission, not in low rents that mean little or no commission. Tourists are routinely shunted to the high–rise gold mines along the beach front.

Another development that means reasonable housing is a change in tourist's habits. Years ago, many people drove their automobiles in from Mexico City, and either built or rented houses up on the hillsides where the views of the bay can make you sigh with ecstasy. Traffic was light, and taxis and limousines were cheap and plentiful, so getting up and down the steep hills was no problem. The "in place" for housing was up on these hillsides, where tourists often stayed a couple of months at a time. But times have changed. Today, most tourists jet in for short, one– or two–week vacations and insist on staying right on the beach. They want to hop out of bed, run to the elevator and be on the beach in minutes. Nobody cares to waste time waiting for a taxi or bus, or––heaven forbid–– walking.

This shift from the hills to the beaches left apartments and hotels up above high and dry. Rents dropped to become competitive, sometimes drastically. Some hotels were forced to practically give away their rooms. Luxury establishments that 30 years ago catered to Hollywood movie stars are now renting rooms for $15 to $20 a day. Many sit abandoned. The last time I was in Acapulco, I rented a room across from the Mirador (where the divers go off the cliffs) for a little over $4 a night for two people. The Mirador itself, once a favorite haunt of Hedy Lamarr and other superstars, was renting rooms nightly for less than $25.

As in other resorts there are the Two Mexicos: One for tourists, one for residents. Since most grocery costs are controlled by the government, your supermarket bills won't be much different in Acapulco than in any other part of the republic. Gasoline and other staples are similarly controlled. So, with low rents, monthly living costs are as affordable as you can find anywhere. Yes, in Acapulco!

Restaurants are on a two-tiered system as well. You can pay plenty for a meal at one of the luxury restaurants, no question about it. But there are only so many people who can afford those meals. The vast majority of the tourists are not rich gringos, but ordinary Mexicans from Oaxaca, Cordoba, Monterrey, and all over the country. Some are wealthy, but most are auto workers, small businessmen—people of modest means. To them a $5 meal is a luxury item. (When they're paying $4 a day for a room, you can see why they would think that way.) Therefore, most restaurants compete for these budget-minded customers. The service is excellent, the food superb, and the prices reasonable. What more can you ask?

Many, many North Americans live here, particularly during the winter months, when French Canadians come in by the thousands, as well as other thousands of people fleeing Minnesota and Montana snows, seeking warm beaches and sun. One problem for year-round living is that much of the population is floating; they stay for a while, maybe two or three months and then move on. Establishing and maintaining a network of friends isn't easy. Then again, maybe you're only escaping the winter and will choose to spend your summers in the cooler parts of Mexico, so it doesn't matter.

PUERTO ESCONDIDO AND PUERTO ANGEL

Since the new highway pushed through the *Costa Chica* country south of Acapulco, some fascinating villages and vistas are available for the first time to tourists. Any one of these villages could make for a unique cultural adventure for those who speak enough Spanish to communicate. One village, Juchitan, is peopled by descendents of escaped black slaves who founded the village years ago. Over the years of isolation they managed to preserve some of their old customs. Another stretch of pavement goes through the only place in Mexico where Indian women go topless. The women weave a beautiful skirt of cochineal–dyed yarn, and wear it around their waist, but nothing on top. However, with the opening of the highway and introduction of city fashions, the younger women have taken to wearing slacks and blouses, leaving the old customs to the grandmothers. So much for that custom. Sigh.

Then, about six hours drive south of Acapulco, is the mecca of the backpacking and surfing set. Somehow, they've done a pretty good job of keeping Puerto Escondido hidden. Appropriately, *Puerto Escondido* means *hidden port*, but it is more of a beach town than a port. It isn't listed on some maps, even though it's grown to a nice–sized village nowadays. Its one main street parallels the beach and is lined with hotels and restaurants. Many of the younger crowd are satisfied with sleeping on the beach or in some rather primitive accommodations, so there hasn't been the pressure for conventional retirement or residential units. This is changing, however, as more North Americans discover the secret of "Hidden Port." This is another location where some building investment might pay off in the coming years. Puerto Escondido is too far off the beaten track to become another Acapulco or Puerto Vallarta, but it's too nice to be ignored for long.

Another drive south, about eight hours worth, is Puerto Angel. This is another unknown paradise, one of my favorites. The town is built on a round bay, ringed by low mountains, and enjoys some of the most beautiful sunsets in the world. Scuba diving and snorkeling are incredible. Yet, despite the picture–postcard quality of the town and the excellent beaches, Puerto Angel has escaped the crush of tourism and awaits your exploration. As far as I know, there aren't any "curio shops" in the center of town, not even a postcard for sale! Housing is available, but not a whole lot of it, since the town is small. It's probably the most remote of all the Pacific Coast resort towns.

The access by automobile takes a long time, and the airplane to Oaxaca only flies occasionally. Puerto Angel is for getting away from it all, not for those accustomed to big–city conveniences.

THE CENTRAL PLATEAU — MEXICO CITY

The contour of Mexico is mountainous, like a crumpled piece of paper, with a relatively flat section in the middle called the Central Plateau. But even here there are ups and downs, mountains, old volcanos and shallow valleys. The largest city on the Central Plateau is Mexico City. It's also the largest capital city in the world, and probably the largest city in the entire world. No one really knows how many live there, since the population grows each day. Estimates run from 17 million to over 20 million. No matter, it's a big city.

I was fortunate to live in Mexico when the capital had less than 3 million population. Needless to say, that was many years ago. In those days, the skies were deep blue with fluffy white clouds continually drifting eastward across the distant twin volcanoes of Popocatepetl and Ixtacihuatl. Many years ago. Today, depending on the way the wind is blowing and upon the strength of the inversion layer, the sky can be so loaded with smog that it's difficult to see the tops of buildings. On the other hand, when the breezes are merciful, the sky looks as gorgeous as ever.

Yet, oddly enough, even though the town has added countless new buildings and about 14 million people since the days of my youth, the downtown section has changed very little. On a clear day (and there are many of them), the 16th– and 17th–century buildings look no different than they did years ago. Then, I feel that same magic I felt when I was young in the Mexico City of yesteryear. The tragic earthquake of 1985 spared this old center of town. Buildings built in the 1600s and 1700s stand just as proudly as the day they were constructed, while modern glass–and–steel monsters twisted themselves into tortured junk piles. They say that 90 percent of the damage in the Mexico City earthquake happened to fairly new, government–built construction. This tells us something about modern–day engineering compared to the common–sense building methods of 400 years ago.

In the days I lived in Mexico City, the "British–American Colony," as they called it, numbered over 100,000. A few people lived in places like Lake Chapala, Acapulco, or Cuernavaca, but most pre-

ferred to live in Mexico City and own weekend houses in those out-
of-the-way resorts.

Today all this has changed. The vast majority of Americans in
Mexico live in smaller towns, away from the capital. Yet, the city has
never lost its charm. About 10,000 Americans still live in Mexico
City, willing to brave smog, traffic and crowded streets, because of
that magical charm. Many would live no place else.

The city boasts outstanding museums and art exhibits, excellent
restaurants, some great opera and smart shops. There is an excited
bustle about the city, even late at night, for late dining is the habit
here. Wide, elegant boulevards criss-cross the city, and modern
buildings stand as towering reminders that something special is going
on around you. The climate is temperate, with cool summers and
winters that are only a little cooler than summer. Air conditioning is
unknown, and you'll sleep under an electric blanket all year around.

It takes a special person to want to live in Mexico City, the kind
of person who loves big cities, the kind who particularly loves New
York City. This kind of person would want to live there no matter
how many recommendations he receives against it. If you're that
type, go right ahead. The good part about the city is that some rather
elegant apartments and condominiums are available at bargain prices.
The place to look is in the Mexico City *Daily News*, either by scan-
ning the classified ads, or placing one yourself.

CUERNAVACA

Cuernavaca's popularity lies in its great climate. About an
hour's drive from Mexico City, the town is 2,000-feet lower in altitude, which translates into a mild, warm climate where temperatures
hover year-round in the 70s. It's a delight for visitors from Mexico
City's coolness. For untold centuries, it was the refuge of the rich and
powerful who live in the capital. Aztec chieftains kept vacation
homes there. When the Spanish conquered the Aztecs, Cortez quite
naturally continued the tradition by building his "Summer Palace" in
Cuernavaca on the foundations of an Aztec temple, which in turn
had been built on the base of a temple even more ancient than the
Aztec nation. Archaeologists have found the remains of five different
pre-Columbian temples at that site.

Cuernavaca is world-famous for its language schools. Innova-
tors in learning techniques, these schools are excellent places for new

residents to perfect their Spanish. Some schools specialize in placing their students in local homes, where learning becomes a round–the–clock affair.

Precisely because of Cuernavaca's superb climate, population began building several years ago. Eventually some industry made it's appearance, and with it, the inevitable smog. Not as bad as Mexico City, perhaps, but a bit disappointing. Also, the city has lost much of its charm with all those added workers and their families crowding the streets and sidewalks. It's still a popular weekend retreat for Mexico City residents, so expect hotels to be packed from Friday through Sunday. Apartment rentals are often located by studying the classified ads in the Mexico City *News*. Since this paper is widely read throughout Mexico, it's a good place to put your own ad if you're looking for something to rent or buy.

CUAUTLA

Now that Cuernavaca has grown to over 350,000 people and is no longer a small town, so many people have moved away from the central City that it now has its own suburbs, the neighboring towns of Lake Tequesquitengo, Tepoztlan, and Ixtapan de la Sal. Another, Cuautla, is becoming popular as an escape from the city. Once the headquarters for General Zapata's revolutionary army, Cuautla is a little lower in altitude than Cuernavaca yet still enjoys a superb climate. Its thermal sulphur springs are reputed to cure everything from rheumatism to liver ailments, thus attracting a group of North Americans interested just in the baths.

GUADALAJARA

The second largest city in Mexico, at 2.5 million people, is Guadalajara. The largest number of North American retirees probably lives around Guadalajara and nearby Lake Chapala. Because of its altitude and mild climate, guidebooks insist on describing Guadalajara and environs as "the land of eternal spring." I've seen it pretty hot in the summer, and have had to wear heavy sweaters in the winter, but all in all, it's as near to perfect weather as you can reasonably expect to find. The evenings usually are balmy, shirtsleeve perfect, and the days are seldom so hot that you wouldn't feel comfortable in a sports jacket at midday if you felt like being dressy.

Guadalajara enthusiasts point out that they average only one day a month when the sun doesn't shine at least part of the day.

A plus about living around here is the large, organized community of North Americans, which has its own newspaper, social clubs, churches, and regular social activities. The Guadalajara–Chapala area is a great place for a North American beginner to break into Mexico living. It wouldn't be a bad idea to start off here on your test visit, and take advantage of all the help offered by the local gringo community.

The residents and retirees seem to be unusually proud of their choice. They point out the unmistakable beauty of the city, the excellent parks, museums and theaters, and the rich cultural life available.

When we were doing research on the cost of living in Mexico, our surveys showed Guadalajara to be an unusually economical place to live. The president of the local American Society and her husband reported a monthly household budget of $357, which included a maid and entertaining. The American Society there, by the way, is very active, with a large membership. It publishes an excellent weekly newspaper, which I recommend to anyone considering to move there.

LAKE CHAPALA, AJIJIC

Artists, writers, sculptors, all seem to be drawn to Guadalajara, especially to the Lake Chapala area, which has gained a reputation as a "culture colony." The bohemian atmosphere is especially evident in Ajijic (a 15–minute drive along the lake from Chapala), but more and more retirees are settling in. Several of the local *supermercados* (supermarkets) have bulletin boards with rentals listed. These are not too hard to find, since it seems that so many people, when building their dream home, add a rental unit or two on the property to supplement their income. While there isn't a surplus, the number available keeps rents fairly low.

An easy drive from Guadalajara, the lake area isn't too far away for those who demand occasional big city life. And then, people from Guadalajara often visit here for a game of golf or a weekend away from the city. The local foreign community is exceptionally active in community affairs, making it a good place to meet people and make friends.

MICHOACAN

Years and years ago, when the volcano Paricutin was in eruption near the village of Uruapan, I spent a couple of unforgettable weeks enjoying the superb weather and soaking up the peaceful atmosphere of Uruapan. Today, it's no longer a village but a city of 105,000. Still, the setting is gorgeous. For my money, the State of Michoacan, 200 kilometers (120 miles) west of Mexico City, is one of the prettiest in all the republic. It receives a fair share of rain, which keeps things green all year around. Gentle mountains, forests, waterfalls and rolling fields, plus low population density make Michoacan a good bet. If Uruapan seems too crowded, you might investigate some of the surrounding towns and villages. I'm not aware of many, if any, North Americans living around here, so this is the place for your Spanish skills. If you are a guitar player, as I am, a particularly interesting village is Paracho. The entire village is involved with guitar making. It seems that every family has something to do with either making some part of a guitar, lacquering and polishing, or assembling guitars or violins.

MORELIA

A medium-sized city of about 240,000, 200 kilometers (120 miles) west of Mexico City, Morelia has managed to retain much of its colonial charm. The city government insists that all new construction conform to the early styles. A university town, Morelia has extensive offerings of music and culture. The town is remarkably clean and comfortable.

The earliest residents decided that its climate and mountainous backdrop made it one of the most desirable in Mexico. Later, North American artists and writers "discovered" Morelia and formed a good-sized community. Its altitude of 6,300 feet makes for brisk evenings and mornings in the winter, but the days are generally delightful. And of course, the summer weather couldn't be better.

OAXACA

A nine-hour drive south from Mexico City is Oaxaca. This is another strikingly well-preserved colonial city. Its population is still less than 150,000, which keeps it from feeling like a city so much as a good-sized town. Beautiful, twin zocalos (plazas) form the center of Oaxaca. Shaded by huge trees and surrounded by sidewalk cafes, the zocalos are popular places to people-watch and relax, the social center of the city. Businesses cluster around, but aren't intrusive on the tranquility of Oaxaca. This is the heart of Zapotec Indian country, and the flavor of this ancient culture pervades the town in the form of distinctive handicrafts and stoic brown faces just in from the countryside to sell their wares in the regionally famous marketplaces.

The altitude here is a bit over 5,000 feet, which means even, spring-like weather all year long. For this reason, it's a favorite place for retirees. Wages are low in this region, making household servants an economic possibility. Because of the unusual-looking greenstone of which many buildings are constructed, Oaxaca is often called "The Green City." This stone is also ubiquitous in the many ancient ruins that surround Oaxaca. For the amateur archaeologist or the history buff, the area is fascinating. Numerous villages throughout the Oaxaca valley are also good prospects as residence or retirement sites.

HIGH COUNTRY -- GUANAJUATO AND SAN MIGUEL DE ALLENDE

Two favorite towns for residents and retirees are Guanajuato and San Miguel de Allende. Both are located in the northern mountains midway between Mexico City and Guadalajara. Both towns have been declared National Colonial Monuments with restrictions on any new construction or remodeling. The results are two jewels tucked into the Sierra Madre range.

Guanajuato sits at 6,500 feet, just a little higher than San Miguel, and has a medieval Moorish flavor that the original settlers brought with them from the southern Spanish province of Andalusia. Set in a gorge, Guanajuato's pastel homes, with their wrought-iron balconies, cling to the sides of the steep canyon. Crooked streets of cobblestone wind around up and down, sometimes so steep that stairs have to be used, sometimes crossing over or under another street. Old fashioned lanterns light the way at night, and three peaceful plazas make for pleasant daytime lounging.

Guanajuato is a university town, proud of its cultural heritage. There are many events, concerts, lectures and the like available to the resident community. There is a considerable population of North Americans living there, most of whom will be angry at seeing their secret paradise exposed in this book. It's okay, because during my next trip there I'll be wearing fake nose–eyeglasses with moustache attached. Summer brings the heaviest tourist traffic here, so you might try to arrive after October or before June to find the best rental deals.

While Guanajuato's origins were in silver mining, San Miguel was founded originally to support the mines. Today its major attraction is as an art and education center. Sturdy old mansions, little changed from colonial days, line cobblestone streets where burros trundle along with bundles of firewood on their backs. A favorite hobby of the gringo immigrant is renovating the old houses, restoring them to the grandeur of past centuries. They've done quite well, but have also driven up the price of real estate in the bargain.

Two institutes teach Spanish, sculpture, oil and watercolor painting, and weaving. These schools draw students from all over, and are popular with the expatriate colony as well. This colony is probably the largest, proportionally, in all of Mexico, representing about one in every 15 inhabitants of the town. Attending an art class or studying Spanish at one of the institutes is an excellent way to begin meeting local residents, as well as interesting visitors. The foreign community is quite active and even publishes a weekly English–Spanish newspaper to keep its members abreast of local news, as well as financial and government regulations that may affect them. Because of their work with health, education and library projects for local people, the gringos in San Miguel enjoy a good reputation. They are seldom seen as "Ugly Americans." Becoming a part of philanthropic action is the best way to make Mexican and American friends plus do something for needy people as partial payment for Mexico's hospitality.

IN THE SOUTH OF MEXICO

This southern part of Mexico, the State of Chiapas, is the most *Indian* of all, in that there are several tribes living here not much differently from the way their ancestors lived before the Spanish conquest. In some towns, like San Juan Chamula, the majority of the people cannot communicate in Spanish except in rudimentary phrases, not much better than the average tourist's vocabulary. A word of caution here: be careful to respect the local customs, particularly the taboo against photos. The one thing that is sure to make the Indians angry is to have a tourist put a camera in their face and start clicking away. There are several things they see wrong with this, one of which is the religious belief that a photo robs something of their soul. Another is that they've seen picture postcards for sale and are convinced that the tourist is taking the pictures to sell and make a profit at their expense.

If you're an anthropology buff, this section of Mexico holds many fascinating adventures. But if not, you might feel excluded and lonely because of the almost impenetrable wall between the outsider and the Indian. It takes special skills to make friends with these people, and the only other North Americans around seem to be anthropologists.

SAN CRISTOBAL DE LAS CASAS

For those interested in anthropology or ethnology, you must at least visit San Cristobal de las Casas, in Chiapas. Set high in the mountains, San Cristobal is another feast for the eyes with architecture little touched by the 20th century. One of the oldest European-style buildings in the hemisphere (1522) is now a hotel on the corner of the main plaza. The city was the first to be laid out according to the traditional plan of old Spain by a priest known as Las Casas. He became the protector and advocate for Indian welfare and did much to protect them from slavery and exploitation. Perhaps for this reason, the area around San Cristobal de las Casas is one of the most "Indian" in Mexico. Two major tribes populate the surrounding mountains, and often visit town to purchase supplies and pay a visit to the many churches.

Many of the foreign residents and retirees here are anthropologists or students of anthropology. They come from all countries, and speak all languages, but share one common bond: the study of indigenous cultures. The tourists who visit San Cristobal aren't typical, looking for gaudy curios or searching out a "good time." They almost all are quietly impressed by the other–worldly aura of the town and its primitive countryside. There is also a permanent colony of artists, sculptors and weavers living here. Almost every one you will meet is interesting to talk to, especially if you share an interest in Native American cultures.

A drawback to living here is cool winter weather. San Cristobal is high, almost 8,000 feet, and morning ice on the streets isn't uncommon. Fireplaces are definitely in order, and often feel good on a cool summer's evening. But happily, just a few miles' drive down to low country brings you to year–round summer, should the cold get to gnawing at your bones.

PALENQUE

Palenque is 120 kilometers (73 miles) northeast of San Cristobal. This little village grown into a town has no reason to exist except for the hordes of tourists who come to visit the famous Mayan ruins a few miles out of town. Two distinct worlds exist side by side here, with the local people almost oblivious to the non–Spanish speaking tourists, and the tourists concerned only with their visits to the ruins. The only spoken contacts are usually commercial, when the tourist needs to buy something or to use the bathroom, or when the local wants to sell something outrageously overpriced to the naive tourist. Still, the town's local world is pure Mexican, and a pleasant world to enter, should your mastery of the language permit.

The town's plaza, shaded by huge trees, is a pleasant social center for townspeople, as well as a gathering place for tourists to discuss their theories on how and why the ancient Mayas constructed the fantastic temples and palaces in such unlikely places as Palenque. Here is where many expeditions begin for trips into the jungles to visit or search for more Mayan ruins. Summers can be hot and humid, but winters are exceptionally beautiful and mild in the lush countryside surrounding the town and in the nearby mountains.

THE YUCATAN PENINSULA

Two of the more sparsely settled parts of the republic, the contiguous states of Yucatan and Quintana Roo have only recently been looked at by North Americans as retirement possibilities. The winter climate is balmy, and in most places, rather delightful. But summer can be very, very hot, particularly away from the ocean breezes. In the interior, the climate can be described as varying from hot to impossible. This is one reason the peninsula is not more heavily settled.

The coastline along the Gulf of Mexico coast is rather uninteresting, with placid, copper–colored water and lots of swampy areas. It isn't until you turn the corner going east, then south, and find your-self on the Caribbean, that the seascape changes into the gorgeous blue waves and white beaches you might expect of the Yucatan. I've often wondered why this change; maybe some oceanographer out there will clue me in someday. The cities of Campeche and Merida are on the Gulf side, Cancun and Tulum on the Caribbean side of the peninsula.

Campeche is a favorite city of mine, at least in the winter. In the 1600s, the town was a favorite of British, French and Dutch buc-caneers. For protection, the townspeople erected some massive walls around the town, many portions of which are still standing. The city is a fascinating blend of the old Spanish Main and modern-day Mex-ico. The old-fashioned streets and colonial buildings seem to ooze history, Mayas, conquistadores, buccaneers, revolutionaries. In the summers, however, Campeche is reminiscent of a huge frying pan with the heat turned to "high."

Merida also is hot in the summer, but large trees line many streets, giving merciful shade and fooling you into believing it's cooler than it really is. Again, winters are great here, and could be enjoyed as an occasional "second summer." My main objection to Merida is that there are more unmuffled autos and motorcycles roaring past per minute than muffled ones, at least it seems that way. Most Mexican towns enforce at least some standards on mufflers, but for some rea-son Merida ignores this problem. The peaceful cast of the town, and the friendliness of the people, more than makes up for this defect, to my way of thinking.

On the Caribbean side of the peninsula, Cancun leads the way in gringo settlement. Condos and hotels are popping up all over. A word of caution about buying a time-share condominium here, or anywhere: You should realize that you aren't *buying* anything. You are laying out your $5,000 or $8,000 simply for the privilege of living there for two or three weeks out of the year and paying maintenance for the rest. The other 50 weeks go to other people who live in *your* condo. What kind of ownership is that? My suggestion would be to invest that money at 10-percent interest, then take the profits, plus the maintenance you've saved, and put that toward a vacation. You'll probably find you can rent a nice apartment or house for *two months* instead of two weeks.

Prices are higher on the peninsula than elsewhere, admittedly, but by looking around, you can usually find affordable housing, and by cooking in your apartment or eating in non-tourist restaurants, you can cut costs. Cancun is so new that it hasn't acquired the charm of Mexico. It probably never will. It seems more like a beach resort town in the United States. The city government has done pretty well, however, in keeping the streets clean and the architecture consistently modern.

The entire coast, all the way through Belize to Guatemala, is beautiful almost beyond description, with long stretches of uninhabited beaches, and azure–blue waters that invite swimming and loafing. All very tempting for North Americans. And the weather is tolerable during the summer, even if it is somewhat warm. But beware of rushing into financial deals, like buying any of the luscious beachfront properties. No matter that they have beautiful stands of coconut trees and lovely buildings, and that the owners assure you that the sale is perfectly legal. It isn't necessarily that they want to cheat you, but too often these people *think* they own the property. But when they sell, they discover that it reverts to the government, not to the buyer. Many titles here are good only as long as the family lives on the property. Then too, few really understand the laws about owning property near the ocean, including some lawyers who claim to.

Cozumel Island is another possible spot for temporary or long–term residency, as well as many small places along the mainland beach as far south as Punta Allen. Beachcombing, fishing, and solitude are the attractions. But when you get into Belize, you must exercise a great deal of caution. I know people who love Belize, particularly the scuba diving and fishing. But these people are street–wise, savvy travelers who know how to keep from being ripped off by the marvelously talented thieves of Belize. I get the impression that a great deal of social status goes with being an accomplished con man or pickpocket in this tiny country. It's worth a visit, but expect to lose something to an expert or two.

OTHER PLACES ON THE MAINLAND

These aforementioned towns and cities are not by any means all of the possibilities for residency. If you can get by without having English spoken every day, the selection is unlimited. Simply choose your climate and go looking. There are other towns where U.S. and Canadian citizens live, and worth checking out. At the moment, I have little current information on the following places, but I have visited most and can vouch for their having pleasant living, should other factors point you in their direction.

Queretero, the capital of the state of Queretaro, about 170 kilometers (105 miles) northwest of Mexico City, and neighboring Tequisquiapan, where I once lived as a youth, are very pleasant, although my impression is that the arrival of industry and good–paying jobs has changed them a lot. "Tequis," for example, has had many of its old–fashioned cobblestone streets paved over for easier driving. Although the asthetics aren't the same, the local people have benefited greatly with higher standards of living. Personally, I'd rather see people living well than see a picturesque little village of marginally existing peasants. Taxco is another town that suffers and benefits from the 20th century, but it still retains much of its original charm. I'm not sure that many gringos live there today.

I understand that Aguas Calientes and Saltillo, both farther north, are plausible candidates for North American residents. Saltillo, particularly, is interesting because of its university and its summer programs directed at English–speaking students. Puebla is another university town, with the University of the Americas at Cholula being one of the better schools nationwide for the study of archaeology. The students have access to the nearby enormous, multi–layered Toltec pyramid for lab exercises. Our respondents say Puebla is inexpensive and has a fine golf club.

BAJA CALIFORNIA

Because "Baja" is so accessible to California and the West Coast of the United States and Canada, it would appear to be an ideal long–term residence or retirement location. For some it turns out that way, for many others it doesn't. Much depends on your personality, what types of activities you enjoy, and how much "foreign" atmosphere you're looking for.

First of all, Baja California is divided both politically and socially into two distinct parts. The northern part is a state, the southern part is a territory. The northern part has its advantage for North Americans because of the *zona libre*, or "free zone" that reaches 60 or more miles down the peninsula. This means that tourist cards are not required, and customs are very relaxed. Although it isn't legal for foreigners to live in these zones, or own permanent homes, many do. Some even commute back and forth to jobs and businesses in California, while maintaining a home in Ensenada or one of the other coastal towns. I'm not advocating this, understand, I'm simply reporting it. There have been problems with subdivisions being sold to retired Americans who were later evicted by the government because of the illegalities of the sales. Still, many people "own" property there.

Certainly, this part of Mexico can be a way of testing whether retirement or long–term residence might be practical for you. Yet, there are many things that, to me, aren't truly Mexico. That is, there are many "Yankee" influences here that diminish the farther south you go from the border. Another thing is that prices and wages are much higher here than on the mainland. Everything must be imported or trucked over the one, serpentine highway that connects the peninsula with the Mexican state of Sonora. Still, a great many gringos swear by Baja.

To love Baja, you must love the desert. Some places here are almost as dry as the deserts of Peru and Chile, with an absence of rain for up to years at a time. Then, when it finally does rain, it can be with a vengeance. To love the desert is essential. For the fisherman, both coasts of Baja California are paradises, with near–record catches common occurrences. To a naturalist, the unique flora and fauna of the peninsula are a wonderland, found no where else in the world. For those seeking solitude, you've come to the right place, for cleaning fish and watching cactus grow are the highlights of the cultural scene.

The 900–mile long peninsula has two climates. The Pacific side enjoys a dry, Mediterranean climate, with foggy overcast and ocean breezes keeping the temperatures fairly pleasant year–round. The fog brings a little winter rain, which decreases the farther south you go. Irrigation is the only way of farming. On the Gulf of California side (which travel writers are fond of calling "The Sea of Cortez") even less rain falls, and few mists ever temper the glaring sun. During the summer months, temperatures rise to incredible heights, often rivaling those of Death Valley. A few very hardy gringos make their homes here for the full year. They're the ones who can't stand the thought of leaving all those fish uncaught. Winters, however, are nice, as you might expect.

The whole peninsula is populated by friendly, peaceful people. But the closer you are to the border, the more bored the natives are with gringos. After all, very few of the thousands of tourists passing through can speak Spanish, so there's little reason to communicate.

By the time you reach Baja California Sur, you'll find outwardly friendly people, and a culture that more closely resembles that of the mainland.

The La Paz and Cabo San Lucas areas attract the most North Americans in Baja Sur. My entry for the most likely place to live in Baja happens to be San Jose del Cabo, some 55 kilometers (32 miles) northeast along the highway from Cabo San Lucas. This little town is immaculately clean, with the charm of Oaxaca and the casual, quiet pace only found in Baja California.

By the way, if you're planning on driving to Mexico from the West Coast of the United States, a real adventure is to drive the peninsula to either La Paz or Cabo San Lucas, and then take an ocean–going ferry to the mainland. The ships load your car, provide you with a first–class stateroom, offer dinner in a fairly good restaurant (and sometimes dancing) for the overnight trip –– all for less than you would expect to pay for an ordinary motel in Phoenix. The roads down are okay, and a bonus is that you not only see Baja, but you avoid a lot of heavy traffic and sometimes boring scenery on Mexico's west coast Highway 15. Going to Puerto Vallarta, you can save over 300 miles of driving.

INVESTIGATE FURTHER

Obviously, a book of this size can't offer you complete information about road conditions, shopping, sports, fishing, golf, tennis, theaters, hotels, television programming and things of that nature. No one book could do all that. If it were possible, you wouldn't be able to lift it. Should you think Mexico might be for you, it becomes your job to go to the library or bookstore and do some heavy research. The bibliography at the end of the book contains a list of helpful publications, but there are many more out there.

Please read the section in the introductory chapter about contacting local residents or realtors. To include addresses here would be an exercise in futility. There would be hundreds of letters going to the people who were kind enough to assist us in producing this book. Never would I impose on their patience to expect them to reply. Could you spare the time and expense of replying to a couple of hundred total strangers?

Instead, pick up a Mexico guide book, such as *Mexico on $25 a Day,* or some similar publication, and find a hotel (or preferably a hotel–apartment) in the area that attracts your attention. Spend a few days orienting yourself. If there's a local English–language newspaper, become familiar with the names of local people, clubs and social organizations. You'll find most people gracious and helpful, once you are there. Check the supermarkets and restaurants for bulletin boards where you can find rentals and other North Americans who might help you. And, should you really fall in love with the area, for gosh sakes, *try it* before you make any drastic, irrevocable moves!

Before you go tossing your household belongings into a U–Haul trailer and heading off for Mexico, remember one word: customs. Not customs as in habits, but customs as in border crossings. The Mexican customs, or *aduana*, will not okay your bringing all that stuff across the border. Particularly not electrical appliances or loads of furniture, books or TVs––namely, everything you've accumulated over the years. When you receive your immigration papers, and not before, you will be given permission to bring in a certain amount of duty–free belongings. Until then, you'd best plan on buying or renting most of your household goods. Most short–term apartments come equipped with everything you need, down to eating and cooking utensils, and often sheets and blankets for the beds.

CHAPTER 16

Financial Considerations

INFLATION

One of the major dangers perceived by Americans considering living abroad is the specter of inflation. "The money isn't worth the paper it's written on," you hear from people who are "experts" in the field of finance. "Stay away from any country with a 25 percent inflation rate, because it's a disaster area," they add.

I submit that either these people don't understand how inflation really works, or else they are looking at inflation from the wrong end of the telescope. Let me give you an example of what I mean:

On New Year's day 1985, I arrived in Buenos Aires. I remember having a beer in a rather nice restaurant and that it cost me two 1-million-peso bills. This meant that I was paying $1 U.S. at the official rate. But the 'parallel market' (where everyone changed dollars) gave a better rate, so I was actually paying only 70 cents U.S. for my beer. Two months later, the same restaurant charged 4 million pesos for the same beer! By the first of June you needed more than *12* of the million-peso bills to buy the same beer.

Sounds like a horror story, doesn't it? But in the parallel market, the 12 million-peso bills I paid for the beer represented a little *less* than the 70 cents I paid in January. Nothing changed for me except that some things became even less expensive.

It should be redundant to state that exchange rates are relative, yet it seems very difficult for some 'experts' to step outside the shell of the dollar and view other currencies in the proper perspective. What is important in a local economy is how many goods and services a U.S. *dollar* will purchase, not how many the local bank note will buy.

But what about the poor Argentinian who had to suffer that loss of purchasing power in six months? Wasn't he damaged by all of that? Not necessarily. Had he kept his money in dollars (as many of them did) he would have earned about 12 percent per annum on his deposits, which was considerably more than a dollar earned in the United States at that time. But had he kept his money invested in pesos, he would have been earning almost 30 percent per month. You read correctly, 30 percent per *month*! So, with an inflation rate that was over 25 percent per month and an interest rate that was almost 30 percent per month, you can see that he was still slightly ahead of the game. If he were a wage earner, his salary was automatically adjusted upward every couple of weeks, and if he were a landlord, the rent ceilings were similarly adjusted by the government. Things generally came out even.

I don't wish to minimize the effect of raging inflation on a country, and cannot deny that some people are hurt. Yet, for every person who is hurt, someone else is helped. In the final analysis, inflation is relative. When I was a child, Pepsi–Cola used to advertise "Twice as much for a nickel, too," but in those days a nickel bought 10 times what it does today. Our dollar has been devalued. Does our devaluation mean we are any less affluent? Aren't we living better in most ways despite inflation?

A few years ago, when the military ran the Argentinian government and the peso was rigidly controlled in relation to the dollar, the peso became overvalued, held at an inviolable 10 pesos to a dollar. The result was that the dollar became so cheap that Argentinians routinely flew to Miami or Los Angeles for their vacations because things were so 'cheap' here. This was a disaster for Argentina because foreign countries couldn't afford to buy its produce or manufactured goods. Imports became so cheap that local people stopped buying anything made at home and went for foreign products instead. Factories and businesses were stifled from lack of demand for their products. Production dropped and workers lost jobs. The economy suffered much more from control than from the cause than from the later deflation.

Suddenly, the value of the peso collapsed. Dollars now became expensive. Consumers had to buy local goods because they couldn't afford imported things any longer. Factory production picked up. Unemployment dropped. Exports boomed, because now Argentinian goods were once again competitive on the world market. Local industry was pressured to produce more and more. The cheaper the peso, the stronger the economy. Inflation isn't all bad!

There's another way of looking at inflation, and that is in the advantage you have as a long–term traveler, an investor or a retiree with dollars in your pocket. Because of the years of hyperinflation, many Latin American investors sold their real estate at sacrifice prices in order to convert their holdings to hard dollars for investment purposes. Everyone was selling, no one buying. The ultimate result is the absurdly low prices on houses, condominiums, beachfront property, and investment property. Property that would have set you back $200,000 a few years ago can be picked up today for $30,000. How long this happy condition will last is anybody's guess, but for the time being, it's possible to find real bargains.

There is another economic development in the wind that you should be aware of and be prepared to take full advantage of. That is: control of inflation is bound to happen once a government decides to do something about it. This is going on now in Argentina, where they've suddenly controlled the collapse of the peso against the dollar! Don't applaud, it's no big trick––it's simply a matter of the government putting a halt to it. Remember, with inflation, the biggest debtors are the biggest beneficiaries, and guess who the biggest debtor of any country is? You've guessed correctly: the government! So, in June 1985, the Argentinian government decided to halt deflation simply by stating it would buy *or* sell dollars at a stated exchange rate, and that in the future, the interest rate would be 7 percent per year as opposed to 30 percent per month. Before, the government would buy all the dollars you gave it, but refuse to sell dollars. This forced devaluation and inevitable creation of a black market because people need dollars for foreign purchases or travel. They had no other place to deal but on the black market.

How this is going to work out is anybody's guess, but so far, the new money, the Austral, which has replaced the peso, has been holding at about $1 U.S. per Austral.

The point here is that anyone thinking about traveling or living in Latin America for more than a short vacation must keep alert to change. Read the local papers and watch for trends. At the moment, countries like Uruguay, Mexico and Argentina are great places for inexpensive living, provided your income is in dollars. But if a strict monetary control is maintained, my guess is that the value of the dollar will drop. My prediction is that monetary controls will never be as strict as in the past, and that the value of the dollar won't drop enough to affect the cost of living in any significant way. My predictions, however, have ways of going awry. If they didn't, I'd frequent the racetrack more often. Still, I'm convinced that stability will last for a long time to come. But don't take my word for it; keep your eye on the dollar at all times.

"Aha," you say, "the value of the dollar could drop, therefore I could lose my shorts!" Not necessarily. If you have investments in a local economy, such as a house or a business, then as the dollar drops, your property becomes more valuable in local currency. This means if you sell, you'll get more dollars for your business. Example: I have a $6,000 investment in a condominium in Buenos Aires (a half–share in a two–bedroom unit) which cost my partner and me $12,000 in 1985. Ten years earlier, before the collapse of the peso, this condo would have been a steal at $100,000. If real estate prices remain as they are, or even drop lower, I will be half owner of a very pleasant apartment which I can use whenever I want, or allow friends and relatives to use. My winter retirement haven. However, if prices should rise to previous levels, I will be a reluctant seller with a half–share in an $88,000 profit. I'm a winner either way. (In the United States a $6,000 investment would buy a two weeks time share in a so–called condominium. Actually, you're merely prepaying the rent and assuming liabilities to boot.)

To sum up, my advice is not to concern yourself with the value of the local currency, except as it affects the value of your dollar. Mentally convert everything to dollars before you buy, and you will see what you are actually paying. However, always keep on top of currency trends, and do as the local people do: take advantage of them. Don't forget, for every loser, there's a winner.

CAN I AFFORD TO RETIRE?

Some questions are foremost in the minds of anyone thinking about retirement. "Can I get by on a reduced income?" "How much will I have to change my lifestyle?" These are all valid questions that each one must deal with individually. But all too often the answers are negative when they needn't be. So retirement gets postponed until that nebulous future when it's "safe."

Florida and Arizona retirement communities are full of once dynamic couples who always dreamed of the positive, exciting things they would do "when it's safe to retire." Finally, it's "safe." But now they're 75 years old, and they discover that it's too late. Life has slipped away and they've avoided adventure for so long that the idea of trying something new is frightening. Life is a one–way journey, and postponing your dreams until the end of the line may postpone them forever.

The major question should be, "What kind of lifestyle will I be satisfied with?" Some people are perfectly comfortable working and they enjoy their work immensely. Maybe they shouldn't think of retirement. I have a friend who goes to work every day, loves what he is doing and does a very good job at it. He is 92 years old. I'm convinced that his attitude and his satisfaction with his life has kept him sharp, alert and physically fit at a time when most of his colleagues are either dead or in nursing homes.

On the other hand, I once met a married couple who were camping next to my wife and me on a Baja California beach. I guessed them to be in their early 60s. When we became acquainted, we were astonished to learn that the man was 84 and his wife had just turned 80. It turned out that when he was in his early 40s, he inherited a small apartment building that produced a modest monthly income, and decided to try retirement, at least for a while. "It was never easy," he explained, "but by budgeting and doing a lot of camping, we've been able to spend the last 40 years traveling about the world, enjoying life." They had driven their VW camper through South America and Europe, and once had spent several months exploring India. Their interest in life and their activity kept them young in mind and in body. (You notice these things in nudist camps.)

Then, of course, we all know of cases where people retire, find nothing to do, and end up disintegrating in a rocker in front of the television set. Perhaps mercifully, their lives don't last too long, because boredom and stultification takes their toll all too soon.

The secret to a successful retirement is to find something interesting, fulfilling and rewarding to do. For many people, these years are full of opportunity. Finally, they have unlimited time to do all those "special" things they've wanted to do all their lives, but for one reason or another couldn't.

Can you afford it? My question to many people is, "Can you afford *not* to retire?" Today's retirement generation is heavily influenced by memories of the Great Depression. Those who were of working age during that time remember how valuable a job was and how important it was to work every day. Today, when they miss a day's work, they think in terms of "losing money" from not working. Even those who saw no hard times often cannot escape the work ethic from those bleak days. Quitting a well-paid job to go on pension and Social Security can be traumatic. "Can I afford to lose all that money?" they ask. They aren't "losing" money, they just aren't working hard to earn money they probably don't need. Can they afford more years of their lives working, just for the sake of working?

IF YOU OWN PROPERTY

How many couples nearing retirement age are living in paid-for homes? Many are, and many have huge equities in their homes because of the appreciation of real estate in the past decade. They think they are living cheaply because their payments are low. If you fall into this category, take your calculator and do some figuring for a moment. See what it actually costs to live in your house. First, figure what you would net if you were to cash in on your house. Now, remember that if you're over 55, the IRS exempts the first $125,000 of your profit, so you pay taxes on only 40 percent of any profit over the $125,000. So, chances are, your tax liability will be very small. Next, take the figure you will net on your house and calculate what that would earn if the money were placed in a safe investment, let's say utility stocks at around 10 percent per year. That return is what it is costing you each year to live in that home of yours, because that is the amount you are losing by not having your money earning money for you. Add this amount to your payments, taxes, utilities and repairs to find out how much it really costs you to live in your "inexpensive" home. There's a possibility that this amount is two or three times what it would cost you to live in Mexico, Costa Rica, or South America.

The next move is to figure how much you could earn by leasing your house to a reliable tenant. See how this amount matches the income from an investment in a safe public utility stock. If you could earn more from stock than rent, maybe your house is not such a good investment. You might be better off selling your place and renting from someone else! If leasing the house brings in more than an investment, then you could think about doing that and using that money for an adventure retirement.

Of course, no one wants to spend all his income just on retirement living. That's one advantage of foreign retirement: You can usually get by on your Social Security (maybe even save some) and put the rest of your retirement income into safe investments.

CAN YOU REALLY LIVE IN A FOREIGN COUNTRY ON YOUR INCOME?

Here's a chart showing what wage earners have to spend each year to provide a middle–class standard of living for their families in various cities around the world. See how your income stacks up against theirs. Note that these figures are net, after all taxes, social benefits, hospitalization, etc. are deducted. If they can make it on that income, you should also, unless there are some complicating factors in your case.

Earnings per year (in U.S. dollars)	Teachers	Electrical Engineers	Secretary	Construction Worker
Zurich	19,800	21,600	13,600	10,300
Chicago	16,700	25,200	17,800	21,500
Los Angeles	18,400	25,400	13,900	18,600
Houston	16,600	26,600	16,200	15,600
New York	20,100	26,000	13,100	14,800
Buenos Aires	2,700	7,400	4,200	1,400
Rio de Janeiro	2,400	10,300	5,900	800
Mexico City	2,500	7,000	3,900	2,400
Lisbon	3,600	4,300	3,400	1,600
Madrid	7,100	11,900	6,200	3,600
London	7,900	11,200	6,600	6,000

(from *Prices and Earnings Around The Globe*, 1985 edition, Union Bank of Switzerland.)

CHAPTER 17

Traveling Abroad

MONEY--CASH OR TRAVELERS CHECKS?

If you watch television commercials promoting travelers checks, you'll notice that people always lose them--at the opera, bullfights, even in Japanese hot tubs. But have you ever seen a commercial about people losing cash? Of course not. Yet they caution you against taking cash. They claim that because travelers checks are so easy to replace, you can feel free to lose them to your heart's content. That may or may not be true. I've heard stories of people having their passports held and being prohibited from leaving the country until the police completed an investigation of the missing checks. One man I met had some stolen checks recovered by the police, but they held them as evidence for the trial. The bank didn't want to replace the checks because they weren't lost any more, and the police would not release them until after the trial. He eventually got his money, but not until after the vacation was over.

Of course, there are times when you might feel a lot safer with travelers checks, and there are many countries where travelers checks are as good as cash. But you could pay a high price for this feeling of security. For example, in many Latin American countries there are two rates of exchange: An official rate, and an unofficial rate or parallel market. You can lose heavily by dealing in travelers checks instead of U.S. dollars. Example: In January 1986, in Argentina, a U.S. 100–dollar bill was worth 80 australes at a bank. But that same $100 bill was worth 91.60 australes on the parallel market. This is a 14.5 percent gain by dealing with the parallel market (all perfectly legal, even though it's sometimes referred to as a black market). But a $100 travelers check brought only the official 80 austral rate minus three australes for cashing it, so it netted only 77 australes as compared to 91.60––a difference of over 18 percent! When you're losing $18 per hundred for the convenience of feeling safe, you're paying dearly.

To make matters worse, the companies up here cheerfully take your dollars and sell you the checks, but when you arrive in South America you find they're not permitted to give you dollars back, only local currency at the deflated rate. To get dollars you have to go to a *casa de cambio* and give a stiff discount of 2 to 7 percent. Sometimes you will find that a branch bank in South America will only accept its own travelers checks, forcing you to run around and find someplace which will take them, again at a discount. If you were traveling in Europe, there would be no problem, because travelers checks are as good as dollars. But that's not the case in many Latin American countries.

It's difficult to give advice on how to handle something like money, so all I can do is tell you my system. I investigate the target country to find out if there is a parallel market, and if travelers checks are freely cashed as dollars instead of pesos, colones, quetzales, or whatever the local currency might be. If there's a question, I take most of my money in cash, maybe enough in travelers checks to bail me out should I lose or spend everything.

There are numerous ways to conceal cash where it is safe (see section on safety). Don't get carried away with bringing too much money, not only because you are tempting fate, but because the U.S. and other countries have currency restrictions, and it's assumed that if you're carrying a suitcase full of money, you're probably doing something illegal. To bring in or to take out $10,000 or more requires registration with customs. Best to take just as much as you will need; with today's costs in most of Latin America, you can easily take three or four months supply without violating any currency regulations. If you are going to stay for a longer time, make arrangements with a bank with branches both at home and in your target country. They can usually set up a dollar account for you, if not in your new country, then in a neighboring country.

According to the Department of State's Bureau of Consular Affairs, "local banks generally give more favorable rates of exchange than hotels, restaurants or stores." That may be true in some countries, but not in much of Latin America. Banks often are only permitted to give you the official rate, which can be as much as 40 percent *less* than a store or your hotel might offer. Ask your desk clerk what the hotel's rate of exchange is and if it is the same as the parallel exchange. If he can't pay the parallel rate, he can advise you where to go. If he won't—wanting to profit at your expense—perhaps you shouldn't stay in a hotel that won't look after its guest's interests, and tell him so.

You might be approached by people on the street wanting to change money at even higher rates than the parallel market. You could be swamped with such offers. Be very careful here. First of all, many of them are short-change or sleight-of-hand artists; you could be left with a handful of worthless currency. I once had a man count out bills into my own hand, and I counted each one carefully as he laid them slowly into my palm, then (after he left) and I counted them again. I was short by 25 percent. To this day I can't figure out how he did it. Another problem in high-crime countries like Brazil or Colombia is: The fact that you are changing money is a tip-off to thieves that you are an interesting character who might be worth knowing better. However, be aware that in some countries the parallel market is actually a black market and is illegal. Costa Rica, for example, is very strict about this and sometimes has undercover agents watching for street transactions.

Since currency markets are changeable, it's impossible to give a list of exchange rates (most would be out of date before the book is printed), and it's impossible to make a definitive statement as to which countries allow the parallel markets. Make local inquiries as to the legality of parallel markets. It's not worth it to take chances for a few extra dollars on a hundred.

Credit cards are accepted almost anywhere. But here again, be cautious about how you use them. In converting the bill to dollars, chances are the official rate will be used. But since the bill is usually written at parallel rate; you will lose in the exchange, from 10 percent to 40 percent. It isn't the merchant's fault, that's just the way it works out at the bank. Since there is a charge to the merchant for using the card, he often adds this to the bill as well. I use my credit card only for dire emergencies.

Taking a handful of single dollar bills is always a good idea because they are great for tips. They're often more valuable than local money in the eyes of the receiver, because they don't depreciate and are always gaining in value compared to local currency. Another idea is to carry a few solar calculators and digital watches (inexpensive here, prohibitively costly there) as a special gift or tip for someone who has been specially helpful to you. A gift of this nature will be accepted gratefully whereas a tip might seem insulting to someone who is helping you because they want to be friends. Some people carry hard candies or small toys for the kids. Ball–point pens and notebooks are always practical and welcome gifts for children.

TRAVELING SAFELY

I've traveled all over Latin America, visited some of the most poverty–stricken areas imaginable, strolled through neighborhoods famous for the skills of pickpockets and criminals. Yet, I've never lost a thing to a thief nor have any of my traveling companions. That isn't to say it can't happen, but I'm confident that the odds are against it. Why? Because I am careful, always aware. By the same token, I've never been robbed or burglarized in North America, either.

Don't get the impression that Latin America is one continual battle of wits between you and the pickpocket. There are places there where I feel as safe if not safer than I do in the United States. Particularly safe–feeling are Argentina, Uruguay and Chile in South America, and Mexico and Costa Rica in the middle Americas. As is the rule anywhere, the smaller the town, the safer I feel. Nonetheless, the watchword is caution. Don't tempt a thief.

There are several safe ways to carry cash. One of the worst ways is to carry it in a purse or a hip–pocket wallet, the next worst is to use a money belt. For one thing, the belt is uncomfortable, hot, and often bulges through your clothing to tip off a serious thief. Much better are the "shoulder holster" type of carriers, which comfortably hold a passport and a lot of bank notes without being obvious. A tip for men (or women wearing slacks) is a kind of stocking top that slips over the calf and and has pockets to hold money and a passport. But the best way to conceal cash is the old–fashioned "pin-on pocket" idea. Buy a couple of pocket replacements from the sewing section of a dime–store, or sew them yourself, and then pin them to the underside of your skirt, your slacks, or the inside of your jacket sleeve or shirt sleeve. Rather than pinning, I prefer to use Velcro, so I can reach inside my waistband and rip the pocket free when I need extra cash. By distributing cash in two or three pockets, you are being discrete and safe. Keep your credit cards in one of these pockets.

I always carry a cheap wallet in the front pocket with a small amount of spending money in it. The rest of my loose cash I keep in a shirt pocket or another pocket in my slacks-- anywhere it won't make a conspicuous bulge. Thus, in case of a pickpocket, the thief is distracted by the decoy wallet. This has never happened to me, but others tell me it's a good idea.

Don't wear jewelry on the street. Don't carry an expensive camera in the open. I use a shabby-looking airline bag, or a plastic sack to conceal my photographic equipment. The camera I own is worth a year's wages to some of the poor in a country like Peru, so I can't blame someone for casting a covetous eye on it. If you are carrying a purse, hold it in front of you so it can't be slashed open. And, be especially cautious in crowds; that's where thieves do their best work.

As one travel writer said, "Don't be cautious, be paranoid." This is good advice. If you travel around Latin America, you will find yourself relaxing your guard in safe-feeling countries like Argentina or Mexico, and then having a difficult time adjusting when you get to places like Colombia or Panama where thievery is practiced as an art form. Cultivating common sense habits and keeping them going is a good practice. But don't let the minor inconvenience of having to be careful keep you from enjoying the more exciting countries in Latin America. There is so much to see, so much to do, that the little risk you face is well worth it. And it's only the unaware, the careless tourist who gets taken, not you.

PASSPORTS AND DOCUMENTS

Each country is a little different on rules for carrying your passport. Costa Rica, for example, insists that you have your passport with you at all times. Being caught without it can mean an unpleasant trip to the police station while everything is straightened out. Other countries, like Brazil, recommend that you keep your passport locked up in the hotel safe, because thieves have figured out ways to use passports and go to great lengths to steal them. In any event, as soon as you receive your visas and permits, make a couple of photocopies of the pertinent parts of the passport; always carry one with you and keep another in your luggage. Should you lose your passport, you will have some identification. It will be much easier to get new documents and to prove to the police how long you've been in the country. It's a good idea to update the photocopies when you enter a new country to keep a record of just when you crossed borders.

VISAS

Some countries require visas, others don't. (See end of chapter). These should be obtained in advance. Your travel agent can send your passports in and have them processed, which saves you some time, but my recommendation is to visit the consulates personally. That way you can speak person–to–person with the consulate people about any problems or last–minute changes in regulations. As an example, in January 1986, Brazil changed the rules to require tourists who've spend 10 days or more in South America to have a yellow fever vaccination. People who obtained their visas by mail weren't advised of this change and it caused lots of problems.

Another reason for applying for your visas in person is that the consulate people often have travel brochures for you, special suggestions of places to visit, and perhaps places to stay *away* from They are proud of their country and anxious that you enjoy your stay. Also, you will generally find a stack of daily newspapers from their country. These are valuable sources of information about the country, particularly the advertisements. You can learn a lot about a country by seeing what kinds of things are advertised and the prices. A study of classified ads is an education in the availability and cost of apartments and homes for rent, the cost of used automobiles and the wages being offered servants. The display ads disclose the cost of groceries, furniture, appliances and other commodities that affect the cost of living. An hour of reading through back issues of the newspapers is an excellent way to prepare for your trip.

CHAPTER 18
Health

Medical care in Latin America varies from excellent to horrendous, depending on the area you are in, the doctors available, and the medical problems you may have. The same can be said for many places in North America, with the added observation that medical care here is outrageously expensive. Sometimes, for travelers, adequate medical care is very difficult to find in the United States because of the reluctance of doctors to treat other than regular patients, and because many small–town hospitals refuse to accept patients other than those referred by local doctors. Catch 22.

I've never run into problems like these in Latin America. Since many countries have socialized medicine, public and private medical care is available to all and at low prices. Once, in a small town in Mexico, I had a slight health problem and wanted a checkup. The local doctor examined me, gave me an ECG, blood–pressure test, and whatever else they do. After telling me that he thought I was okay, he said, "If you were a citizen, I wouldn't have to charge you. But as a foreigner, you must pay a fee."

The fee was about 80 pesos, at that time about 50 cents U.S. I gave the doctor a dollar bill and he was pleased when I told him to keep the change. When was the last time you tipped your doctor?

Recently, an article in the *San Jose Mercury News* (San Jose, Calif.) stated that the average hospital bill for patients in that area topped $1,000 a day. Reading that, I couldn't help but recall an occasion when I was in a hospital in San Jose, Costa Rica. There, a private room––including nursing care and some of the best meals I've found anywhere—cost less than an ordinary first–class hotel in that city, less than $40 a day. Compare that with the average of $1,000 a day in San Jose, California hospitals!

Of the North Americans interviewed, almost all said they were satisfied with the medical treatment available in Latin America. However, most added that for something really serious, they would probably return home and check with doctors there. This makes good sense, too, if the patient is under Medicare, since Medicare isn't applicable outside the country. Meanwhile, medical care is so inexpensive in most of Latin America that ordinary ailments needn't be given any special thought. The American or Canadian Embassies can refer you to a qualified physician, should you have doubts about who to choose. Remember that local doctors have experience treating locally–occurring problems.

On the other hand, if your health is fragile, or if you are in constant need of special care, you might think twice about leaving your home for any foreign country.

MEDICINES

It's important to have a prescription for all drugs you intend to carry with you into Latin American countries. This is particularly important if you take medication containing habit–forming or narcotic drugs; make sure you carry a doctor's certificate to that effect. All drugs should be in their original labeled containers. Customs officials have been known to confiscate anything that looks suspicious. You can't blame them. A Lomotil pill looks very much like some of the "speed" drugs out on the illicit market.

Once you are in Latin American countries, you find that prescriptions are not required for most non–addictive drugs. Antibiotics and painkillers are sold over–the–counter almost anywhere. Since most drugs are either imported from American or European countries, or else manufactured under license, the trade names are often the same as you are used to at home.

Occasionally a drugstore insists on a prescription, but if you know what you need and don't have the prescription with you, just go to another drugstore. If you have some kind of chronic problem or disability, it's a good idea to carry a letter with a Spanish translation explaining what your problems are and what kind of medication you are taking.

It isn't a bad idea to keep up on your inoculations, no matter if you travel to Latin America or if you stay home. Of course, smallpox shots are no longer required anywhere, but tetanus and typhoid boosters ought to be considered if you plan on visiting any out–of–the–way places. Some areas have problems with yellow fever and malaria, but these aren't too common. As a routine thing, you need yellow fever inoculation for Brazil if you are going to do a lot of traveling in other South American countries before you enter Brazil. They seem to be particularly worried about the jungle areas of Peru and Bolivia. If you plan on getting off the normal tourist trails, it would be a good idea to check with the U.S. Health Service, and while you're at it, get your tetanus and typhoid boosters. Tetanus immunity is for three years and yellow fever lasts 10 years. Have your immunizations recorded in the International Certificate of Vaccinations, Form PHS–'31. Carry that, or another proof of vaccination, with your passport.

A doctor I met while traveling in Guatemala advised me to take high doses of vitamin B and not to drink alcohol when in a malaria zone. Presumably, vitamin B keeps insects from biting you (it makes you smell offensive to them) and alcohol dissipates the effect of the vitamin B. Still, if you are going to be in an area of malarial contamination (generally lowland, swampy places), you should consult a local doctor, since there seems to be different varieties of the disease, some of which are resistant to ordinary drugs.

TOURIST DISEASE

Can you drink the water? It depends on where you are. Some countries, modern ones like Costa Rica and Argentina, have excellent public health agencies that oversee water treatment, sewage disposal and other hygienic matters. There's no problem at all in this case. Other countries leave it to local option. Sometimes there is good drinking water, provided the source of the water is safe or if purification is done. But some localities just don't have enough public funds to do anything about impure water. It's up to each family to take care of the problem on its own.

The problem with drinking water usually arises when the source is a shallow well rather than a central water system. Combine this with extensive use of septic tanks and cesspools which allow sewage to seep into the water–table, and you have trouble.

Some water systems, particularly in Brazil and Peru, do an adequate job, but they use a different method of water treatment than we're used to, which is said to make some tourists ill. I'm not sure what this means, because I drink tap water in Rio or Cuzco, and have never felt any bad effects, nor have I spoken with anyone who has. You know that the water is bad when hotels and apartments provide bottled water for their tenants.

When you're living or traveling in an area of questionable water, you simply develop a common-sense system of dealing with the problem. For one thing, you don't avoid tap water all day long and then use it to brush your teeth at night. You make sure leafy vegetables are thoroughly cleaned and soaked in a purifying solution (one hydrochlorizone tablet to a pint of water--15 minutes will do it). Most households have purified water delivered daily in five-gallon jugs, but if that isn't convenient, you can do it yourself simply by bringing your water to a boil. A quick boil is all that is necessary. Just heating water to 150 degrees F. is enough to kill any known organism outside of some rare creatures that live in volcanic springs.

Another method of water purification is to use two or three drops of household bleach or one drop of tincture of iodine per pint, letting the water stand for 15 minutes. Since I can't stand the taste of either bleach or iodine, I simply use the readily available bottled water. Cooking, of course, solves any kind of bacterial or amoebic problem. And things don't have to be cooked to a black crisp; 150 degrees F. will do it, but heated all the way through.

You've probably heard people say that the natives naturally develop an immunity to dysentery. I've even heard health professionals claim the same thing. Not true. In Mexico, where much of the water is tainted, *dysentery is the leading cause of death!* More people die from "bad water" every year than from heart failure or cancer combined. Does that sound as if people develop an immunity? Granted, these casualties are mostly poor folks who can't afford bottled water. Many are young children of poor families. But these people are the most exposed to poor water and food, and would be the first to develop an immunity if this were possible.

Fortunately in the countries this book recommends for long-term living or retirement--except Mexico--you won't have to worry much about food or water, at least not in the major cities. And in Mexico, since you'll likely be doing your own cooking or be eating in safe restaurants, you'll have no problem there. After a while, these precautions become second nature, just as they are with the natives.

When eating out or when traveling on the road, you might take extra precautions. To be sure about the water, order mineral water with your their meals. Make sure you order *gaseosa* (with carbonation), so that you know the bottle has been freshly opened, not simply refilled with tap water. Yes, that happens, particularly in the nice "touristy" places where they know you won't be back.

If you actually get sick, not just the "runs" but the real thing, amoebic dysentery, go and see a doctor. You'll know when you have it: It's very much like being seasick—you have difficulty maintaining consciousness and you feel extremely nauseated. This won't happen if you are careful.

The best preventative is good, common sense. The only prescription preventative I'm aware of is a mild anti–biotic known as doxycycline (also known as vibramycin). You probably should consult your doctor about it before you leave, although many doctors don't seem to know much about it. It doesn't require a prescription in most countries. Few drugs need prescriptions anyway, outside of addictive or highly dangerous compounds. A drug that has traditionally been used is Enterovioforma, which is supposed to be especially good for amoebic dysentery. Personally, I wouldn't touch it, since it was banned in Japan for causing brain damage among regular users.

ALTITUDE

A sure way to feel bad is to take an airplane to Cuzco or someplace where the altitude is 9,000 feet or more. Altitude sickness, or *soroche*, can really lay you out if you don't get enough rest until you become acclimatized. Mexico City is high enough to cause you problems. The only remedy is to take it easy. Don't drink alcohol and don't overeat. In Peru and Bolivia, you can order *mate de coca*, a tea made from coca leaves. Too bad this drink is illegal in most countries. It really works as a mild stimulant.

CHAPTER 19

Must I Learn Spanish?

Of course there are people living and traveling in Latin America who have never bothered to learn the language. And in the United States and Canada there are foreigners who never learn English. But it's a definite handicap, like being a partial deaf–mute. When you have to communicate with sign language, you miss out on a lot of the world around you. If you plan on living in a foreign country––renting a house, shopping, making friends––you had better count on learning the language.

You often hear people affirm: "No matter where you are in Latin America, there's usually someone around who's studied English in school." This is probably true in the more advanced countries where education is valued and literacy rates are high. But most people living in the more backward places not only haven't studied English, they haven't even mastered Spanish, preferring to converse in their native, pre–European languages.

Besides, even if many speakers have studied English, you must not depend on their being fluent. If they've learned the language from a teacher who was not a native speaker of English, but who learned *his* English from a teacher who learned it from a book . . . well, you can see the problem. Anything you say in English sounds to them like one long word of rapid–fire syllables. They may read English well, but reading a language is not the same as speaking it.

This is precisely the problem with Americans learning Spanish. They concentrate on reading and writing, learning from books, and instructed by teachers who have never mastered spoken Spanish. Despite what many teachers think, language is not simply reading and writing. A language is a system of meaningful sounds that can be understood and interpreted by a listener who is familiar its the sound system. The written word is merely a symbolic representation of that sound system. Too many students have been subjected to learning that is almost useless when it comes to being fluent in a foreign language. When they go south of the border and discover that while they may be able to speak some meaningful phrases, they are unable to understand anything that's said to them. It does precious little good to be able to ask where the bathroom is if you can't understand the reply.

MISCONCEPTIONS ABOUT SPANISH

The most common mistake is thinking that Spanish, or any foreign language, is easy to learn. People commonly say, "Oh, I won't bother studying Spanish now, I'll pick it up pretty fast when I get there." Unless the speaker is a child (they do learn languages quickly), or is a genius, the chances of his "picking up" any foreign language are almost non–existent. Work and study are essential!

Another misconception is that there are many different dialects of Spanish around the world, and that if you study "Castillian" Spanish, you will only be understood in the central part of Spain. The fact is, Spanish is amazingly uniform wherever you go. This is due to conscious efforts on the part of the academic community, working through the Royal Academy in Spain, to keep the language as standardized as possible. The basic differences among Spanish–speaking countries are usually less than the differences in the English–speaking world. In England, there is a "BBC accent" which is the standard for radio and TV announcers, and is considered "standard" English for Britain. In the U.S.A. and Canada, we hear an "ABC" accent that is considered neutral by announcers, so the newscaster from Atlanta sounds very much like his counterpart in Seattle. It might come as a surprise to many people to know that the "Mexican Spanish" they cannot understand is the standard neutral accent that is used by Spanish–speaking communicators world wide. Radio announcers and cultured people throughout the world tend to use this neutral speech. The difference between Mexican and Castillian Spanish are so slight that unless you've had training in linguistics, you'll seldom be able to detect them. The vast majority of people in Spain don't use the Castillian pronunciation anyway.

The bottom line is that there is no such thing as "Mexican Spanish," as opposed to "College Spanish" or "Castillian Spanish." Mexicans, Argentinians and Spaniards communicate just as easily as do Americans, Australians and Englishmen. So, don't use that as a cop-out.

The reason for this homogeneity is historical. The early Spanish adventurers who came to this hemisphere came mostly from the provinces of Valencia and Estremadura. Their accents and vocabulary became the standard for the New World. During the ensuing centuries, intellectuals made a concerted effort to keep the language "pure." This is not to say that there aren't differences between countries. Slang words, and fashionable phrases will vary from country, but native speakers are conscious of these, so when speaking with a foreigner, they are usually careful to use standard Spanish.

There is, however, one structural variation between Spanish spoken in some countries, a very important difference to be aware of. That is the use of the familiar form. As you probably remember from your high school Spanish class, there are two ways of addressing a person: the polite form, *usted*, and the familiar form, *tu*. To further complicate matters, there is another familiar form that is seldom taught in our schools: The *vos* form. When you studied Spanish you probably learned that you use the polite form with strangers and the familiar form with family, friends and people you deal with on an everyday basis. Be careful—this is not always true!

For example, in Costa Rica, it's okay to use the familiar *vos* form with friends, but never the familiar *tu* form. One only uses *tu* when talking to animals or people one wishes to insult gravely. In Chile, the *tu* form is used as a signal of solidarity among the working and the poorer classes, and is seldom used by the middle class. In Argentina, the *tu* form is almost never used because the *vos* form is preferred. And, since the retirement of the military government there, the use of *vos* has become such a popular statement of egalitarianism that it threatens to wipe out the formal *usted* form entirely—it's used with strangers, without class distinction. For an American, it's always safer to use the polite usted until you are sure, very sure, of the customs.

LEARNING SPANISH

Yes, you can learn to speak a foreign language. You just have to go about it sensibly. To learn a language, any language, you must speak and listen. Listening to a tape or record that repeats the words very clearly, distinctly, with each individual word separated from the others, is all but a waste of time. You must hear the language as it's spoken, at the speed that a native speaks. Memorizing lists of verbs and parsing them over and over is also non–productive, as well as a pain in the neck. People learn to use verbs by using the language. But don't despair––that Spanish course you took in high school will be helpful because it gave you a basis for understanding why some verbs are irregular, and why there are different forms of verbs. You can build from there.

If you are planning a trip for the future, you should get a head start by working on your Spanish now. Get a good set of cassette tapes that provide oral–lingual drills, at normal speed. Work on them daily. If there's a Spanish–speaking person around, try conversing with him or her. Listen to all of the Spanish radio you can, and see Spanish movies if they are available in your area.

My favorite learning method is that used by the U.S. National AudioVisual Center, with the text by the Government Printing Office. This system is used in training diplomats and military personnel for diplomatic duties around the world. The first set of 15 cassette tapes goes with a manual that is oriented towards listening and speaking. You use the manual for reference only, and don't worry about how a word is spelled, or what tense the verb is. You learn the appropriate verb by hearing it used, then copying. That's the way you learned English verbs, right? (Another system, also sold by the AudioVisual Center, is a programmatic course, which uses different principles, and perhaps arrives at fluency even faster than the older method.) The book and cassettes can be ordered from National AudioVisual Center, 8700 Edgeworth Drive, Capitol Heights, MD 20743–3701. (Phone 800–638–1300 for credit card orders.) The cost is $80 for the first 15 units including a text and 15 cassettes. Units 16–30 contain 21 cassettes and the text for $105. The texts can be purchased separately at any U.S. Government Book Store or from the Superintendent of Documents, Government Printing Office, Washington, DC., 20402.

Once you are in Latin America, your learning will begin in earnest. You will now be forced to learn, and you'll progress at a very rapid rate by having to use the language. Almost anywhere, you'll find local teachers who give private Spanish lessons in their homes. This is a great way to not only learn, but to meet local people and to begin gathering a network of friends.

GOING TO SCHOOL

The very best way to break into the language and culture of a foreign country is to go to school and study the language in that country. A bonus is that it's inexpensive. Several places come to mind that are reknown as language learning centers: San Jose, Costa Rica, and Cuernavaca, Mexico, for starters.

An example: A class at an excellent school in San Jose, with four hours of daily classroom study, will cost you as little as $600 for a month. That not only includes registration, tuition and text materials, but also pickup at the airport upon arrival, plus a private room in a middle–class family's home, all meals, and even laundry! Six hundred dollars total for a month! This is a real bargain, one worth investigating closely. My understanding is that the schools in Cuernavaca cost even less for the same deal.

The advantage of living with a family which speaks no English––taking your meals with them, watching Spanish–language TV with them, having them help you with your homework––is that you are totally immersed in the language and culture at the same time. You will learn Spanish much more quickly, and you will learn to adapt to new situations and customs. Plus, should you decide to stay in the town where you go to school, you have a chance to make friends with the natives.

Almost any larger town, particularly ones with many American residents, will have a language school or two. Most will try to provide you with comfortable homes for board and room. But my two favorites are in Costa Rica. Since I am familiar with them and am convinced their system of teaching is effective, I'll pass along information about them. The first is Centro Linguistico Conversa (Apartado No. 17 Centro Colon, San Jose, Costa Rica). The cost for a month's instruction is $1080 for one person, with a discount for a couple. A jeep picks you up at your house early in the morning and takes you up the mountain to a beautiful Costa Rican farm where classes are held, usually on outdoor patios with gorgeous views of the valley. Classes start at 8:30 in the morning and last until 3:30 in the afternoon, with a break for lunch (included in the cost). Classes are from two to five students, and teachers are rotated for optimum learning.

Another good school is Instituto Interamericano de Idiomas Intensa (P.O. Box 8110 1000, San Jose, Costa Rica). This school charges $600 for the same four–week session, but for a four–hour a day class time. Six hours a day is available for $740. Since the classrooms are in town, you walk to school, and the private home where you will stay is close by.

Many towns, particularly if there are lots of Americans living there, will have language institutes. Sometimes the class sizes are much larger, but there is an advantage to this: The larger the class size, the more acquaintances you'll make. Many institutes offer other cultural classes as well, including art, sculpture, weaving and academic courses. This is great for making valuable social contacts.

IT'S NOT IN THE DICCIONARIO!

While Spanish is amazingly uniform from country to country, some words its speakers use are not. This shouldn't be too surprising, if you look at the different words we use for the same item. Depending on where in the United States or Canada you live, a davenport becomes a sofa or a couch and a frying pan becomes a skillet. In England, a truck becomes a lorry, an elevator a lift and so forth.

It's the same way in Spanish speaking countries. Once when traveling in Central America there were several occasions when I found myself needing safety pins. But the word for safety pin in Guatemala was different from the word in Nicaragua or Costa Rica. I solved the problem by drawing a picture. I collected three words meaning safety pin.

If you are going to be traveling in South America, try to find a Spanish dictionary printed in Buenos Aires or Bogota. You need a Spanish–to–Spanish dictionary, one which recognizes the lexical differences in South America. For travel in Mexico and Central America, the University of Chicago Spanish Dictionary is fairly good, since it recognizes Central American idioms, and in Costa Rica, there are several good English–Spanish dictionaries put out for the numerous Americans living there.

Even a good dictionary won't help when it comes to reading restaurant menus. Apparently, the Royal Academy doesn't concern itself with standardizing the names of dishes. A word for sausage in

Costa Rica means porterhouse steak in Argentina. The word for scallops in some countries means cow stomach in others and veal cutlet in still others. A tortilla in Mexico is a thin, flat corncake, but in South America a tortilla is an omelette with chunks of potato in it, sometimes without the egg, sometimes without the potato. Don't ask me, I've never figured it out, either. In Mexico, the word for station wagon translates to pickup truck in Chile. The common word for bus in some countries means truck in others. So don't rely on a dictionary printed in Madrid or St. Louis to help you in Bolivia. Make a collection of small, locally printed dictionaries if you plan on traveling extensively.

But even though some words vary from country to country, most people, particularly educated people, are fully aware of the differences. If you ask "What time does the next truck leave the station?" they know you mean "bus", and probably won't even smile. If you order "frijoles" instead of "achuelas," the waiter knows you want beans. It would be the same thing if an English tourist in the United States were to ask you about the "underground," you'd know he was talking about the "subway," wouldn't you? By the way, the subway is called the "subte" (short for subterranean) in Buenos Aires, and the "metro" in Mexico.

WHAT ABOUT PORTUGUESE?

In Brazil, as you probably know, the language is Portuguese. Brazil and Portugal have never maintained the close intellectual ties as have the former Spanish colonies and Spain. The result is that Brazilian Portuguese shows a lot of original development. This is particularly true in that Brazilians have evolved some odd ways of pronounciation. Although the written language looks very much like Spanish, and many words are spelled exactly the same, it turns out that the pronunciation is so different it's almost impossible to pick out meaning from a conversation--unless you've done some preparation.

The Foreign Service Institute's tapes (also distributed by the National AudioVisual Center) are very good, and cost $130 for 23 cassettes and a text. This is called Portuguese Programmatic Course--Vol. I. There is also a short course for those who have a good command of Spanish and want to transfer their skills to Portuguese: Portuguese--from Spanish to Portuguese. This costs $20 for a text and two cassettes. You might look in your local university book stores for language courses offered at that school.

If you know Spanish, careful attention to pronunciation differences is most helpful in understanding Portuguese. I've always found that by speaking very slowly in Spanish, and having the other party speak very slowly in Portuguese, we communicate. We can't discuss philosophy or politics, but we enjoy being understood as we found out each others' families, jobs, and lifestyles.

Incidentally, if you don't speak Portuguese, it can be useful to start off speaking Spanish, then switching to English if the speaker knows something of that. The reason being that in tourist spots, an English speaker is usually a richer tourist and might be expected to pay more for goods and services than the less affluent Spanish-speaking South American tourist. This isn't always true, but I do it anyway.

A question commonly asked is "Will studying Portuguese interfere with my Spanish?" Some believe so, but I disagree. Because of the structural similarities, it is easy to build on your Spanish skills by concentrating on the phonetic and lexical differences. Because the pronunciation is so different it would be all but impossible to get them confused.

Portuguese is closely related to Spanish. If you look at a Portuguese newspaper, you'll realize that you can understand much of it, provided you're familiar with Spanish. This is because almost 85 percent of Portuguese vocabulary consists of words with cognates in Spanish. But the problem comes when Portuguese is spoken. Because Portuguese has so many different vowel and consonant sounds, you begin to believe there is no correlation between the written and the spoken language. Certainly, those 85 percent of the cognates sound little like Spanish. The secret is understanding the pronunciation differences, listening to the tapes and analyzing the new sounds.

The most striking pronunciation differences are: The ending 'o' is usually pronounced as a 'ooh' sound; the 'r' sound comes out as a harsh 'h' sound; 'te' or 'de' comes out like 'chi' or like the 'j' of 'judge'; and the nasal sounds are sometimes slurred. There are five nasal vowel sounds in Portuguese ('ẽ' 'ĩ' 'õ' 'ũ' and 'ũh').

So, don't let the sounds of Portuguese throw you. Get some tapes and get started!

DON'T BE AFRAID TO SPEAK THE LANGUAGE!

You will find Latin American people unusually helpful and patient with strangers trying to learn their language. They seldom laugh or make fun of a beginner. (I've seen Parisians go into hysterics at my horrible French, and on two occasions, French–Canadians informed me that my butchery of their language was offensive to their ears.) Those Latin Americans who've studied a little English in school usually love the opportunity of practicing English with you. You'll often find yourself in a situation where you are using broken Spanish, and your friend replies in equally broken English. You both have a great time! I'm convinced that one of the best learning situations is having a friend who speaks just a little English, just enough that once in a while, when you can't find the right word to use, you can throw in an English one. This takes the tension out of speaking, and gives you the chance to talk about subjects way beyond your normal range of ability. You will find yourself arguing politics, exchanging philosophies, and being part of the scene. At this point, learning accelerates.

Once you've acquired some skills in a foreign language, you'll find an exciting new set of opportunities open to you. It's like opening a door into a new world, where you can make new friends and suddenly become part of a totally different universe. As your learning accelerates, so will your experiences. Your new language can make the difference between an ordinary life and a full and stimulating adventure in living.

CHAPTER 20

The Ugly American?

It's interesting to watch American tourists and residents in a foreign country. Too often their personalities undergo an inexplicable change and you find them behaving as they would never dream of doing at home. With some, it's simply a matter of being relaxed and enjoying their surroundings, so their natural exuberance and enthusiasm surfaces. They have a great time. But others undergo some radical changes, becoming arrogant, demanding and rude. Being aware of how a foreign setting affects others, and yourself, will help you avoid some of the mistakes that can lead to an unpleasant stay, or contribute to the stereotype of the "Ugly American."

The worst mistake is to be continually comparing your host country unfavorably with "back home." So the food is different, the customs bewildering, service infuriating, and red tape impossible. If you want everything to run as smoothly as "back home," then the obvious solution is to stay "back home." Things happen in different sequences in foreign countries, with different speeds and rhythms--sometimes for the best, and sometimes for the worst. Just remember there is always a reason, perhaps an obscure reason, for things being as they are. Because you can't understand or accept the reason does not matter. All of your coaxing, pleading, and threatening, will be wasted. Nothing is going to change, so you might as well accept it and smile.

One example is the telephone system. At home, we've been spoiled rotten--just drop a coin in the slot and dial. It's not quite that simple in some Latin American countries. Some pay systems are ridiculously cheap, with the coin required worth only a fraction of a penny. But the problem arises when you discover that they haven't minted that coin for years, and they are as rare as square–cut diamonds. Some places you need to purchase a *ficha*, a brass slug that works instead of a coin in pay phones—maybe it will and maybe not. But when do you put in the ficha? Before you dial the number? After you dial? When the other party answers the phone? How many fichas do you use? There are so many systems that the mind grows numb. Long distance calls can also be an Alice-in-Wonderland experience. Sometimes you have to make a reservation with the long–distance office, and you might wait an hour or more for your call to go through. I spent three days trying to call the States from a small town in the Yucatan once. On the other hand, I called Denver from Huehuetenango, Guatemala one time as easily as if I were in Denver. Cussing the system or taking it out on the telephone clerk doesn't help a bit.

In the United States, when you want a telephone installed, you simply notify the phone company and you'll usually be hooked up in a matter of hours, days at the worst. Not so in most of Latin America. If you're lucky, it's a matter of only a few months, but it can be as long as a two–year wait. It won't do you any good to complain. The problem is that the telephone companies have so much trouble keeping phones working that there isn't time for new installations. Sometimes the problem is with the telephone workers, who find it much more profitable to *repair* telephones than *install* them. Their interest fades when it comes to your problem of getting a phone installed. Usually these are government workers, with strong union protection, and it's often claimed that they split the repair money with their superiors.

There is nothing you can do about situations like this, short of embarking on a vociferous campaign to reform labor relations and change the entire system (and making a fool of yourself in the process). It isn't your country and it is up to you to accept conditions as they are. I remember a tourist in Acapulco who caused raised eyebrows all over the restaurant when he bitterly complained because the establishment didn't sell Budweiser beer.

Most Latin Americans have a different way of viewing time, a way that is very difficult for the time–oriented North American to understand. When we invite someone to our house for dinner, or make a business appointment for a certain hour, we are insulted if the person arrives late. There, they would be astounded if you came at the precise hour. The reasons for this (to us) warped time–sense are buried in centuries of social relations and customs to the point where it seems normal to Latin Americans. If you ask why people cannot be punctual, you will simply receive a blank stare; it's like asking a fish why he swims. Ultimately, it has something to do with the class consciousness of Latin America. Social scientists have measured the differences between the stated and actual time of appointments in Latin America and have come up with correlations that measure the distance in social classes. The more social standing a person has, the later he will be for an appointment. Since this is the way things are in Latin America, it will do you no good to become angry and try to change the system. I've seen Americans create lots of frustration for themselves and puzzled resentment among their neighbors and friends, by trying to instill an American sense of time on the world. The easiest way to determine what time a party is actually going to begin is to ask your host: "Is that 8 o'clock Latin American time, or American time?" They understand perfectly.

Americans have the reputation for being brisk and businesslike, even in personal relationships. But the Latin American's reputation is for courtesy and measured politeness. This politeness is not something they put on for special occasions; it's a habitual way of relating to friends and strangers alike. They view Americans as cold and unfeeling—all "business." In business relationships, Latin Americans often place negotiations on a more personal basis. Before undertaking a piece of business, it's customary to inquire about the other's family, his health, or his golf game.

One behavior pattern that is sure to be destructive is what I call the "priority game." This is played between fellow expatriates and reminds me of games played by animals to establish dominance. The participants mentally circle each other like roosters, determining how long the opponents have been in the country, how many stamps they have in their passports, or other things that might establish one as the superior expert on the country. It's as if they are jealous of the intrusion of a fellow countryman into their domain. The winner gets to look down his nose at the loser, and speak to him in the most condescending terms.

Don't be lured into playing this game, but don't immediately write off the other person as an insufferable boor. My advice is to allow him to win, and then see if deep inside the "priority winner" might not be someone you might want to add to your network of friends. Sometimes even boorish friends can be valuable if the "Gringo Gulch" community is small.

Living in an Anglo–American community has been compared to living on a small island. You are stuck with your compatriots, and you had better make the best of what is available. Being an "Ugly American" won't help a bit. It will not only turn away the local people, but will also hurt your standing with the Anglo–American community. Some people can get along without the company of other North Americans, but almost all will need help from time to time. Best keep in good graces with everyone.

LOVE, HATE AND FEAR

My first experience with Latin America came when I was a teenager. My father accepted a position with the U.S. government and was headquartered in Mexico. At that time, the British–American colony was a rather close–knit group with lots of social activities, cocktail parties, dinners and the like. I immediately noticed something odd. Most of the expatriates fell into two distinct classes. Either they loved Mexico passionately, irrationally refusing to see any faults, or they *hated* everything Mexican, refusing to recognize anything good about the country, its people, its institutions.

It's the same way with tourists. Have you ever noticed that friends who return from a Latin American vacation usually fall into one of two categories? On the one hand there is the enthusiastic traveler who insists on telling you every detail of the trip, and who loves everything about the country. On the other hand, is the tourist who hated every moment, and who can't think of anything good to say about the country. They've visited the same place, haven't they? Yes, but they saw it through different eyes.

"What was wrong?" you ask. "Everything. You couldn't turn around without someone wanting a bribe, customs officials, cops, cab drivers." Or they might say, "The poverty was heart–wrenching. I couldn't have a good time knowing so many people around me were poor." "I got the Aztec Two–Step," others will say, "you can't trust the food or the water there." These people cannot understand how their fellow countrymen noticed nothing wrong.

What's the reason for these opposite viewpoints? I feel that the answer lies in the psychological phenomenon known as *projection*. Simply stated, projection is a gut–feeling that everyone shares the same kinds of fears and prejudices as you. Thus if you feel negatively toward an individual or group, projection convinces you that others feel negative toward you. This reaction feeds upon itself until the feeling of rejection becomes overwhelming.

For a moment, let's assume you are racially prejudiced (perhaps even unconsciously), or that you link foreigners with anti-American terrorism, bandidos and the like. It's very possible to get the feeling that a dark-skinned stranger on the street corner senses your ill will and holds similar prejudices against you. You assume he is full of hate and resentment, and is, therefore, dangerous. His eyes glitter with hate and a thirst for revenge. In fact, his eyes are probably glittering with innocent curiosity about you as a human being.

If you have an acute awareness of the shabby treatment that dark-skinned aliens sometimes receive in our country, your projections can easily trigger these crippling feelings of paranoia. Your guilt feelings about living so well at home, make you very uncomfortable at the sight of people living below your standards and you expect resentment from these people, whom you think are probably planning on robbing you at any moment.

The reverse of this gut-reaction occurs in those who adore everything foreign. They've managed to repress their feelings of racial prejudice and project an aura of fondness and brotherly love and they expect to receive the same in return. To them, the stranger's glittering stare is one of shyness and goodwill. A wave of the hand and a smile brings one in return. Since politeness is an essential part of the Latin American's personality, he is forced to smile and wave back, thus reinforcing the feelings of love and euphoria in the gringo. How could anything be ugly about a country where the people smile at me, wave at me, love me?

RESPECT THE CUSTOMS

It shouldn't be necessary to remind a visitor to respect the customs of the host country. All but the most boring of the "Ugly Americans" try to blend in. But what if you don't know or understand the customs?

The matter of "bribes" for cops or government officials is a case in point. We are used to policemen getting paid good money, $20,000 or $30,000, maybe $40,000, a year. To accept money for doing the job that already pays pretty well, is criminal. It's as simple as that. But in many parts of Latin America, this isn't the case at all. Cops are paid minimal wages and are expected to make up the rest in *mordidas* ("bites").

"Crooked!" the outraged gringo complains. "Bribery!" Not so at all. Look, a policeman in Tijuana, Mexico receives $80 a month in salary. Does anyone seriously expect him to support a family on that? He must make up the difference by catching speeders or collecting parking fines. If the government gave him a living wage, this wouldn't be necessary. But if you ask a Mexican taxpayer why he doesn't pay cops better, you will hear an indignant, "What? Take my tax money to pay someone to chase speeders? I never speed. Let them get it from the speeders. If I ever get caught speeding, *then* I'll pay the cop, but not before!" I have to admit, there is a certain logic in that. In our countries, it's the law–abiding citizens who foot the bill while the lawbreakers receive a warning slap on the wrist.

This philosophy of the lawbreaker paying the costs carries through into the punishment system. This is the reason you've heard so many horror stories about harsh treatment of American prisoners in some Latin American countries. We read news articles about someone sentenced for narcotics violations having been denied decent food, a bed, even denied blankets. But it isn't that he has been denied anything, it's just that the Mexican taxpayer refuses to spend his money on criminals. "Let them buy their own blankets, let them pay for their food," he'll say. "If they can't afford to buy, let 'em work for it." Actually, most Americans do quite well in prison, because they can usually have access to funds that allow comparative luxury.

When you've been caught doing something wrong, don't complain if the cop suggests that you might want to pay him the fine instead of going down to the municipal offices to pay. He is actually doing you a favor, because otherwise he would have to take your license plate and turn it into the police station until you come to pay your fine and retrieve it. He is saving you from having to waste a day running around from one office to another, filling out forms, just to pay the fine. You don't call the tip you give a waiter for good service a bribe, do you? This is precisely the same, tipping a man for doing a service for you. And often, a police officer in Latin American countries has about the same social status as a waiter.

A word of warning: Don't try to tip your way out of a serious offense where others are involved, an automobile accident for example. It usually cannot be done. And don't go flashing money around.

Wait until the subject of *mordida* is broached by the cop. If he does not bring it up, you subtly ask, "Is it possible for me to pay the fine to you? To save me a trip to the police station?" If he agrees, you can then bargain with him as to the amount of the fine. Never pay the asking amount without an argument (unless it is a trifling amount). There are exceptions to this situation, where police officers are expected to be professional and are paid a living wage even in countries where *mordida* is the norm. In this situation, you would receive about the same reaction as if you were to attempt to bribe a cop in most U.S. or Canadian cities.

The same thing applies to dealing with bureaucrats. A very subtle question about the possibility of paying an extra fee to expedite a red–tape–tangled procedure can often put you at the top of the list. But sometimes not. Be very subtle about this. The *mordida* system isn't as strong in some Latin American countries, and is all but absent in others. Generally, the more prosperous a country, and the more middle–class, the higher–paid the public servants and the less likely a tip would be accepted. You have to feel your way on this.

PERSONAL BUSINESS

We in the north are famous for our no–nonsense, brusque manner of doing business. We enter a store, point at what we want, throw down the cash and *adios*, we're gone. Not so in Latin America. Businessmen and customers like to feel that they have a more personal relationship. It doesn't hurt to know something about the people you're dealing with, and ask about their children from time to time. It will pay off in the long run, and in the meantime, it makes business dealings easier.

In some countries, the simple matter of getting waited on in a store can be misunderstood by gringos who don't understand the local custom. For example, in Costa Rica, it can be frustrating to see people shoving their way in front of you and getting waited on first, even though the clerk knew perfectly well that you were next in line. What is happening here is that the people are obeying a local custom (occasionally a sign will remind them) that says the first people to be served are, in this order, handicapped people, pregnant women, elderly women, then elderly men. The same goes for bus seats. If one of the above gets on a bus, you are expected to get up and offer your seat to him or her. I've seen arguments on a bus where a man

227

thought he was elderly enough to demand a seat, and a woman claimed priority because she was almost as old and a woman, too. Don't be surprised if you get on a bus and some youngster gets up for you. Up here, if a youngster gets up, he may be getting ready to mug you.

In Chile, on the other hand, you can be waiting to be served and someone behind you calls out, and he gets served first. Why? Because there it's considered bad manners for salespersons to force themselves on a customer until he is ready to buy. At that point the customer calls out, and the transaction takes place.

Each country differs in the way things are done and it pays to be very observant. In Mexico, people push and shove to get on a bus or subway, sometimes so strongly that the people shoving and pushing to get *off* the subway have a hard time leaving. (Never ride a subway at rush hour!) But in Costa Rica, there is an orderly queue and no one would dream of cutting in front of a line unless that person is handicapped or pregnant. The same thing is true in Argentina.

EL QUE SE MIDE, SE MUERE

"He who is measured, dies." A few years ago I was teaching English in an adult education class and was demonstrating English survival skills to a beginners' class of Latin Americans. To demonstrate the use of inches instead of centimeters, I took a yardstick and was going to measure the height of a student. The reaction from the class was a collective gasp of horror.

This was a new one on me, so I asked, "What's wrong?" "El que se mide, se muere," came the reply. It turns out there is a superstitious taboo against measuring a person, because that's what they do when you die—measure you for a coffin. You won't be going around measuring people, but there are some things that we do, part of our North American personality, that are absolutely insulting to Latin Americans, and we aren't even aware of them.

Here's another that involves measuring: When we talk about a child and want to indicate its age, we hold our hand, palm down above the floor to indicate how tall a child is. From that we infer their age. Latin Americans do the same thing, but, with the palm *up*. With the palm facing down, as is our custom, you are indicating how tall an *animal* is. In effect, what you are saying, when you measure children this way, is that they are nothing more than animals. Insulting.

Another habit we have is that of pointing our index finger at someone when we are talking to them. We do this to emphasize a point, or when we are particularly excited about something. This can make some Latin Americans very uncomfortable. It stems from an ancient superstition that when you want the Devil to notice an enemy, you point at him. Over the years the custom has evolved to where you only need point at someone when you want to insult someone.

Another confusing gesture to the North American is a hand signal that means "thank you." If you invite someone to have a drink, he might hold his hand in front of his face, then nod or bow slightly. Sometimes he may say *gracias* at the same time. You think that means you should order a drink, and when you do, the astonished friend says, "But I told you I didn't want a drink!" His signal was shorthand for, "Thank you, but no." Gestures have a way of changing meaning, or disappearing from one country to another. You must become a keen observer of gestures and nuances.

It would be difficult to list all of the possible *faux pax* due to ignorance of Latin American customs. Even if it were possible, they wouldn't all be valid for all countries. Some countries, like Mexico, Peru, Bolivia and Guatemala are heavily influenced by indigenous beliefs and superstitions, while countries like Argentina, Costa Rica and Uruguay have European traditions. It will be your job to try to discern what is going on around you and to conform.

LIVING OR RETIRING ABROAD

Should you be one of those individuals who savors the new, who can cope with the occasional drawbacks of foreign living, then your life of adventure lies ahead. You'll find that friendships forged in a foreign setting have a way of becoming remarkably solid. You have in front of you an enviable opportunity of changing your lifestyle, of entering an exciting new world. I urge you to do a thorough self–examination, to see if you have the temperament and the openness to try this adventure. If so, check your finances to make sure you can afford it, then plunge right in!

A final word of caution, one that has been given several times in this book, but worth closing on: *Try it before you buy it!*

bibliography

AAA. *Travel Guide to Mexico*. Falls Church, VA: American Automobile Association, 1986.

Arthur Frommer's Guide to Mexico City & Acapulco. New York: Frommer-Pasmantier, 1984.

Birnbaum, Stephen. *Mexico 1986*. Boston: Houghton Mifflin, 1986

Bureau of Consular Affairs, *Travel Tips for Senior Citizens*, Govt. Printing Office, 1983.

Cassell's Colloquial Spanish New York: Macmillan, 1980.

Epstein, Jack *Along the Gringo Trail*, And/Or Press, Berkeley Calif. 1977

Flandrau, Charles Macomb. *Viva Mexico!* Campaign, IL: University of Illinois Press, 1964.

Fodor's Budget Mexico 1985. New York: McKay, 1984.

Insight Guides. Mexico. Englewood Cliffs, NJ: Prentice-Hall, 1983

Lemkowitz, Florence. *Mexico 1985*. New York: New American Library, 1984.

Prices and Earnings Around the World, Union Bank of Switzerland, Zurich, 1985.

Sierra, Justo. *The Political Evolution of the Mexican People*. Austin, TX: University of Texas Press, 1975.

South America on $25 a Day Arthur Frommer, New York, 1985.

South American Handbook 1986, Rand McNally, 1985

Sunset Editors. *Mexico: Travel Guide*. Menlo Park, CA: Sunset-Lane, 1983.

United Nations *Monthly Bulletin of Statistics*, September 1985.

Wallace, Jean *The Key to Costa Rica 1985* Editorial Texto Ltd., San Jose, Costa Rica.

index

COMMENT AND ORDER FORM

TO: **GATEWAY BOOKS**
66 Cleary Court • Suite 1405
San Francisco, CA 94109
(415) 821-3440

FROM: _____

_____

_____

_____

COMMENTS _____

(In this space we'd welcome your gripes as well as your kudos, but most of all we want your suggestions as to how we can make the next edition of *CHOOSE LATIN AMERICA* more helpful.)

Please send me _____ copies of *CHOOSE LATIN AMERICA* at $9.95 per copy. (Plus 6% sales tax for California residents.) My check or money order includes $1.25 for shipping. I understand that orders will be shipped Book Rate and should arrive in three or four weeks.